MODEL ROCKET
DESIGN AND CONSTRUCTION

How to create and build unique and exciting model rockets that work

Timothy S. Van Milligan

KALMBACH BOOKS

Publisher's Cataloging in Publication
(Prepared by Quality Books Inc.)

Van Milligan, Timothy.
    Model rocket design and construction : how to create
and build unique and exciting model rockets that work. /
Timothy S. Van Milligan.
        p. cm.
    Includes bibliographical references.
    ISBN 0-89024-561-4

    1. Rockets (Aeronautics)—Models. I. Title

TL844.V36 1995   629.4'750'228
                                  QBI95-20096

Printed in the United States of America.

About the Book

This book has been written for modelers who have experience building rocket kits, but want to build their own designs. It covers a variety of topics in a manner that most readers will easily understand. In this book you'll learn some of the techniques that real aeronautical engineers use to design and build aircraft and rockets. Many simple guidelines are presented that will allow the model rocket designer to construct successful rockets without proceeding through an extensive trial-and-error process. These guidelines are very broad, and allow the designer to create a wide variety of models, not limiting them to a small category of rockets that seem to all look alike.

The book is the most up-to-date ever written on the subject of model rocket design. It is illustrated with drawings and photographs to help the reader understand the topics being addressed. This book discusses how to get modeling ideas, how rockets are designed to be stable in flight, how to make them fly higher, and the basic construction techniques needed to make the rockets strong, yet lightweight. The different types of rocket recovery systems are extensively discussed, with extra emphasis on the more challenging types—gliders and helicopters. This book contains the first and only guidelines ever written on the subject of helicopter recovery.

Through this book, you'll also learn how to design scale model rockets, payload carrying rockets, and the techniques of successful clustering and staging of rocket engines. Finally, this book also contains information on the special techniques needed to build larger and higher-powered rockets. Whatever your design desires, this book is for you!

About the Author

Tim Van Milligan has been designing and flying his own model rockets since 1976. After obtaining his degree in Aeronautical Engineering from Emby-Riddle Aeronautical University in 1988, Tim worked as a launch operations engineer for McDonnell Douglas Corp. In this position, he helped assemble and launch the highly successful Delta II rocket for NASA and the U.S. Air Force. The author has also worked as a model rocket designer at Estes Industries. A few of the many rockets he has designed include: CATO, Skywinder, Terrier/Sandhawk, TurboCopter, and Omloid.

Tim has written many articles on the various types of model rockets for a number of magazines and newsletters, and been an active competitor in national and international model rocket competitions as a member of the F. A. I. Spacemodeling team.

The author is very interested in the success of your rocket designs. If you have any comments about this book and how it might be improved in future editions, or if you have designed a unique model rocket, send a photograph and description of the rocket to him in care of Kalmbach Books.

Dedication

For the many forward-thinking model rocketeers who desire to have more fun flying their own designs.

Acknowledgments

This book took years to develop, as there were many areas of rocketry that I had to learn first myself. I would like to thank all those modelers who went before me, blazing trails of their own into the sky, yet who took the time to point other rocketeers, like me, in the right direction. Without these people, model rocketry would not exist as it does today.

Special thanks goes to those who helped with this book—Patrick McCarthy for technical review of the text and help in selecting photographs, Mark Lavigne for encouragement and for providing photographs, and Ed LaCroix and Steven Bachmeyer for taking specific photographs.

Thanks also to Sig Manufacturing Co., Inc., for use of the information on the grading and selection of balsa wood. Similarly, thanks to Gerald M. Gregorek for allowing the reprinting of his boost glider design rules.

Additional thanks goes to those people at Kalmbach Publishing for expediting this book with quality and speed.

Finally, thanks and love to my wife, Cindy, who allowed me the time to write this book.

Contents

1

Getting Started

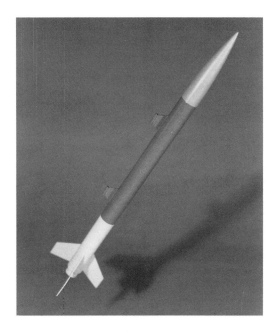

A basic sport model. (photo by Steven A. Bachmeyer)

Designing and building successful model rockets is a step-by-step process with several phases. This book will discuss each part in sufficient depth to help you develop successful rockets, but first it is important to know what makes a successful rocket flight—the goal of every rocketeer.

A flight is considered successful when it safely completes the five individual phases: ignition, lift-off, stable flight (including the coast phase), recovery system deployment, and safe landing. Without any one of these phases the flight is termed unsuccessful.

Successful Flight Criteria

1. Ignition
2. Lift-off
3. Stable ascent
4. Recovery system deployment
5. Safe (damage free) landing

The Design Process

The design process begins with an idea. This is usually the hardest step of the process because every rocket builder wants to create a unique model that no one has ever thought of before. Ideas are easy to copy, but new and different ones are difficult to come up with. If you have an idea, sketch it out on paper. If you don't, turn to the section in this book that describes the different types of model rockets (page 9). You can also find ideas in the section on the various methods of returning your model to the ground (page 10). These methods are called recovery systems. Other places to get ideas are in the "payload rockets" (page 92) and "styling" (page 12) sections of this book. If you've already paged through this book, you have noticed that it is full of ideas for new rockets. Many great models are developed by selecting the best parts from several different rockets. Whatever your idea, first sketch out the model or at least write down a paragraph describing it or its purpose.

Second, determine the size and general layout of the rocket. At this point, go directly to Chapter 2 and familiarize yourself with all the ways to make your rocket fly straight. This is the most important part of the design, as it will directly affect whether or not your model is successful. Choosing the size of the rocket is completely up to you, but you might want to consider some design constraints that affect how big your rocket is. These include what engines the model will be powered by, the size of the field you plan on using to launch your rocket, and the materials you will use to build the model.

At this point you should be getting into the specifics of what the model should look like or how it should function. Several sections in this manual should help you refine the design. "Parts of a Model Rocket" (page 15) shows the basic layout of a typical model rocket, which will help you determine which components you'll need to build your model; "Drag Reduction and Aerodynamics" (page 21) describes ways to streamline your rocket to achieve very high altitudes; and "Rocket Recovery Systems" (page 65) tells how to determine the size of the recovery system so the model will return safely to the ground. This last section also gives tips on designing gliders and models that return to the ground using the helicopter recovery method.

When you've decided on the size and shape of the model, develop a list of materials you'll use to build it. From this list you may want to order specialized parts from your favorite rocket kit manufacturer, or you may want to build these parts from materials you have on hand. If you choose the latter, the section on "Creating Custom Parts" (page 51) will help you.

You are now in the final stage of rocket design. Some additional chapters to read are "Constructing Higher Powered Rockets" (page 52), "Clustered Engine Rockets" (page 101) or "Multi-Stage Rockets" (page 95) if your design will include any of these special features.

If you haven't already done so, make a good drawing of your model rocket design. If your model is complex this drawing should be to scale, but otherwise it can be a simple sketch.

Design

1. Generate concept or idea
2. Determine size and general layout of rocket
3. Select components and final appearance
4. Determine type and size of recovery system
5. Generate list of materials to be used
6. Make final drawing of rocket

Construction

1. Gather all parts to be used
2. Make patterns and templates
3. Construct model

4. Apply finish or paint model
5. Apply decals

Launch

1. Select proper rocket engine
2. Prep rocket
3. Launch and recover rocket

Construction

Gather all the materials you will need. Now is the time to make any patterns or templates and order or construct special parts. Actual construction should proceed smoothly now that you are armed with your drawing and a complete set of parts. Reading all of Chapter 6 will help you with the actual assembly.

Painting and decorating your model is the final phase of construction. Chapter 8, "Painting and Decorating," describes how to obtain a smooth, high-quality appearance, which in itself will make your rocket unusual.

When the rocket is complete, prepare for launch. Selecting the proper engine is very important to a successful flight. Read Chapter 15, "Rocket Engines," to find out how to properly select an engine.

"Repair Techniques," Chapter 9, tells how to bring back that "showroom-new" appearance to older rockets.

The above chapters form a cycle in which several steps are repeated. In reviewing your design, you will constantly see ways to improve it. Once a change has been made it may be necessary to repeat a step or two to make sure one change didn't affect other parts of the design. Take your time designing your rocket; it takes a lot longer to repair a problem than to do it right the first time.

To help you understand an unfamiliar word or phrase, the final section of this book is a glossary of terms. It is one of the most extensive rocketry glossaries in print, covering not only rockets, but gliders, too.

If everything is done right, your rocket will be the envy of all who see it. If you come up with a truly unique rocket and want to share it with others, send a photo of the model to me, in care of Kalmbach Publishing Co., with a description of how it works; maybe the next edition of this book will display your model. I wish you success in your building endeavors!

An assortment of unique rockets designed and built by Randall Redd (photo by Marc Lavigne).

Safety

The most important design constraint while you're designing and building your rocket is safety. You are the only person who can make sure it will function safely. It is your responsibility to see that it is designed, constructed, and flown so that nothing is damaged when the rocket takes off.

To help all model rocket designers and flyers, the National Association of Rocketry (NAR) has developed a code to guide and promote safety in the hobby. The safety code was developed over a period of 30 years. Please do not skip this important section. Read it, understand it, and commit yourself to following it.

NAR Safety Code

1. Materials: My model rocket will be made of lightweight materials such as paper, wood, rubber, and plastic suitable for the power used and the performance of my model rocket. I will not use any metal for the nose cone, body, or fins of a model rocket.

2. Engines: I will use only commercially-made NAR certified model rocket engines in the manner recommended by the manufacturer. I will not alter the model rocket engine, it parts, or its ingredients in any way.

3. Recovery: I will always use a recovery system in my rocket that will return it safely to the ground so it may be flown again. I will use only flame-resistant recovery wadding if required.

4. Weight Limits: My model rocket will weigh no more that 1500 grams (53 oz.) at lift-off, and its rocket engines will produce no more than 320 Newton-seconds of total impulse. My model rocket will weigh no more than the engine manufacturer's recommended maximum lift-off weight for the engines used, or I will use engines recommended by the manufacturer for my model rocket.

5. Stability: I will check the stability of my model rocket before its first flight, except when launching a model rocket of already proven stability.

6. Payloads: Except for insects, my model rocket will never carry live animals or a payload that is intended to be flammable, explosive, or harmful.

7. Launch Site: I will launch my model rockets outdoors in a cleared area, free of tall trees, power lines, buildings, and dry brush and grass. I will ensure that people in the launch area are aware of the pending model rocket launch and can see the model rocket's liftoff before I begin my audible five-second countdown.

8. Launcher: I will launch my model rocket from a stable launching device that provides rigid guidance until the model rocket has reach a speed adequate to ensure a safe flight path. To prevent accidental eye injury, I will always place the launcher so that the end of the rod is above eye level or I will cap or disassemble my launch rod when not in use and I will never store it in an upright position. My launcher will have a jet deflector device to prevent the engine exhaust from hitting the ground directly. I will always clear the area around my launch device of brown grass, dry weeds, or other easy-to-burn materials.

9. Ignition System: The system I use to launch my model rocket will be remotely controlled and electrically operated. It will contain a launching switch that will return to "off" when

released. The system will contain a removable safety interlock in series with the launch switch. All persons will remain at least 5 meters (15 feet) from the model rocket when I am igniting the model rocket engines totaling 30 Newton-seconds or less of total impulse or less and at least 9 meters (30 feet) from the model rocket when I am igniting model rocket engines totaling more than 30 Newton-seconds of total impulse. I will use only electrical igniters recommended by the engine manufacturer that will ignite model rocket engine(s) within one second of actuation of the launching switch.

10. Launch Safety: I will not allow anyone to approach a model rocket on a launcher until I have made certain that the safety interlock has been removed or that the battery has been disconnected from the ignition system. In the event of a misfire, I will wait one minute after a misfire before allowing anyone to approach the launcher.

11. Flying Conditions: I will launch my model rocket only when the wind is less than 30 kilometers (20 miles) an hour. I will not launch my model rocket so it flies into clouds, near aircraft in flight, or in a manner that is hazardous to people or property.

12. Pre-Launch Test: When conducting research activities with unproven model rocket designs or methods I will, when possible, determine the reliability of my model rocket by prelaunch tests. I will conduct the launching of an unproven design in complete isolation from persons not participating in the actual launching.

13. Launch Angle: My launch device will be pointed within 30 degrees from vertical. I will never use model rocket engines to propel any device horizontally.

14. Recovery Hazards: If a model rocket becomes entangled in a power line or other dangerous place, I will not attempt to retrieve it.

This is the official Model Rocket Safety Code of the National Association of Rocketry. Note: The largest model rocket engine defined by the CPSC is an F (80 N-s). To launch rockets weighing over 1.36 kilograms (3 pounds) including propellant, or rockets containing more than 62.5 grams (2.2 ounces) of propellant, you must obtain a waiver from the Federal Aviation Administration (FAA). Check your telephone directory for the FAA office nearest you. They will be able to help you get permission to operate larger rockets than those listed above.

A large scale model of the Saturn 1B is ready for launch (photo by Tim Van Milligan).

Model Classification

There are several types of model rockets you can design and build. They are usually classified according to their specific purpose. The list below describes several types, some of which are more complex than others. This book contains special sections of additional design criteria to consider when you're dealing with those models.

Sometimes a rocket may not fit perfectly into one category. It may be a combination of one or more different types—for example, it might be a combination glider and cluster model. The purpose of this section is to give you many different ideas, so you can build your own fleet.

Sport Rockets: A sport rocket is any rocket built strictly for the fun and enjoyment of model rocketry. It usually serves no purpose other than to make you or others happy. This category is broad and can be divided into subcategories based on how the rocket is powered.

Single Engine Sport Rockets: This is probably the most common type of model rocket built and flown. As the name describes, it is powered by a single engine and usually recovered by a

Two different types of futuristic or fantasy type models (photos by Steven A. Bachmeyer).

Functional Rockets: Functional rockets have a secondary purpose or unique feature that gives additional value and enjoyment over the basic sport model. There are several categories of functional rockets, as there are of sport rockets, but here they are differentiated by their secondary purpose or feature. Functional rockets can include gliders and helicopter models, which are described in Chapter 10.

Scale Model Rockets: A scale rocket is a miniature replica of an actual flying missile or rocket. The level of detailing and the exactness of dimensions determines whether or not the model is actual scale or semi-scale. Some tips on building scale models are given in Chapter 11.

Fantasy Model Rockets: Rocket models that look as though they belong in outer space or on some distant world are called *futuristic* or *fantasy* rockets. Many times these rockets are replicas of spacecraft or rockets from movies. Fantasy rockets also include those designed to resemble actual scientific or military missiles. These rockets are sometimes known as *pseudo-scale* model rockets because they look as though they were modeled after a real rocket, even though the larger, full-scale versions do not exist.

Competition Model Rockets: Competition rockets are models used in games or contests. Rules for different events vary but can include contests such as highest altitude for a given type of rocket engine or longest duration aloft with a specific type of recovery device. For more information on rocket competitions, contact the *National Association of Rocketry*, whose address is listed at the end of this book.

Payload Model Rockets: A payload model rocket is designed to carry some type of special cargo into the air. The cargo, or payload, is usually placed in a module called a payload section, which protects the delicate cargo from the heat of the engine's ejection charge. For additional help in designing payload rockets, read Chapter 12.

streamer or parachute. Most rocket kits sold in stores are this type.

Cluster Engine Sport Rockets: A cluster engine sport model uses two or more engines ignited simultaneously and designed to operate as a single propulsion unit. Because of the extra power, cluster models fly higher than single engine models, or they can be used to carry heavier payloads into the sky. Chapter 14, "Clustered Engine Rockets," describes the design criteria for this model.

Multi-Staged Sport Rockets: Multi-staged rockets use two or more rocket engines stacked one on top of the other and ignited in sequence. The purpose of these rockets is to achieve very great altitudes. See Chapter 13 if you are designing multi-stage rockets. It explains how to get the models to stage reliably at the proper time.

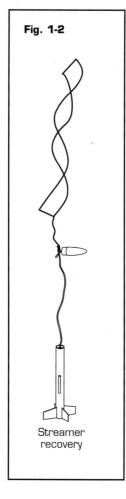

Fig. 1-1

Parachute canopy

Shroud lines

Parachute recovery

Fig. 1-2

Streamer recovery

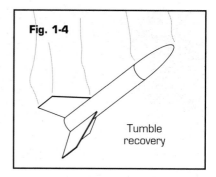

Fig. 1-3

Nose-blow recovery

Fig. 1-4

Tumble recovery

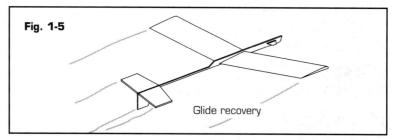

Fig. 1-5

Glide recovery

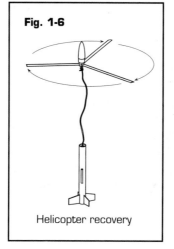

Fig. 1-6

Helicopter recovery

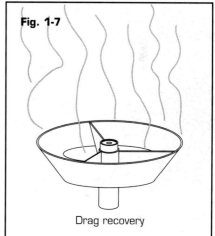

Fig. 1-7

Drag recovery

Rocket Recovery Systems

A recovery system is any device incorporated into the model for the purpose of returning it safely to the ground. All recovery systems work by developing either lift or additional drag to counteract the force of gravity. You may get an idea for a rocket from the way the model is returned to the ground. Below are the main ways to return a rocket to the ground safely.

Parachute Recovery: A parachute is an umbrella-like device used to retard the descent of a falling body by offering resistance to its motion as it moves through the air. Parachutes are the most common recovery method because of the relative ease of constructing a chute and because they make very slow descent speeds possible. Larger and heavier rockets are almost exclusively returned to the ground by parachute.

Streamer Recovery: Streamers are strips of material, generally rectangular,

used to slow the rocket down by fluttering in the wind. They are used only on smaller models under 56 grams (2 ounces) because they do not create as much drag as a parachute. Streamers are very easy to make and to prep for flight.

On very light rockets it may be possible to eliminate the streamer altogether and have the shock cord act as the drag-producing device. If this is done, it is typically called *nose-blow recovery*.

Tumble or Featherweight Recovery: Small, low-mass rockets often tumble or flutter to the ground. If the speed of the rocket is slow enough during its fall, it may not need any other type of recovery device. This is termed tumble recovery. The tumbling action is achieved by changing the relationship of the *center-of-pressure* (CP) and the *center-of-gravity*

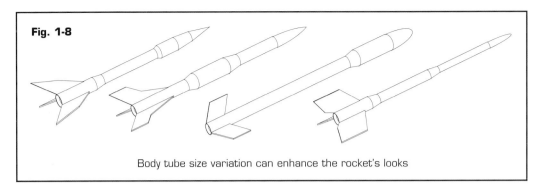

Fig. 1-8

Body tube size variation can enhance the rocket's looks

(CG) of the model. When the CP is forward of the CG, the rocket becomes unstable and begins to tumble. This may be accomplished in two ways: sliding the rocket engine rearward after engine burnout, or ejecting it entirely from the rocket. If you plan to use this type of rocket, always check its stability before flying it; your rocket may be stable even without the rocket engine installed. Read Chapter 2 to understand how the stability of a rocket can be altered.

Typically, tumble recovery is applicable only for small and short rockets that are built to withstand the forces of a hard landing on the ground. An important use of tumble recovery is for recovering the lower stages of multi-stage rockets.

Sometimes this type of recovery is called featherweight recovery. In this variation, the engine is ejected entirely from the rocket and the model still descends in a stable manner. Because the model has such a very low mass in relation to its drag, its terminal velocity is limited and it falls very slowly. Its descent is similar to the slow, stable flight of a badminton shuttlecock.

Glide Recovery: When the recovery method relies on lift created by wings to act against the force of gravity, and the model flies like an airplane, you have glide recovery. These models need to be carefully designed, as they are more susceptible to damage during launch than regular models. A special section in Chapter 10 will help you make great flying gliders.

Helicopter Recovery: Like glide recovery, this method relies on lift produced by the blades to counteract gravity and slow the rocket's descent. However, in this recovery method, the rocket also rotates, resembling a helicopter in its flight characteristics. A special section is also provided in Chapter 10 to help you design your own helicopter models.

Drag Recovery: Drag recovery uses the large frontal area of the model to increase the air resistance and thus the drag force of the descending model. This method does not require any other recovery device, as the slow speed of the falling model prevents damage.

Styling Ideas

If you'd like to style your rocket to give it a unique appearance, here are some ways to make it look distinctive. For more styling ideas, check books on airplanes and rockets and, by all means, look at other people's designs. Another good source is the product catalogs all model rocket manufacturers produce. The larger your stock of ideas, the better your rocket will look.

Paint Pattern and Decals: Paint and decals are the easiest ways to improve the appearance of an otherwise typical-looking model rocket. The paint should be smooth and without runs or sags. You can purchase decals from hobby stores or order them from your favorite model manufacturer. Don't limit yourself to decals from rocket manufacturers; try some made for plastic models, too.

The two major types of decals are pressure sensitive and water transfer. Pressure sensitive decals are sometimes called "crack-and-peel" because they have a sticky back side protected by special paper. To apply the decal, just peel the back paper off and lay the decal in place on the rocket. The sticky glue will adhere easily to the finish.

Water transfer decals must be soaked in water prior to application. They then slide easily off the special backing paper and onto the model. When you have the decal properly positioned, soak up excess water with a paper towel and let it dry. You'll find more information on applying paint and decals in Chapter 8.

Body Tube Diameter Variation: A typical model rocket has a tube, a nose cone, and fins. Just by varying the diameter of the tube, you can make the rocket look completely different. Make the transition from a body tube of one diameter to another with body tube adapters. Adapters can be made out of a variety of materials, including plastic, balsa wood, or paper. You can buy them from model rocket manufacturers or make them yourself. Chapter 6 has more information on construction of adapters.

Tunnels and Wire Conduits: Tunnels and wire conduits are used on the outside of real rockets and missiles to protect wires and small pipes that run from the front of the rocket to the back. You can simulate these tunnels on your rocket by cutting small body tubes in half lengthwise or by sanding wooden dowels to shape and gluing them to the side of your rocket's body tube. An added benefit

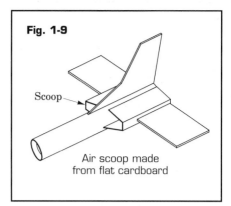

Fig. 1-9

Scoop

Air scoop made from flat cardboard

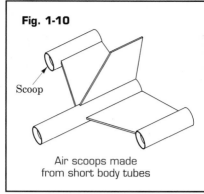

Fig. 1-10

Scoop

Air scoops made from short body tubes

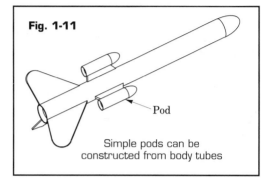

Fig. 1-11

Pod

Simple pods can be constructed from body tubes

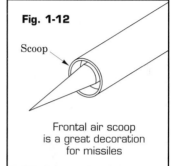

Fig. 1-12

Scoop

Frontal air scoop is a great decoration for missiles

of using simulated tunnels is that they add strength to the tube.

Equipment Pods and Air Scoops: Equipment pods are used to store and protect delicate cargo, and air scoops allow air inside the aircraft. Adding either of these features to your rocket can dramatically change its appearance. Construction of these components is fairly easy, as they can be made out of cardboard, plastic, or balsa wood.

Forward Fins and Stabilizing Vanes: In addition to having fins at the rear of the rocket, they can placed at the nose, middle, or tail. Vanes are the same as fins, but are usually much longer. Although they add a distinctive

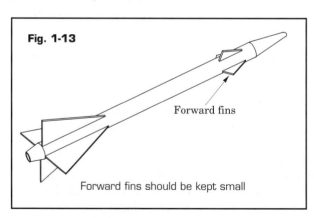

Fig. 1-13

Forward fins

Forward fins should be kept small

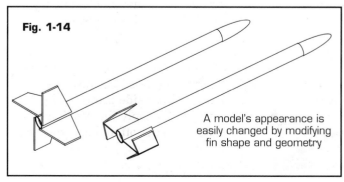

Fig. 1-14

A model's appearance is easily changed by modifying fin shape and geometry

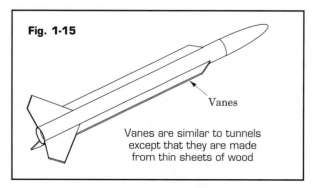

Fig. 1-15

Vanes

Vanes are similar to tunnels except that they are made from thin sheets of wood

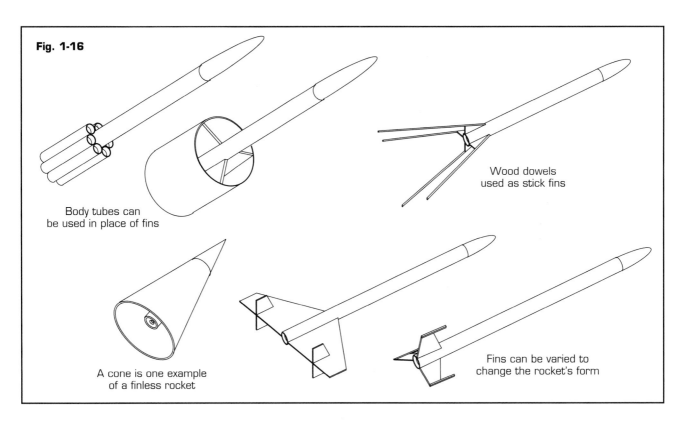

Fig. 1-16

Body tubes can be used in place of fins

Wood dowels used as stick fins

A cone is one example of a finless rocket

Fins can be varied to change the rocket's form

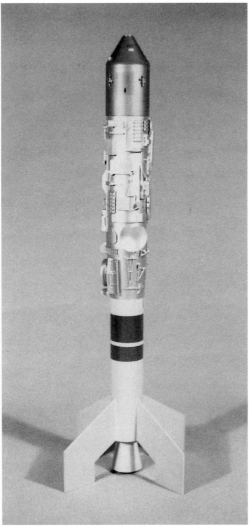

This complex looking rocket was constructed by gluing plastic model parts to the side of rocket tube (photo by Steven A. Bachmeyer).

look to the model, forward fins and vanes should be small because they can cause the rocket to become unstable. Always perform a stability check before flying a model equipped with forward fins or vanes.

Fin Geometry and Shape: By changing the geometry, the number, or the size of the fins, you can completely change the overall appearance of the model. Fins are usually made out of flat balsa sheet, but you don't have to limit yourself to that material—or to a flat shape. You can make stabilizing fins out of plastic, paper, wood dowels, or even hollow body tubes. The model does not even have to use any fins if you use cone stability, as described in Chapter 2.

Extraneous Details: Like adding a different paint pattern or using a lot of decals, adding three-dimensional components to the outside can enhance the look of a basic rocket. These details can be simple pieces of wood or extra parts from a plastic airplane kit. Adding them to the rocket is as easy as gluing them to the side of the body tube.

Body Tube Shape: You can vary not only the diameter but the shape of the body tube as well. Why not change the

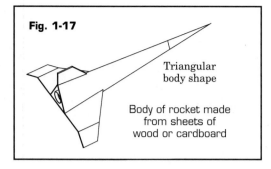

Fig. 1-17

Triangular body shape

Body of rocket made from sheets of wood or cardboard

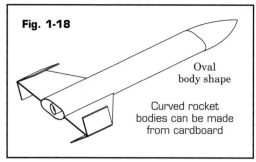

Fig. 1-18

Oval body shape

Curved rocket bodies can be made from cardboard

shape from a circle to an oval or to a square? Materials for the body of the rocket need not include only paper. You can carve the body out of a block of balsa and build it up using sheets of cardboard, plastic, or balsa wood.

Parts of a Model Rocket: The Basic Building Components

Figures 1-19 through 1-21 show the basic parts used in most all model rockets. Use the illustrations and definitions below during the design phase of your project.

Body Tube—A specially wound and treated cardboard or plastic cylinder used to make the fuselage or main body of the rocket.

Centering Ring—A circular frame or bulkhead that concentrically aligns and firmly secures one body tube inside another of larger diameter.

Engine Block—A bulkhead placed directly in front of a rocket engine to prevent the engine from sliding forward into the rocket.

Engine Hook—A bent piece of metal with a small angle at one end that holds the rocket engine securely in the engine mount.

Fig. 1-19

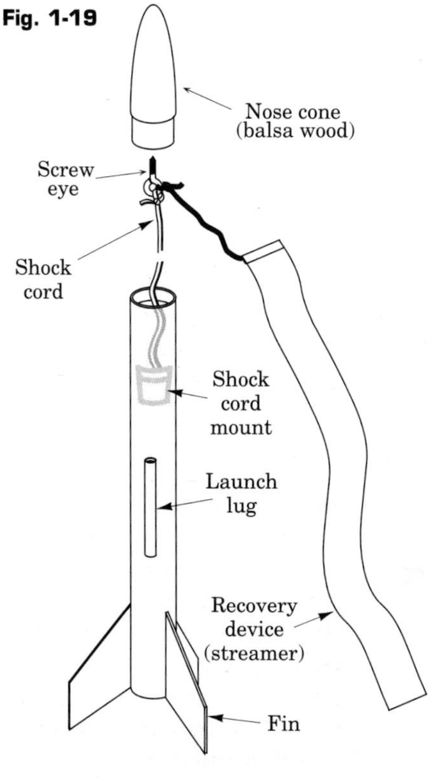

Nose cone (balsa wood)

Screw eye

Shock cord

Shock cord mount

Launch lug

Recovery device (streamer)

Fin

The basic parts of a model rocket

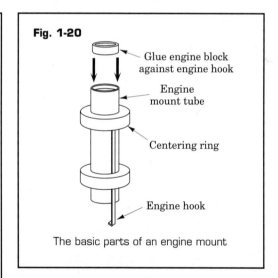

Fig. 1-20

Glue engine block against engine hook

Engine mount tube

Centering ring

Engine hook

The basic parts of an engine mount

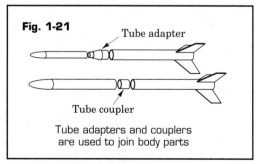

Fig. 1-21

Tube adapter

Tube coupler

Tube adapters and couplers are used to join body parts

2

Stability: Getting Rockets to Fly Straight

This is a tower launcher actually used by NASA to impart spin to a small sounding rocket (photo by Tim Van Milligan).

Stability is the ability of a rocket or airplane to maintain its attitude or resist displacement, and if displaced, to develop forces that restore the original condition. A stable rocket travels in a relatively straight line, while an unstable rocket constantly turns its nose away from the intended flight path. An unstable rocket has a good chance of crashing at a high velocity.

The difference between a stable and an unstable rocket can mean the difference between a safe and an unsafe rocket. This is why stability is so important, and why we talk about it here at the beginning of this book. You can almost equate stability with safety.

Two properties of the rocket are used to determine its stability—the location of the rocket's center-of-gravity (CG), and the location of its center-of-pressure (CP). The relationship between these two entities determines if the rocket will be stable or unstable. Simply stated, for a model to fly in a stable manner, the location of the center-of-gravity must be forward of the location of its center-of-pressure.

Center of Gravity

The CG is the point where the rocket will balance. It is also the location about which the model will rotate if unrestrained. It is easy to picture the center of gravity and just as simple to locate it on your rocket.

To find the location of the CG, simply balance your rocket on the edge of a ruler.

⊙ **CP Symbol**

⊕ **CG Symbol**

When it balances without falling one way or the other, the edge of the ruler is at the rocket's CG. When you perform this test, balance the rocket in its flight-ready condition—that is, install the parachute, recovery wadding, and an unused engine. You don't need to install the igniter because that will no longer be attached to the rocket after liftoff. After you find the CG, mark the position on the rocket, either by labeling it "CG," or by using the symbol for center-of-gravity (⊕).

Fig. 2-1

Balance point = CG

Ruler

Engine and recovery system installed

Locating the rocket's center-of-gravity

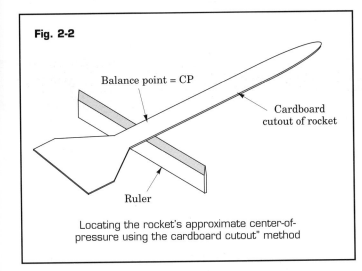

Fig. 2-2

Balance point = CP

Cardboard cutout of rocket

Ruler

Locating the rocket's approximate center-of-pressure using the cardboard cutout" method

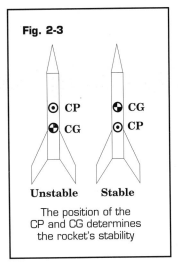

Fig. 2-3

CP

CG

CG

CP

Unstable   **Stable**

The position of the CP and CG determines the rocket's stability

Center of Pressure

The location where all the aerodynamic forces acting on a rocket balance is called the center-of-pressure (CP). In an airplane it is often referred to as the aerodynamic center (AC). At this point the aerodynamic forces acting on the front of the rocket are equal to the forces acting on the back. Every rocket moving through the air has a CP, just as it has a CG.

The hard part is determining the location of the CP. The most accurate method is to test the rocket in a wind tunnel and measure the forces trying to rotate the model. By moving the pivot point holding the rocket and measuring the forces, you can find the CP at the point when the forces acting on the pivot become zero. Not many people have a wind tunnel, so this method may be impractical.

Since the CP is based on the shape of the model and the size and location of the fins, the next method of determining its location is to solve a series of mathematical equations. If you plan to create a lot of rockets with the classic rocket shape, you might consider computerizing these equations or buying a computer program for it. Information on these equations is available from the National Association of Rocketry, whose address is listed at the end of this book. At present, the equations and computer programs used to determine the CP location are limited to models that are generally long and slender and have the classic rocket shape. If the model has wings, pods, vanes, or a different shape, the equations are no longer valid and can

not accurately determine the CP location.

If you want a quick way to determine the approximate location of the CP, the cardboard cutout method will work. Make a cutout of the outline of the rocket from of a piece of stiff cardboard and balance this cutout on the edge of a ruler. The balance point will be at the approximate CP location. This method is not exact, but it will give you a starting point for determining the location of the CP, so you can fly your rocket.

When you know the location of the center-of-pressure, mark it on the model either using the letters "CP" or its symbol (⊙). Compare this location to that of the center-of-gravity. If the CP is behind the CG the model should be stable. But because of the uncertainties in determining the location of the CP, build a safety factor into the rocket before you fly it: make sure the CG is at least one body-tube diameter ahead of the CP. This is called one-caliber stability. If the CG is two body-tube diameters ahead of the CP, you will have two-caliber stability.

A final check of stability can be done prior to flight by performing a swing test of the model in its liftoff condition (with

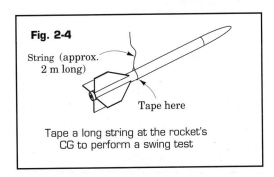

Fig. 2-4

String (approx. 2 m long)

Tape here

Tape a long string at the rocket's CG to perform a swing test

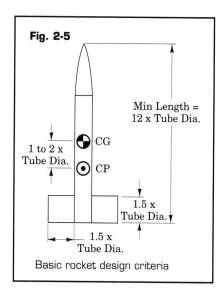

Fig. 2-5

Min Length = 12 x Tube Dia.

CG

CP

1 to 2 x Tube Dia.

1.5 x Tube Dia.

1.5 x Tube Dia.

Basic rocket design criteria

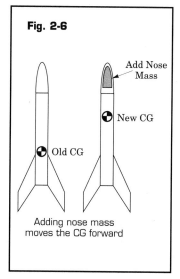

Fig. 2-6

Add Nose Mass

New CG

Old CG

Adding nose mass moves the CG forward

unproven model, fly it in complete isolation from persons not participating in the actual launch. Also, try to find a very large field from which to launch your rocket. Always follow the model rocket safety code.

Correcting Rocket Instability

There are two ways to correct instability: moving the CG forward, and/or moving the CP rearward.

You can move the CG forward a couple of ways. First, look for ways to remove mass from the rear of the rocket. Maybe your design calls for a pod near the fins. If your rocket suffers from instability you could remove this weight.

If you can't remove any mass from the rear of the rocket, you might add some to the front. Just remember, adding mass lowers the altitude the model will reach. When adding extra mass, always check to be sure the model's lift-off mass does not exceed the mass the selected rocket engine can safely lift.

The best place to position extra mass is as close to the tip of the nose as possible. If your design calls for a model with a plastic nose cone, you could push some modeling clay directly into the hollow area. For balsa nose cones, attach washers to the base of the nose with a small steel screw eye.

You can also move the CG forward by lengthening the body tube. This has the same effect as adding nose cone weight, and you will probably add less mass by increasing the length of the tube.

Recessing the engine into the body tube can also move the CG forward, but be careful not to place it too far forward,

parachute, wadding, and unburnt engine installed). Make a loop in a long piece of string of the same diameter as the body tube of the rocket. Slip the loop over the rocket and tape it at the CG location you marked. Now swing the rocket horizontally while holding the free end of the string. It should fly straight if it is stable and therefore safe to launch. If it flies in some position other than nose first, it is unstable or at best, neutral stable. Correct these conditions before launching.

The swing test is conservative and sometimes doesn't work even though the rocket was shown to be stable by other methods. The string may not be long enough for the rocket to fly straight, or the velocity may not be high enough for the fins to generate sufficient restoring forces. The purpose of the swing test is to give confidence in a design, not to prove it unstable.

Finally, as the model rocket safety code dictates, on the first flight of an

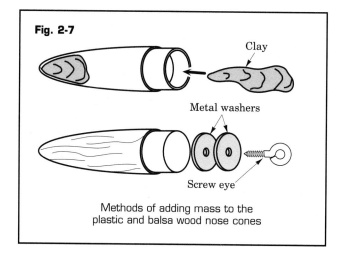

Fig. 2-7

Clay

Metal washers

Screw eye

Methods of adding mass to the plastic and balsa wood nose cones

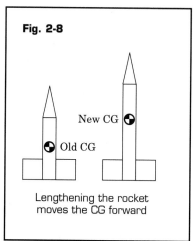

Fig. 2-8

New CG

Old CG

Lengthening the rocket moves the CG forward

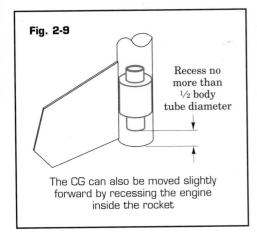

Fig. 2-9

Recess no more than ½ body tube diameter

The CG can also be moved slightly forward by recessing the engine inside the rocket

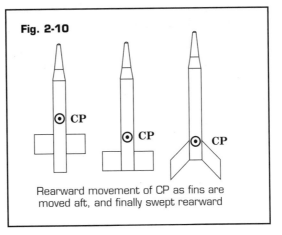

Fig. 2-10

CP CP CP

Rearward movement of CP as fins are moved aft, and finally swept rearward

or it may burn the aft end of the body tube and cause a loss of thrust. This loss of thrust is termed the Kushnerik effect. The nozzle of the motor should be no more than one half body tube diameter into the tube.

You can move the CP rearward by moving the fins rearward on the body tube or sweeping them toward the rear. Another way is to increase the area of the fins. As a rule of thumb, the fin size should be at least 1.5 body tube diameters wide and long. If you need more area, it is more effective to increase the span than to increase the length.

If your design has small forward wings or fins forward of the CG, you may want to remove them too. Forward fins are destabilizing and should be used with caution. If the rocket proves unstable, reduce the size of these fins or remove them completely.

If your motor is canted, or off the centerline of the model, the fins must be much larger to provide the restoring force needed to overcome the unbalanced force of the engine. This is why you should always keep the thrust forces concentric around the centerline of the model. If you do not, the rocket may become unstable as soon as it clears the launch rod.

Besides moving the CP or the CG, you might be able to correct instability by causing the rocket to spin on the way up. This is called spin stabilization. The spinning action creates angular momentum, which provides inherent stability (think of a toy spinning top or a gyroscope) and cancels out any unbalanced forces acting on a rocket, such as that produced by one fin creating more lift than the other fins.

Spinning the rocket can be accomplished in four ways. You can cant the fins on the body tube at some small angle; you can add small canted tabs to the bottom of existing fins; you can sand each of the fins so they have a cambered airfoil shape; or you can use a specially designed tower, such as the one shown in the photo at the beginning of this chapter, to impart a spin to the model.

The drawback to spinning is the amount of drag it produces. This increase in drag will reduce the overall height the model is capable of achieving.

Rockets with small fins have a harder time producing the necessary forces to restore the model to the correct flight path. To help increase these forces you can increase the velocity. More air flowing over the fins will produce larger restoring forces. You can increase speed by reducing drag or selecting an engine that produces more thrust. Both of these topics are covered elsewhere in this book.

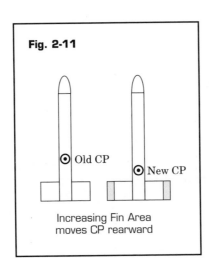

Fig. 2-11

Old CP New CP

Increasing Fin Area moves CP rearward

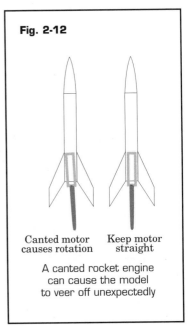

Fig. 2-12

Canted motor causes rotation   Keep motor straight

A canted rocket engine can cause the model to veer off unexpectedly

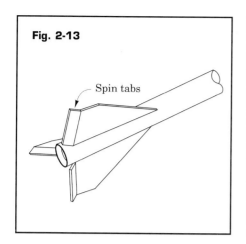

Fig. 2-13

Spin tabs

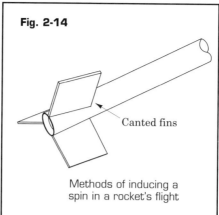

Fig. 2-14

Canted fins

Methods of inducing a spin in a rocket's flight

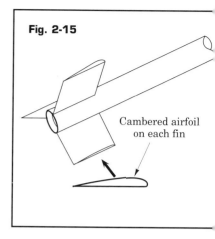

Fig. 2-15

Cambered airfoil on each fin

How to Increase Rocket Stability:

A. Move CG forward
1. Decrease mass at rear of rocket
2. Add mass to nose cone
3. Lengthen rocket body tube
4. Recess engine inside body tube

B. Move CP rearward
1. Move fins rearward
2. Eliminate any "forward" fins
3. Sweep fins to the rear
4. Increase fin area
5. Increase number of fins

C. Other methods
1. Insure proper alignment of rocket engine
2. Cause rocket to rotate with spin fins
3. Use a higher thrust motor
4. Make rocket fly faster by minimizing aerodynamic drag

Cone Stability: The shape of the rocket also plays a role in its stability. If the rocket is generally cone-shaped, it may not need stabilizing fins at all. Cones have an inherent stability, and the CP is located ⅔ of the way back from the tip toward the base of the cone. So if the CG is forward of this location, the rocket will be stable. To move the CG forward, add mass to the nose in front of the recovery device and/or recess the engine into the base of the cone.

Things to Avoid That May Cause Instability:

Fins forward of the CG

Fins that are too small

Short rockets

Off-center or canted motors

Heavy, slow-moving rockets

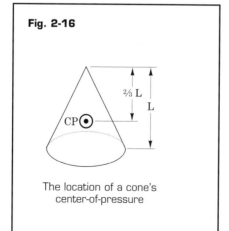

Fig. 2-16

⅔ L

L

CP

The location of a cone's center-of-pressure

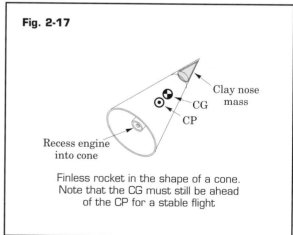

Fig. 2-17

Clay nose mass

CG

CP

Recess engine into cone

Finless rocket in the shape of a cone. Note that the CG must still be ahead of the CP for a stable flight

3

Drag Reduction and Aerodynamics

Aerodynamics is the science that deals with the motion of gases and with the forces acting on solid bodies when they move through gases. Why is aerodynamics so important in rocketry? First, an understanding of aerodynamics allows you to control the forces acting on a rocket. In Chapter 2 you learned why it is important to keep your rocket stable. Studying the forces acting on a rocket allows you to determine whether or not it will be stable and how you can correct any problems.

The second reason for understanding aerodynamics is that by controlling the forces you can increase the performance of your rockets. This will allow the rocket to travel higher, or enable you to launch heavier payloads in existing rockets. This chapter deals chiefly with drag. The greater this force, the more it robs rockets of maximum altitude or the ability to carry heavier payloads.

Rocket Drag

Aerodynamic drag, or simply drag, is the resistance or friction force experienced by any object moving through air. All rockets have a drag force, and although it cannot be eliminated, it can be reduced. Knowing what factors cause an increase in drag will allow you to make rocket designs that will minimize it.

The factors that affect the drag force are velocity, air density, the frontal area exposed to the oncoming air, and a unitless factor called the coefficient of drag.

Mathematically the drag force experienced by a rocket can be expressed by the following equation:

Bob Koenn helps his son, Matthew, place a rocket into a tower launcher. Using a tower eliminates the need for a launch lug, which produces a lot of drag on the rocket (photo by Tim Van Milligan).

$$D = \tfrac{1}{2}\, C_d \rho V^2 A$$
where:
D = Drag force on the rocket
A = Frontal area
V = Velocity of rocket
ρ = Density of air
C_d = Coefficient of drag

If you look at each of the factors contributing to the overall drag on the rocket, you can search for those you can control. Once you know how to reduce drag, you can design more efficient rockets.

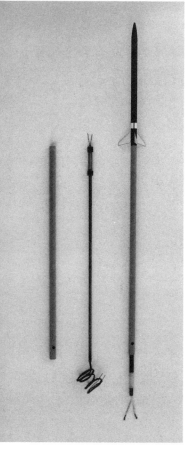

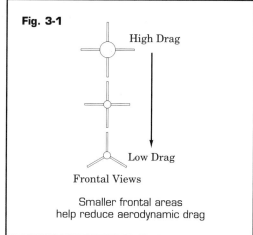

Fig. 3-1

High Drag

Low Drag

Frontal Views

Smaller frontal areas
help reduce aerodynamic drag

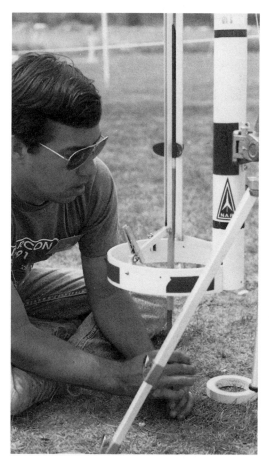

Above left: The main components of a piston launcher in unassembled form (left), and a small rocket on a piston in launch configuration (right). (photo by Ed LaCroix) **Above right**: Bob Koenn centers a piston launcher under a high performance rocket. A piston launcher is used to increase the lift-off velocity of a rocket, allowing it to fly higher. Typically, piston launchers are used with tower launchers for extra safety during liftoff. (photo by Tim Van Milligan)

Frontal area: The frontal area is what you would see if you were looking directly down on a rocket as it sits on a launch pad. If the frontal area is small, the total drag on the rocket is small.

The frontal area is dictated by several factors. If you have a payload vehicle you might be limited by the size of the cargo you intend to launch. Similarly, if you are launching a glider, the wings may project far out and you may not be able to reduce this area. But if you want a rocket that will use every amount of available power from the engine in the most efficient

manner, you'll want to use the smallest diameter body tube in which the engine will fit. This is called a minimum diameter model.

The other way to reduce frontal area is to decrease the number of fins to the minimum necessary to keep the model stable. This means using three fins. You'll also want to eliminate any extraneous protuberances from the rocket, such as pods, scoops, pylons, any extraneous details, and the launch lug. Studies have shown that the launch lug contributes up to 30 percent of the total rocket drag. This drag can be reduced by streamlining it, but for maximum performance it will have to be eliminated.

With the elimination of the launch lug the model will still requires support during launch until it reaches a speed great enough that the aerodynamic forces on the fins are large enough to stabilize it. Two ways to supply this support are the tower launcher and the pop-off launch lug. Figures 3-4, 3-5, and 3-6 illustrate how each of these methods

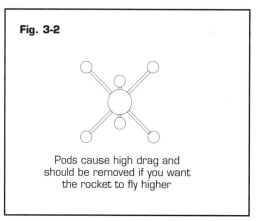

Fig. 3-2

Pods cause high drag and should be removed if you want the rocket to fly higher

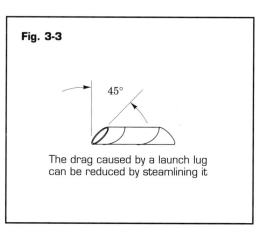

Fig. 3-3

45°

The drag caused by a launch lug can be reduced by steamlining it

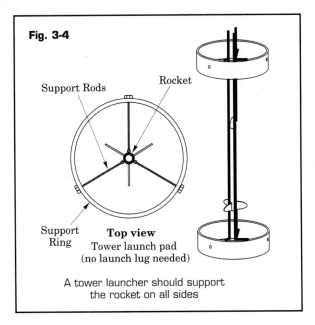

Fig. 3-4

Support Rods

Rocket

Support Ring

Top view
Tower launch pad
(no launch lug needed)

A tower launcher should support
the rocket on all sides

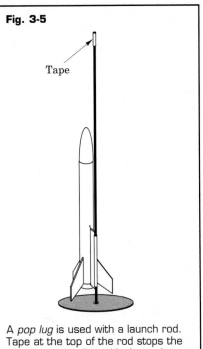

Fig. 3-5

Tape

A *pop lug* is used with a launch rod.
Tape at the top of the rod stops the
lug from traveling with the rocket

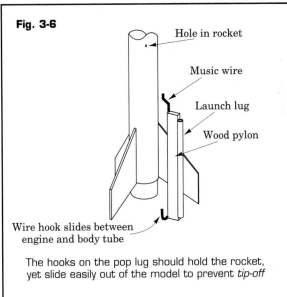

Fig. 3-6

Hole in rocket

Music wire

Launch lug

Wood pylon

Wire hook slides between
engine and body tube

The hooks on the pop lug should hold the rocket,
yet slide easily out of the model to prevent *tip-off*

works. A third alternative, the piston launcher, is also available but should only be used on small models with liftoff masses of under 150 grams (5.3 ounces). A piston launcher uses gases produced by the engine to create a large pressure under the rocket that kicks it into the air at a high velocity. It works like a cannon. A diagram of a piston launcher is shown in Figure 3-7.

Making the rocket stable also reduces its frontal area. When a rocket is unstable the nose turns to the side, exposing the side to the oncoming airstream. Keeping it stable eliminates the possibility of this happening and minimizes the drag force.

Velocity of the Rocket: In reviewing the drag equation you can see the detrimental effect of having a rocket flying very fast. If you have two exactly similar rockets, but one flies twice as fast as the other, the faster one will have four times as much drag as the other. This extra drag will reduce the maximum altitude of the rocket. So if you want a rocket that goes to the highest altitudes, you want it to travel as slowly as possible while still stable and safe.

The velocity is determined by the type of rocket engine you use and can be controlled by the designer. The best altitude is achieved when the sustaining thrust level is two times the weight of the rocket. See Chapter 15 on rocket engine selection for more information.

Are there times when you want the rocket to go as fast as possible? Yes. Some people just like to see rockets that are visible one second and disappear the next. A lot of times this can be great fun. You may also want the rocket to go fast so it becomes aerodynamically stable. Flying very fast can make a marginally stable rocket more stable by increasing the amount of air flowing over the fins.

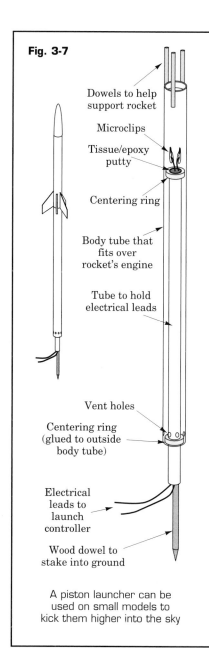

Fig. 3-7

Dowels to help support rocket

Microclips

Tissue/epoxy putty

Centering ring

Body tube that fits over rocket's engine

Tube to hold electrical leads

Vent holes

Centering ring (glued to outside body tube)

Electrical leads to launch controller

Wood dowel to stake into ground

A piston launcher can be used on small models to kick them higher into the sky

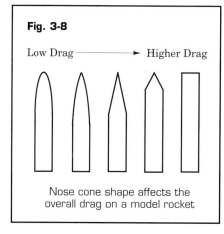

Fig. 3-8

Low Drag ⟶ Higher Drag

Nose cone shape affects the overall drag on a model rocket

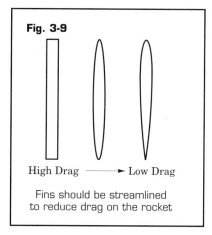

Fig. 3-9

High Drag ⟶ Low Drag

Fins should be streamlined to reduce drag on the rocket

Density of Air: The number of air molecules per unit volume is called density. According to the drag equation, as the density increases the total drag force increases. Likewise, when the density decreases, the drag force decreases. Can the density of air be controlled by the rocket designer? Unfortunately, no. The only way you can decrease the density is to launch on a hot, dry day or from the top of a mountain.

Drag Coefficient: As I mentioned, the drag coefficient is a unitless number that is difficult to determine without actual wind tunnel tests. This number takes into consideration several factors that contribute to the overall drag of the model—form drag, induced drag, interference drag, and skin friction drag.

Form drag is related to the shape of the rocket. For example, a rounded shape has less drag than a blunt shape. Figure 3-8 shows which nose cone shape will have lower drag. Similarly, streamlining the fins into a teardrop shape—that is, making them round at the leading edge and tapering them to the trailing edge as shown in Figure 3-9—will also lead to a lower value of form drag.

A smooth transition between body tubes of different diameter is essential to minimizing form drag. This is

accomplished with the aid of a tube adapter. Adapters are given special names corresponding to their orientation. When the smaller tube is toward the front of the model the adapter is called a shoulder; when the smaller tube is to the rear the transition section is called a boattail, or reducer.

Boattails greatly reduce form drag and should be used wherever possible. For example, if you have a small engine mount tube inside a large body tube, use a boattail transition, as Figure 3-11 shows. Hollow boattails can be made from paper, balsa, or plastic. Paper transitions are the least expensive and are relatively easy to construct. See Chapter 6 for the steps necessary to create a properly fitted paper adapter.

If you want an even greater reduction in form drag, consider using a transition in the shape of a parabola, since it will produce less form drag than a cone. To

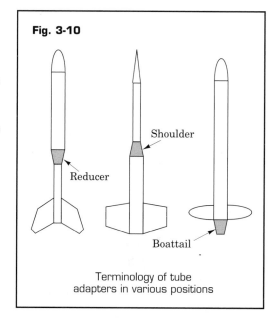

Fig. 3-10

Shoulder

Reducer

Boattail

Terminology of tube adapters in various positions

create a parabolic adapter, start with a nose cone of balsa wood or plastic. Plastic nose cones are easily modified by cutting off the base and the tip. Balsa nose cones are somewhat more complicated: you have to split the piece in half, cut off the tip, hollow out the inside, and glue the halves back together again (Fig. 3-13).

Skin friction drag occurs when air particles in the airstream are slowed down by the surface of the rocket as it travels through the air. It can be reduced by making the surface of the rocket slick and smooth. A good paint finish will help keep skin friction drag low. To make this component of the total drag force as low as possible, fill all seams in the body tube, fill and sand all the balsa wood to a smooth finish, and remove all thick decals and decorative tape. You might even buff the rocket with a rubbing compound to smooth and deburr the paint. If it looks dull after this step, apply a coat of wax over the top of the finish.

The gap between the nose cone and the body tube usually is insignificant, but for optimum performance, eliminate this gap. Glue the nose cone onto the body tube and fill and smooth the gap. The recovery system on such a model has to come out of the back end. This is called rear ejection. An alternative is mid-body ejection. Although the gap persists, it is located farther aft of the nose, where it doesn't create as much drag. Figure 3-4 shows how mid-body ejection is accomplished.

Sometimes people combine the skin friction drag and the form drag. This combination is called profile drag.

When two parts of an airplane or rocket are in close proximity to each other their combined drag is greater than their respective drags if tested individually. It is called interference drag. Reduce this type of drag by eliminating all the unnecessary parts on the rocket, including the launch lug. Additionally, when two parts come together on a rocket they should be faired in so there are no sharp corners. For example, a fillet of glue applied between the fin and the body tube where they join not only reduces drag, it increases the strength of the glue joint (see Fig. 6-21).

Induced drag is produced whenever an airfoil produces lift. It is a result of air

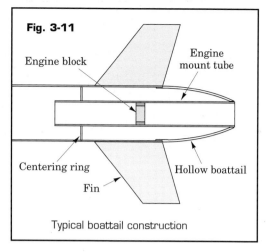

Fig. 3-11

Engine block

Engine mount tube

Centering ring

Fin

Hollow boattail

Typical boattail construction

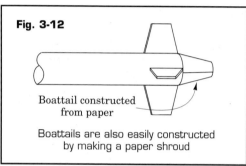

Fig. 3-12

Boattail constructed from paper

Boattails are also easily constructed by making a paper shroud

flowing around the corners of a wing or fin tip from the high-pressure side to the low-pressure side. Making the air change direction to flow around the corner takes energy, and this robbing of the rocket's kinetic energy is called induced drag. On airplanes or gliders it is impossible to eliminate induced drag because you want to produce lift. You can reduce it, however, by modifying the shape of the wing or fins. Figure 3-15 shows what wing shapes will yield lower values for induced drag. Winglets—small, nearly vertical plates mounted to the tips of the glider's main wing—can also help reduce induced drag (Fig. 3-16).

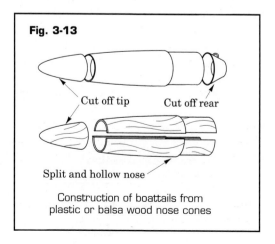

Fig. 3-13

Cut off tip

Cut off rear

Split and hollow nose

Construction of boattails from plastic or balsa wood nose cones

Rear ejection pops the engine and recovery device out the back end of the rocket. This permits the gap between the nose and body tube to be filled and sanded smooth. This photo shows streamer recovery, but parachute recovery is also possible (photo by Steven A. Bachmeyer).

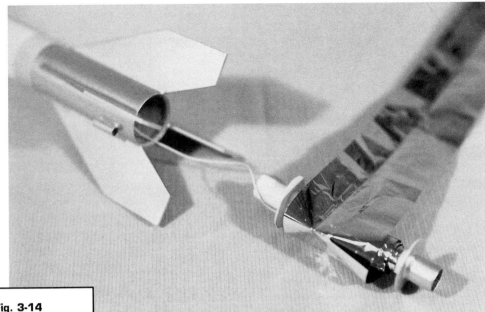

Fig. 3-14

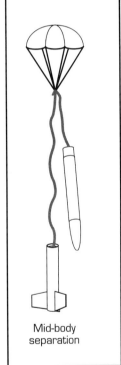

Mid-body separation

Fig. 3-15

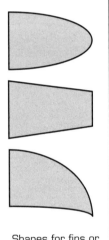

Shapes for fins or wings that have low induced drag values

On rockets, you can also lower induced drag by using proper fin shape and by making the rocket stable. A stable rocket does not tend to wobble, so the fins do not have to create a restoring force to correct that tendency. Because of this, the induced drag is very low. It is important that all fins be perfectly aligned along the rocket body and that each has a perfectly symmetrical airfoil section (streamlined shape) (See Fig. 3-9).

Methods of Reducing Aerodynamic Drag

A. Decrease frontal area of rocket
1. Use smaller diameter body tubes
2. Decrease number of fins
3. Eliminate nonessential protuberances

B. Reduce Velocity of Rocket
1. Use a low-thrust rocket engine

C. Reduce the Rocket's Drag Coefficient
1. Reduce form drag by streamlining rocket
2. Streamline fins
3. Give the rocket a smooth painted surface
4. Add fillets to fins and other parts that protrude away from body tube

Fig. 3-16

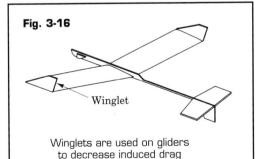

Winglet

Winglets are used on gliders to decrease induced drag

Construction Tools

Construction will go much faster and the parts will fit more closely if you have the proper tools for the job. The following list describes the basic tools you'll need to build your rocket design and explains why you need them. You probably already have most of these tools; if not, you can find them easily at hobby shops, hardware stores, and craft stores.

Essential Construction Tools

Hobby knife. The hobby knife has a very sharp, pointed blade. It is used for cutting cardboard, balsa wood, and body tubes. You will find it almost indispensable in the work of building model rockets. It's very sharp, so be careful with it, as it will easily cut through flesh, too. The blades can be brittle, and it's possible for the tip to snap off; so always wear safety goggles when cutting anything with a hobby knife.

Adhesives. Adhesives are used to join things together. There are several types, and each has a particular area where they work best.

Wood glue. It is much stronger and dries faster than ordinary white glue. Once dried it does not soften when exposed to moisture. Sometimes this glue is called aliphatic resin. It is used for any paper-to-paper, paper-to-wood, or wood-to-wood bond. It works by penetrating into the fibers of the paper and wood and creating tiny fingers that grasp the fibers. This requires that the glue come into direct contact with the fibers of the material, so remove any paint, filler, or other substance from the surfaces being joined. This glue does not work on plastics. Wood glue shrinks slightly when it dries, and

this may affect the appearance of your rocket if you use it for fin fillets. To improve the appearance of wood glue shrinkage, apply a second fillet of ordinary white glue on top of dried wood glue. Although not as strong, the white glue does not shrink when it dries.

Super glue. Technically known as cyanoacrylate, this glue can be used on a variety of materials. It creates a very strong surface bond, so it works best when the materials being joined have smooth surfaces. It will bond most materials and is probably the best adhesive to use when bonding plastic to wood. As the name implies, this glue hardens very quickly and sometimes almost violently, bubbling up instead of turning hard. This happens when the application is too thick or when it is accelerated too fast. The accelerator is sold as a non-aerosol pump atomizer and is sometimes called kicker. It makes the adhesive harden nearly instantaneously.

(photo by Steven A. Bachmeyer)

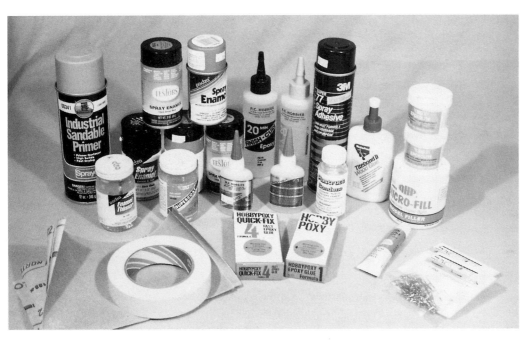

Plastic model cement, glue, epoxy, fillers, primer, and paints each have a specific use during the construction of a model rocket. (photo by Steven A. Bachmeyer)

wing cores. It is usually sold in an aerosol can.

Epoxy. Epoxy is a two-part adhesive that is mixed together before it is applied. It is a chemical cure, which does not rely on evaporation of solvents to complete the hardening process. It works well in the same places as instant glue but gives a much stronger bond although it takes longer to harden. You can buy it in thick or thin viscosities, as well as in various cure times from 5 minutes to 24 hours. In general, the longer the cure time, the stronger the bond. You can accelerate the cure time slightly by warming the epoxy with a hair dryer (no open-flame heating devices) after application. Heat will cause the epoxy to thin out and become runny before it hardens. Be sure to anticipate this, because it could run off the model.

Tape. Tape is used to hold parts together temporarily. Two types of tape are used in construction: masking tape and cellophane (clear plastic) tape. Masking tape is used extensively during general-purpose construction, while cellophane tape has a more specific purpose. It is used during painting to create sharp lines between colors. Masking tape does not work as well for this because the paint seeps under the edges, leaving a jagged edge between colors.

Ruler. The ruler makes length measurements of parts and serves as a straightedge for marking and cutting. I recommend a steel ruler over wood because it is usually more accurate and the edge will stay straight for years. You won't be slicing off parts of a steel ruler with your knife when you use it as a straightedge, either.

Scissors. Scissors are used to cut cloth, thin paper, thin plywood, and plastic sheet. Buy a good sharp pair and they will last you a long time.

Use caution with this glue because it instantly bonds to skin. Wear safety goggles to protect your eyes from accidental splatters.

Super glue comes in a variety of viscosities, from water-thin to syrupy thick. The thin kind works well on close-fitting parts, while the thick fills gaps between loose-fitting parts. Some super glues are compatible with expanded styrene foam, but before you try gluing styrene foam, make sure the bottle says it can be used for this purpose. Also, don't use any kicker on foam, because it will melt the foam. The foam-safe variety of cyanoacrylate is sometimes known as odorless glue, because it does not give off any odor when it hardens.

Plastic model cement. Use this glue only on styrene plastics. It works by melting the surfaces of the parts being bonded and fusing them together. It will not work on plastic-to-paper or plastic-to-wood bonds. Plastic model cement comes in two varieties, a water-thin type and a clear paste. Apply the thin variety with a paint brush; it works best when the parts being joined have no gaps between them. The clear paste is sold in a small tube.

Contact cement. This is another surface bonding agent, as it does not penetrate the fibers of paper or wood. You can use it to bond paper to plastic, but the bond will be very weak. The best time to use this type of adhesive is when you're laminating paper sheets together or bonding thin balsa skins onto foam

Pencil. Use pencil instead of ink or marker when building rockets. Ink will bleed through paint and mar the finish of an otherwise great-looking rocket.

Wood sealers. Use wood sealer to fill the voids and grain of balsa wood. Apply it in liquid form with a paint brush and sand it smooth when dry. Most times, use several applications of sealer to completely fill the wood and give it an even surface.

Paint and primer. Paint the rocket when construction is complete. Apply primer first, as it is formulated to bond to most surfaces. Choose a primer that is sandable. You may have to remove it by sanding to fix the flaws. Apply paint after the primer has completely dried. For the best finish choose an aerosol paint.

Solvents. Solvents are used to clean up after the painting is finished. Soak paint brushes in solvent for a few minutes to rid them of excess paint. Most solvents will work with only a certain type of paint, so always read the labels carefully. All solvents should be used with care, since they can cause chemical burns if they come in contact with your skin. When you're using solvents, always wear safety goggles to protect your eyes. Always use solvents in a well-ventilated area and follow the cautions printed on the container.

Sandpaper. Sandpaper is used to shape or smooth a part. It is graded by its grit number. A low number means the surface of the paper is very rough, while a high number means the paper has a smoother surface. Low numbers, under 150 grit, are used for rough shaping. Intermediate numbers, from 150 to 320, are for initial smoothing of a surface. High numbers, over 400 grit, are for final smoothing and polishing.

Paint brushes. Use paint brushes for more than applying paint. You can also use them for cleaning parts and applying liquid plastic cement. For rocket work, you'll want at least three brushes—small, medium, and wide. Choose a brush with good natural bristles that don't pull out easily.

Filler paste. Use filler paste to fill wide gaps between parts and to make fillets along the joint where the fins meet the body tube. It is sold in either a tube or a

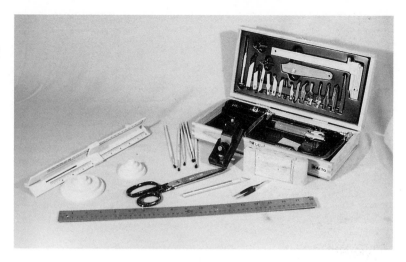

Proper tools make rocket construction more accurate and decrease assembly time. (photo by Steven A. Bachmeyer)

small jar. Many of the newer pastes are water soluble. They can be thinned with water if they start to dry out and have no unpleasant odors. Select a paste that is sandable, because you always have to sand a filled surface to prepare it for priming. An alternative is carpenter's spackle, found at hardware stores.

Work surface. The table on which you build your rocket should be large enough to spread out your parts and should have a smooth, even surface. Protect the surface of your work area with a large piece of plastic sheet. When cutting with a hobby knife, lay a piece of heavy cardboard over the plastic to prevent the knife from scoring through the plastic and into the table.

Optional Construction Tools

Razor saw. For cutting plywood, thick wood, and plastic.

Sanding block. A flat block of wood to which sandpaper is attached; use it to accurately shape or smooth any parts or surfaces.

Razor planer. Use a razor planer to shave thin layers of wood off a larger piece of wood, dramatically decreasing the time it takes to rough-shape a piece of wood. Great for making airfoils on fins and glider wings.

Tweezers. For holding small parts.

Files. Use files to rough-shape wood or plastic parts. They are available in a variety of sizes, shapes, and surface textures. Small files, typically called jeweler's files, are great for model rocketry work.

5

Basic Raw Materials

Materials—*My model rockets will be made of lightweight materials such as paper, wood, rubber, and plastic suitable for the power used and performance of my model rocket. I will not use any metal for the nose cone, body, or fins of a model rocket.*

This is the very first paragraph in the safety code used by all rocketeers. The founding members of the National Association of Rocketry knew the materials used in rocketry could affect the overall safety of the hobby. Before this safety code was written people thought it was normal to launch metal projectiles from their back yards. This rule was implemented to keep you safe.

Many materials are used in model rocketry. When choosing them, try to use lightweight materials with good strength characteristics. You want your rockets to be strong to survive the forces that occur during launch and landing so they can be used time and again. Keeping the mass of models low allows them to fly to high altitudes and accomplish other great feats; moreover, low mass means less potential for damage to people and property around your launch ranges. Below are some of the many materials available to the model rocket designer and their chief characteristics.

This rocket was made from a plastic model kit of a USAF Bomarc. These rockets are called "plastic model conversions." (photo by Marc Lavigne)

Balsa wood

Balsa wood is the miracle material of the hobby world. It has the best strength-to-weight ratio of any readily available material. Known for its high strength and low density, it can be easily shaped, sanded, glued, and painted. It is nontoxic, biodegradable, and absorbs shocks and vibrations well. Balsa wood is imported from plantations in South America; don't worry about destroying the rain forests by using this wood—it grows incredibly fast; an average of 60 to 90 feet tall in 6 to 10 years, with a diameter of about 45 inches. Because of its versatility and strength, balsa wood can be used extensively in your rockets. Typical uses include nose cones, wings, fuselages, and fins.

Balsa can be purchased in almost any hobby shop, and it comes in strips, sheets, planks and blocks. Strips sizes can range from 0.79 mm (⅟₃₂") x 0.79 mm (⅟₃₂") to 2.5 cm x 2.5 cm (1" x 1"); sheets are available in thickness up to 6.35 mm (¼"), and widths are typically 7.6 cm (3 inch) or 10.1 cm (4"). Anything larger is considered a plank or block of balsa.

You can use strips for making surface details and general reinforcing such as making fin fillets, or for reinforcing the leading edges of glider wings. Use sheet balsa for making fins and wings. And use large blocks for making nose cones, transition sections, nose blocks, or anything that is carved or shaped.

Typically, balsa is identified in two ways. The first is by the density of the wood. The denser the wood, the stronger and harder it is. Densities can range from 5 to 20 pounds per cubic foot (80 to 320 kg/m³), with 10 to 12 lb/ft³ (160 to 192 kg/m³) considered medium weight. Extremely lightweight balsa with a density under 6 pounds per cubic foot (96.1 kg/m³) is considered "contest grade" and is used on competition models where mass must be kept to a minimum and where durability is not a top priority.

The second way to classify balsa is by the direction of its woodgrain, which is determined by how it was cut from the log. Grain direction determines the rigidity or flexibility of a balsa sheet more than density does. For example, if the sheet is cut from the log so that the tree's annular rings run across the thickness of the sheet (A-grain), the sheet will be fairly flexible edge to edge. If, on the other hand, it is cut with the annular rings running through the thickness of the sheet (C-grain, quarter grain), it will be very rigid edge to edge. When grain direction is less clearly defined (B-grain), the sheet will have properties intermediate between A- and C- grain. B-grain is the most common and is suitable to use on most jobs.

Whenever you come across pure A-grain or C-grain sheets, learn where to use them to take best advantage of their special characteristics:

A-Grain sheet balsa has long fibers that show up as long grain lines. It is very flexible across the sheet and bends around curves easily. It also warps easily and is sometimes called "tangent cut."

Do: Use for sheet covering rounded fuselages and wing leading edges. Planking fuselages, forming tubes, strong flexible spars, hand-launched glider fuselages. Fins for small, ultra-light competition model rockets.

Don't: Use for sheet balsa wings or tail surfaces, flat fuselage sides, ribs, or formers.

To make A-grain balsa wood more pliable and easier to bend without breaking, soak it overnight in a bucket of water with a small amount of ammonia (or bleach) added. Shape it while it's wet, then hold it in the correct shape until it is completely dry.

B-Grain sheet has some of the qualities of both type A and type C. Grain lines are shorter than type A, and it feels stiffer across the sheet. It is a general purpose sheet and can be used for many jobs. It is sometimes called "random cut."

Do: Use for flat sheet fins on most rockets; for flat fuselage sides, trailing edges, wing ribs, formers, planking gradual curves, wind leading edge sheeting.

Don't: Use where type A or type C will do a significantly better job.

C-Grain sheet balsa has a beautiful mottled appearance. Some people say it looks like fish scales. It is very stiff across the sheet and if bent it splits easily. When used properly it helps build the lightest, strongest models. This is the most warp-resistant type, but it is difficult to sand. It is sometimes called "quarter grain."

Do: Use for sheet balsa fins on larger model rockets. Can also be used for sheet balsa wings on larger gliders, tail surfaces, flat fuselage sides, wing ribs, formers, trailing edges. Best type for wings on larger boost gliders and hand-launched gliders.

Don't: Use for curved planking, rounded fuselages, round tubes, hand-launched glider fuselages, or wing spars.

Plywood

Plywood is made by gluing thin sheets of hardwood (called veneer) together so the grain direction of each layer is perpendicular to the adjacent layers. This material is only available in sheets, which vary in useful sizes from 0.4 mm ($\frac{1}{64}$") to 6.35 mm ($\frac{1}{4}$"). It is used where the part needs maximum stiffness. This material is heavy and should be used sparingly. Another of its drawbacks is that it is hard to cut with typical modeling tools, except for 0.4 mm ($\frac{1}{64}$") ply, which is easily cut with scissors.

Spruce

Spruce is a wood native to North America and is available in a variety of sizes. The most useful sizes for rocketeers are in strips or dowels. If you need a stiff part like the main spar on a large built-up wing or the fuselage boom on a glider, spruce is an excellent choice. You can also use it to reinforce weaker structural members of the rocket.

Basswood

Basswood is a medium-density wood that can substitute for balsa wood. Its chief characteristic is that it has a tight grain, and because of this it takes very little filler to achieve a smooth finish. This makes it excellent for models that need a smooth surface, such as fins on a scale model. You can find basswood at hobby stores that carry balsa wood.

Plastic

Plastic, a very versatile material, is relatively strong and light. It has been used extensively in model rocketry because it can be molded into a variety of shapes: nose cones, transition sections, fins, etc. Modelers building rockets from scratch usually buy plastic in sheets called sheet styrene. Styrene can be easily glued, cut, shaped, and painted.

Thin, flexible plastic is often used to make parachutes. You probably already have this plastic at home in the form of trash bags and dry cleaner's bags.

Polystyrene is also available in a rigid foam called expanded polystyrene, often mistakenly called Styrofoam®. This material is easy to cut and shape. A thin metal wire heated to a high temperature can cut through the foam like a knife through butter. Use this technique to cut accurate shapes such as wing airfoils. Because expanded polystyrene foam is not very strong, you must use it with other materials such as balsa, plywood, or fiberglass. Usually the foam is sandwiched between two thin skins of the secondary material to make a strong, lightweight part.

You might find some expanded polystyrene around your house. Of its many uses, the most common are as packaging for delicate equipment and as

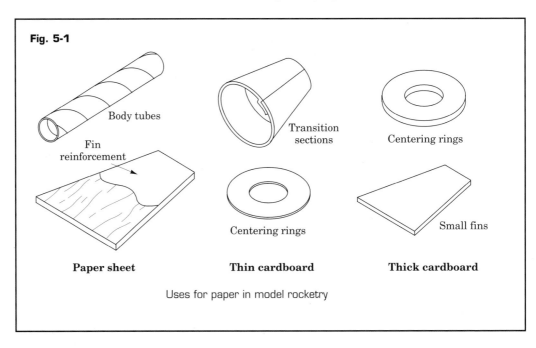

Fig. 5-1

Body tubes

Fin reinforcement

Transition sections

Centering rings

Centering rings

Small fins

Paper sheet

Thin cardboard

Thick cardboard

Uses for paper in model rocketry

heating insulation. Don't use the "peanuts," but the solid blocks of foam.

Take care when gluing anything to foam, as many adhesives will dissolve it. Don't use any styrene cements or polyester-based resins. Epoxy-type resins work very well. If you are unsure about a glue, test the compatibility of the adhesive on a scrap piece of foam first.

Paper

Paper is another miracle material for model rocketry. As a wood product, it shares a lot of wood's characteristics. It is easily cut, sanded, painted, and glued. Paper is also available in several thicknesses, which you can use in a variety of ways. Roll thin paper to make tubes, and apply it over other materials as a smooth skin. Use medium-thick paper to make centering rings, or roll it to make transition sections. Use cardboard make centering rings or fins for small rockets. Avoid using heavy cardboard to make fins with swept-back planforms, as they are easily bent on hard landings.

Fiberglass

Fiberglass, as its name implies, is made from very thin strings of glass that are usually woven together to make a lightweight cloth. Although fiberglass is a relatively old product, it is considered exotic in model rocketry because it is not often used and requires special methods of application. It is available from hobby stores that sell radio control airplanes.

Fiberglass is always used with some type of resin; it can be epoxy, a polyester resin, or even instant glue. When the resin hardens it holds the individual fibers together, creating a strong material.

Sometimes fiberglass is sold in thin sheets with the resin already hardened. This type is used to make lightweight fins and centering rings.

In rocketry, fiberglass is more commonly used to reinforce fins and sometimes is wrapped around body tubes for higher strength. Many competition rockets are made entirely out of fiberglass. When using fiberglass in this way, the rocket builder must create special forms or fixtures to wrap the fiberglass around until the resin hardens. These forms are then carefully removed, yielding a stiff pre-shaped part. I have not covered the construction of these highly specialized parts in this book because you probably won't need them.

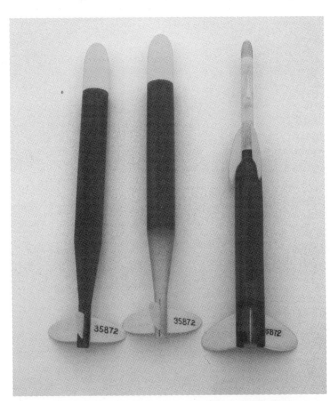

Ultra low-mass rockets can be made using fiberglass. These rockets require extra forms and construction jigs to hold the fiberglass while the epoxy hardens. (photo by Tim Van Milligan)

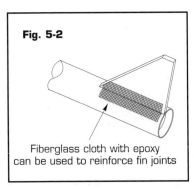

Fig. 5-2

Fiberglass cloth with epoxy can be used to reinforce fin joints

6

Construction Techniques

This chapter contains descriptions of almost all the techniques you will need to build rockets from scratch. When building a model this way you may have to make every part or modify purchased parts in some way. The methods described here will help you make accurately shaped pieces and parts, which will ensure properly assembled rockets. If you follow these methods, your finishing and painting should be easier because your model will not need a lot of extra filling, sanding, or shaping between ill-fitted parts.

Cutting Body Tubes

You may cut body tubes to length two ways. The first is to cut a long strip of paper and wrap it around the tube several times with one straight edge next to the location to be cut. Tape the paper down and make a line around the tube so you can double-check the location of the cut line. Take a sharp hobby knife, press the point into the tube on the line, and slowly rotate the tube into the cutting edge. Hold the knife against the paper so the cut line is straight around the tube. Make several light cuts around the perimeter so the tube isn't deformed by the pressure of the knife.

The second method is to lay the tube into a right-angle channel, as shown in Figure 6-2. One end of the channel should have a stop on it so the tube can be butted up against it. Lay the blade of the hobby knife on the channel at the location for the cut and rotate it downward, so the point cuts into the tube. Now rotate the tube into the cutting edge, holding it firmly against the stop in the channel. Make several

Fin positioning fixtures like this one help align and hold the fins while the glue dries. (photo by Steven A. Bachmeyer)

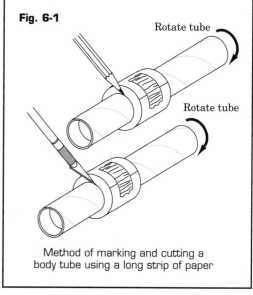

Fig. 6-1

Rotate tube

Rotate tube

Method of marking and cutting a body tube using a long strip of paper

light cuts around the perimeter before cutting completely through.

After you've cut the tube you may need to clean up the cut end to rid it of burrs or uneven edges. Do this by sanding the edge on a piece of sandpaper taped to the table.

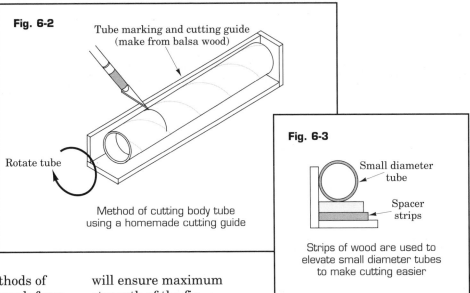

Fig. 6-2

Tube marking and cutting guide
(make from balsa wood)

Rotate tube

Method of cutting body tube
using a homemade cutting guide

Fig. 6-3

Small diameter
tube

Spacer
strips

Strips of wood are used to
elevate small diameter tubes
to make cutting easier

Designing and Constructing Fins

Fins must be able to withstand the forces of flight. The materials and methods of construction determine how much force they can withstand. Small models do not need very strong fins, and simple cardboard or balsa fins will suffice. Large models and those intended to fly at extremely high velocities need more strength. The following list gives several materials and construction methods in order of increasing strength:

Thick cardboard (not corrugated)
Balsa wood fins
Plastic fins
Balsa wood with paper reinforcing
Balsa with spruce wood reinforcing
Built-up fins
Foam core fins
Fiberglass reinforced fins
Plywood

Cardboard is suitable for small rockets using up to a full A rocket motor. Straight balsa wood can be used for rockets of 3 feet (.91 m) or less in height, using a maximum of a D engine. Larger rockets or higher-power models should use one of the other techniques or materials. Most of these methods will be described below. Since balsa is a predominant material, the chart (right) describes the uses for the various thicknesses of balsa available.

If you plan to construct your fins from a solid sheet material such as cardboard, plastic sheet, or balsa wood, first make a template of the fin shape so it can be transferred to the material. Before marking around the outside of the template with a pencil, orient it so that the direction of the wood grain is parallel to the leading edge of the template. This

will ensure maximum strength of the fin.

Fins with straight edges are the easiest to cut because you can use a ruler to help guide the knife. Lay the ruler on top of the fin to protect it if the knife blade should stray while you're cutting. Keep the blade at a 90-degree angle to the wood to avoid beveling the edges of the fin. When making cuts, make several light passes instead of one heavy cut.

Curved fin shapes are only slightly more difficult to cut. To ensure maximum uniformity between fins, make a

Uses for Different Thicknesses of Balsa

0.79 mm (1/32"):	Hollow built-up fins
1.59 mm (1/16"):	Typical small rockets
2.38 mm (3/32"):	Medium-size rockets
3.18 mm (1/8"):	Large rockets or clusters C or larger engines
4.76 mm (3/16"):	Large cluster engine or heavy models
6.35 mm (1/4"):	Generally too thick; high drag

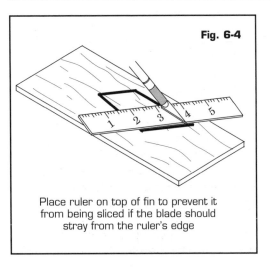

Fig. 6-4

Place ruler on top of fin to prevent it
from being sliced if the blade should
stray from the ruler's edge

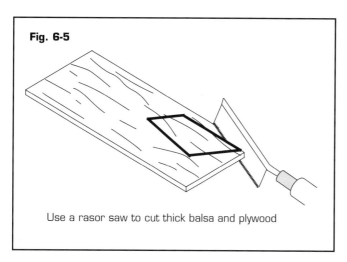

Fig. 6-5

Use a rasor saw to cut thick balsa and plywood

To keep all the fins uniform in size, stack sand them together. (photo by Steven A. Bachmeyer)

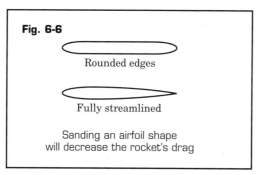

Fig. 6-6

Rounded edges

Fully streamlined

Sanding an airfoil shape will decrease the rocket's drag

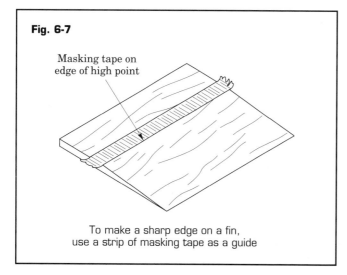

Fig. 6-7

Masking tape on edge of high point

To make a sharp edge on a fin, use a strip of masking tape as a guide

template out of thick styrene sheet and use it to guide your knife blade.

Thicker or harder materials such as plywood are more easily cut with a razor saw. Use care with a razor saw, since it is much harder to guide the blade and keep the edges straight.

After you've cut all the fins, stack them and sand them all together to ensure uniformity of size and shape. Pay particular attention to the edge that will be glued against the body tube (the root edge). It should be perfectly straight to maximize the bond strength of the fin. Also at this time, sand the airfoil into the fin. You might just round the edges, but for minimum drag the fins should be streamlined. Using a small wood planer will drastically cut your sanding time on thick fins

If you want a definite high point on the fin, as you would on a scale model, lay a piece of masking tape along the dividing point as shown in Figure 6-7. If you sand into the tape, remove it and lay a new piece down. This will give a sharp line on the fin.

Finally, give the fin a thorough surface sanding. Remove any lines you drew with pens, as they sometimes bleed through the paint on the rocket and ruin its appearance. You may apply sealer at this time, too. You'll find it easier to sand the fins before they are attached to the body tube.

Reinforced balsa fins: Balsa fins can be strengthened by providing reinforcement. The additional strength will increase their stiffness and make them more resilient during hard landings. To do this you may either apply skins or add stiffer structural members to the fins.

Skins are the easiest to apply, since you usually bond them directly to the fins with wood glue, instant glue, or epoxy. You can make them from a variety of materials, including tissue paper, ordinary notebook paper, cardboard, plastic sheet, very thin plywood, or fiberglass.

Stiff skins are usually applied to flat surfaces, as they are difficult to apply to fins that have airfoils sanded into them. To prevent a balsa wood fin from warping while the glue is drying, place it between two sheets of waxed paper and lay a book

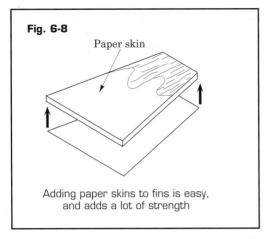

Fig. 6-8

Paper skin

Adding paper skins to fins is easy,
and adds a lot of strength

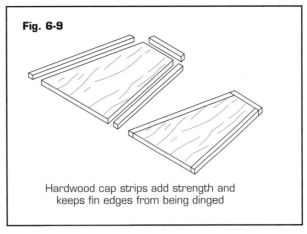

Fig. 6-9

Hardwood cap strips add strength and
keeps fin edges from being dinged

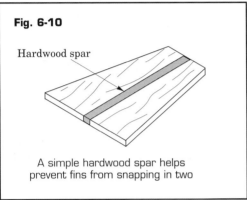

Fig. 6-10

Hardwood spar

A simple hardwood spar helps
prevent fins from snapping in two

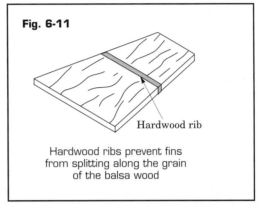

Fig. 6-11

Hardwood rib

Hardwood ribs prevent fins
from splitting along the grain
of the balsa wood

or other weight on top of it. The waxed paper will protect the table and the book from glue that might ooze out.

Flexible skins that drape, such as tissue paper or fiberglass cloth, are better for curved airfoil sections. Apply tissue paper to fins or wings that need only a little reinforcing or to cover the grain of the wood, and use fiberglass cloth for maximum strength. The methods of application are similar but the adhesives differ. Tissue paper is commonly applied with model aircraft dope or wood glue thinned with water. Fiberglass is almost exclusively applied with epoxy, polyester resin, or instant glues.

You can also reinforce balsa fins is by strategically adding stronger members to stiffen them. Members placed around the perimeter are called caps, while those placed inside the perimeter are called spars, or ribs, depending on their orientation. Ribs lie parallel to the centerline of the rocket, while spars are nearly perpendicular from the centerline (see Figures 6-9 to 6-11).

Built-Up Fins: A strong and lightweight hollow fin created by judicious placement of high-strength structural members

inside an outer skin is called a built-up fin. The advantages (if it is built properly) are low weight and high strength. Built-up structures are mainly used on large wings or fins, where weight reduction can be substantial.

Figure 6-12 shows the key parts of a built-up structure. The spars carry bending loads, the ribs give support and contour shape to the skins, and the skin gives the wing an outer cover. When the skin is used to give strength to the structure the wing is said to have a semi-monocoque construction. Skins that can

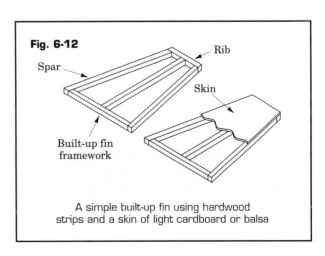

Fig. 6-12

Spar

Rib

Skin

Built-up fin framework

A simple built-up fin using hardwood
strips and a skin of light cardboard or balsa

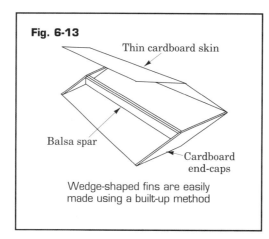

Fig. 6-13

Thin cardboard skin

Balsa spar

Cardboard end-caps

Wedge-shaped fins are easily made using a built-up method

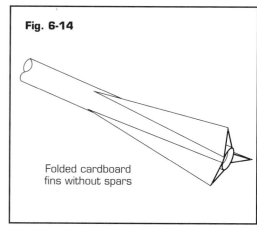

Fig. 6-14

Folded cardboard fins without spars

be used this way include thin cardboard, balsa sheet, thin plywood sheet, or fiberglass sheet.

This construction is also suitable for fins with sharp leading or trailing edges. The skins on these have to be very thin and stiff: light cardboard, thin fiberglass sheet, or thin plywood 0.39 mm ($\frac{1}{64}$") or 0.79 mm ($\frac{1}{32}$") work well. Figures 6-8 through 6-13 illustrate how they could be constructed.

Foam Core Fins: To increase the strength of a built-up wing without significantly increasing its mass, you can insert expanded polystyrene foam into the hollow areas. This will add strength and stiffen the skins. The added strength may enable you to eliminate many structural members inside the skin and decrease the mass of the wing.

Constructing a foam core structure is similar to building a built-up structure. Create a skeleton framework around the fin and cut a piece of foam to fit any hollow area. Shape the foam using a sanding block so it exactly matches the perimeter defined by the skeletal framework. Bond the skin directly to the foam and any structural members. Remember, epoxy is usually a safe adhesive to use on foam, while other glues may melt it.

Again, the type of skin should be appropriate for the expected loads and the shape of the fin. Flat and stiff skins such as light cardboard, thin balsa, thin plastic, or thin plywood are suitable only to fins with flat surfaces. For curved surfaces, fiberglass cloth soaked in epoxy is generally better. Several layers of fiberglass can be added to give extra strength to the fin. This technique is

especially applicable to larger and higher-powered rockets.

Plywood Fins: Plywood is not usually used as fin material because it is difficult to cut and shape and its density is too high for the strength it gives. For small fins that need accurately shaped airfoils, however, plywood does have some nice characteristics. Use only 0.39 mm ($\frac{1}{64}$") or 0.79 mm ($\frac{1}{32}$") thick wood. For fins thicker than this on small rockets, balsa is superior.

Plywood is also acceptable for use as a skin on a built-up or foam core fin. When used this way, only thicknesses of 0.39 mm ($\frac{1}{64}$") or 0.79 mm ($\frac{1}{32}$") are acceptable. Many rocketeers think they need thick, solid plywood fins on larger and higher-powered rockets. This is not true. You can make strong and stiff fins with many of the methods described above. The density and weight of plywood outweighs any benefits it might have. Just take your time and do the job right. Plywood doesn't have the strength-to-weight characteristics to make a really good fin. Even more important, plywood is so heavy it reduces the safety margin in your rocket designs.

Fin Positioning and Attachment: Marking the body tube is the first step in attaching the fins. Since most typical models have either three or four fins, use the fin guide (Figure 6-15) to mark the end of the body tube. Extend the line upward along the tube using a door jamb or a 90-degree angle as shown in Figure 6-17.

If the fins are located with the trailing edge not near the bottom of the tube, draw a line around the perimeter of the

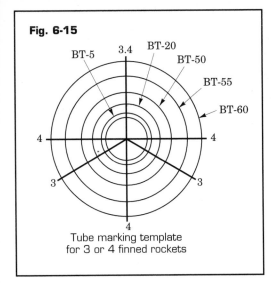

Fig. 6-15

BT-5
3.4
BT-20
BT-50
BT-55
BT-60

4
4

3
3

4

Tube marking template
for 3 or 4 finned rockets

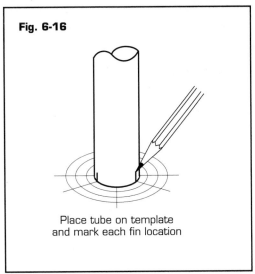

Fig. 6-16

Place tube on template
and mark each fin location

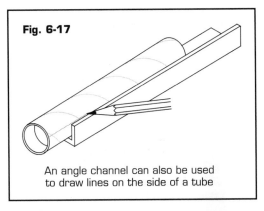

Fig. 6-17

An angle channel can also be used
to draw lines on the side of a tube

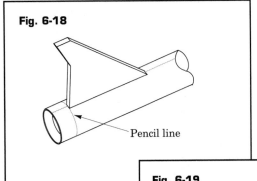

Fig. 6-18

Pencil line

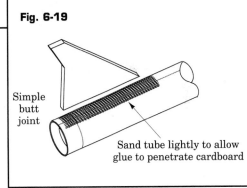

Fig. 6-19

Simple
butt
joint

Sand tube lightly to allow
glue to penetrate cardboard

tube by wrapping a long strip of paper around it, as shown in Figure 6-1. This will make it easier to align the fin edges at the same location on the tube.

There are a couple of ways to attach fins to withstand the forces of both launch and landing, and a few ways to reinforce the joint created once the fin is attached.

The butt joint is the simplest, most common way to attach fins to small models. In this method the root edge of the fin is glued directly to the body tube. As you might expect, this is the weakest type of joint.

To increase the strength of this simple joint make sure the glue grabs tightly to both the body tube and the fins. To accomplish this, lightly sand the surface of the body tube where the fins will be attached and make sure no balsa filler is on the root edge of the fin (Fig. 6-19). Also make sure the root edge is perfectly straight, so the fin will lie level against the tube.

Glue the fin to the tube by running a bead of wood glue along the edge of the fin and then pressing it against the tube along the fin line you drew earlier. Hold it until it hardens enough to maintain its position when you release it. Before it hardens completely, check its alignment with the same guide you used to mark the body tube. You can build yourself a holding tool with a couple of scrap pieces of balsa like the one in Figure 6-20. This frees your hands for other tasks while the glue is drying.

A stronger way of attaching the fins using the butt joint is to use a double glue bond. Apply a thin film of glue to the two parts being joined and allow them to dry almost completely. Apply another line of glue and join the parts, holding them in place until the glue sets. Finally, allow the glue to dry completely before continuing or reinforcing the fins. Attach plastic fins the same way, but

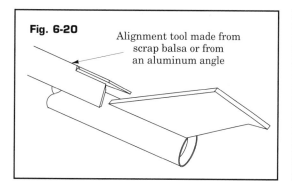

Fig. 6-20

Alignment tool made from scrap balsa or from an aluminum angle

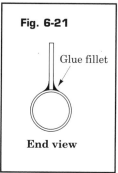

Fig. 6-21

Glue fillet

End view

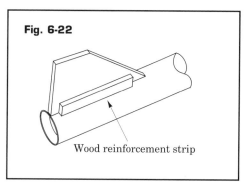

Fig. 6-22

Wood reinforcement strip

with slow-setting super glue instead of wood glue.

You may reinforce the butt joint in several ways. The first is to run a fillet of glue along the joint. Smooth the glue fillet with the tip of your finger. Do not use hot-melt glue for fillets, since you can seriously burn your finger. Lay the rocket on its side until the glue hardens enough so it will not sag when the model is upright. Repeat this for all the fins. Figure 6-21 shows the relative size of the fillet to the body tube size. Fillets larger than this add extra mass without adding any significant strength. Well-made fillets reduce the interference drag of the model, so add fillets no matter what method you use to attach fins.

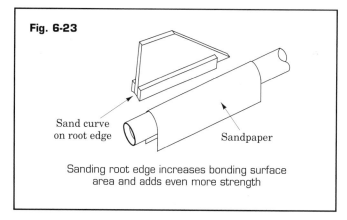

Fig. 6-23

Sand curve on root edge

Sandpaper

Sanding root edge increases bonding surface area and adds even more strength

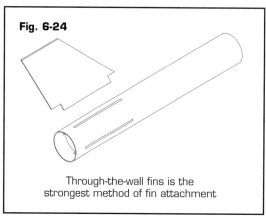

Fig. 6-24

Through-the-wall fins is the strongest method of fin attachment

Use extreme care when making fillets out of instant glues or epoxy. Instant glues harden very quickly and you may find your finger stuck to the rocket. Epoxies sometimes cause allergic reactions in some people, so avoid direct skin contact. Wear rubber or plastic gloves when working with either of these adhesives.

Adding strips of wood along the fin joint is the second way to increase the strength of the butt joint. This increases the contact area of the fin root to the surface of the body tube—and the larger the area in contact with the body tube, the stronger the joint (Fig. 6-22).

I suggest applying the strips of wood after attaching the fin, otherwise the wood may not be positioned properly to make maximum contact with the tube. If you want to attach the strips to the fins before gluing them to the tube, sand a curve into the root edge before gluing the fin to the tube. This can be done by laying the sandpaper over the body tube as shown in Figure 6-23. After the fins are attached, apply glue fillets to reduce interference drag.

The final method of reinforcing the simple butt joint is to pierce the body tube and the root edge of the fin with the point of a pin. This increases the penetration of the glue into both the tube and the fin. The holes in the tube will allow the glue to flow all the way into the tube and create tiny "rivets" that further increase the strength of the joint. You can then strengthen the joint further with wood strip or fillets.

Finally, the strongest way of attaching any fin to the rocket is a method called "through-the-wall." When you make the fin pattern, add an extra tab to the fin. This tab slides through a slot cut into the body tube. The mere fact that the tab extends into the rocket changes the type of forces the fin can withstand. Butt joints can withstand shear forces but are not as resistant to the stronger bending forces. That is why fins snap off models. Through-the-wall fins are much better at withstanding bending forces without a loss of strength in resisting shear forces.

The joint can be even stronger if the tab is long enough to extend down to the surface of the engine mount tube inside the main body (Fig. 7-15). Use this joint on any model using engines larger than a D, or models of large size—more than .91 m (3 feet) tall.

After installing the fin, remember to apply a fillet along the joint to reduce interference drag. Fillets also hide gaps or voids created along the body tube slot.

Engine Mounts

An engine mount holds the rocket engine firmly in place and aligns it concentrically with the centerline of the model. This is critical to successful operation. If the engine were to come free it could fly through the rocket during its thrust phase and destroy the interior of the model, or it might be kicked out the rear of the model at ejection. In the latter case, the recovery device wouldn't be deployed and the model would come back down to earth at a high velocity.

If the engine isn't concentric with the centerline of the model, the off-axis thrust line will cause the model to do flip-flops during the thrust phase of the burn. So you can see the engine mount is a flight critical part of the model—if it should fail the rocket flight would be unsuccessful.

Models that are just large enough in diameter for the engine to barely fit inside the tube are called minimum-diameter models. Their usual purpose is to fly to extremely high altitudes. The most common way to secure engines in these models is to wrap masking tape around the engine so the friction created when it is installed is enough to prevent the motor case from sliding fore or aft during flight.

This method is not totally reliable. If the friction between the engine and the inside of the tube is not great enough, the motor may slide during the flight. Often, after the flight the expended engine case is hard to remove because

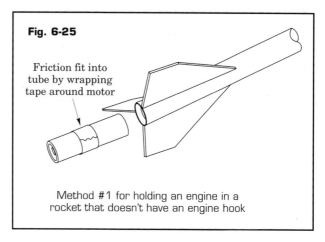

Fig. 6-25

Friction fit into tube by wrapping tape around motor

Method #1 for holding an engine in a rocket that doesn't have an engine hook

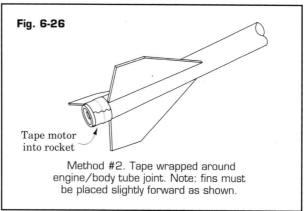

Fig. 6-26

Tape motor into rocket

Method #2. Tape wrapped around engine/body tube joint. Note: fins must be placed slightly forward as shown.

the hot engine case swells, increasing the friction between parts.

A better way is to modify the position of the fins and tape the engine differently. On your next minimum-diameter rocket design, mount the fins slightly forward on the tube so a gap of about 13 mm (½") exists at the rear of the rocket. Then install a thrust ring inside the body tube (Fig. 6-26). Position it so the motor will extend about 13 mm (½") out the rear of the model. This ring prevents the motor from sliding forward into the middle of the rocket.

When inserting the engine, wrap tape around it so it overlaps both the engine and the body tube. Now the engine is not held by friction, but by a more secure tape joint. Additionally, it is easy to remove after a flight.

Remember two things about this method. First, by moving the fins forward you are also moving the CP forward. This may affect the stability of the model, so be sure to check it before flying. (See Chapter 2 on rocket stability.) Second, don't use this method on higher-powered models above G engines. The heat generated by the

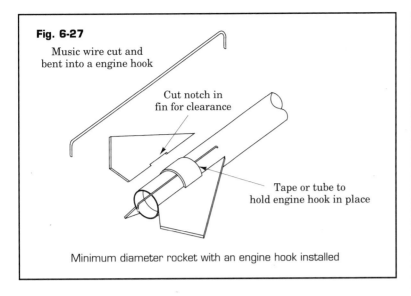

Fig. 6-27

Music wire cut and bent into a engine hook

Cut notch in fin for clearance

Tape or tube to hold engine hook in place

Minimum diameter rocket with an engine hook installed

Upper right: Lightweight engine restraint made from a flexible wire, which was bent and epoxied to the outside of the body tube. (photo by Steven A. Bachmeyer)

Middle right: The engine restraint holds the engine inside the body tube. (photo by Steven A. Bachmeyer)

larger motors could melt the glue on the tape and cause the engine to be spit out at ejection.

For easiest installation and removal of the rocket motor, use an engine hook to securely hold it inside the model. An engine hook is simply a bent piece of metal for holding the engine in the engine mount tube. You can easily make one by bending a stiff piece of music wire as shown in Figure 6-27.

To insert the engine hook into the model, first cut a slit in the tube at the farthest forward location of the engine. Make sure the engine will extend out the back of the tube a short length. Insert one end of the hook into the slit and secure it by positioning a short tube over the midpoint of the hook. When you attach fins to this model you will have to cut a notch in the root of the fin to fit over the ring. Figure 6-27 shows how the model will look when completed.

Another optional engine hook on minimum-diameter rockets is to bend a small diameter, *flexible* wire in a U shape and glue the ends along two adjacent fin roots. Square the corners of the U to fit over the edges of the engine as in the photos (right). With this method, glue an engine block inside the body tube directly forward of the engine to prevent it from sliding forward. For extra security, wrap tape around the wire and engine to prevent the wire from slipping off the rocket case.

On most rockets the engine is smaller than the main body tube, so you will have to build up the engine mount to fit. An engine hook is usually used to hold

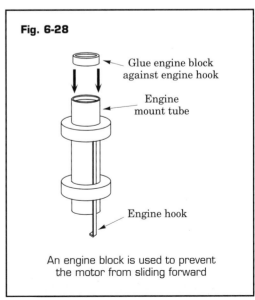

Fig. 6-28

Glue engine block against engine hook

Engine mount tube

Engine hook

An engine block is used to prevent the motor from sliding forward the motor in place, although you may want to delete the hook and tape the motor in the rocket. If you use an engine hook, insert a thrust ring ahead of the motor so engine thrust isn't pushing only against the engine hook. Sometimes the hook can slide forward if it isn't properly restrained. A thrust ring will prevent this from happening (Fig. 6-28).

If you want to use parts from a kit manufacturer, you may purchase engine mount kits or the parts needed to design your own engine mounts. Select the parts carefully and check the dimensions to be sure they will fit together properly. Figures 6-29 to 6-32 show a couple of ways to make engine mounts using purchased parts. The short, thick-walled, cylinders used to center one tube inside another are called adapter rings.

You can make your own centering rings from heavy cardboard. Centering rings are similar to adapter rings except

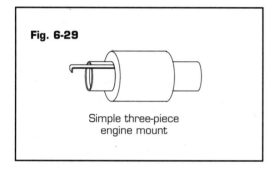

Fig. 6-29

Simple three-piece
engine mount

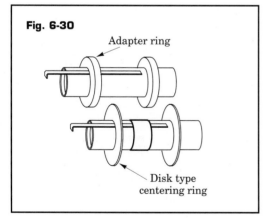

Fig. 6-30

Adapter ring

Disk type
centering ring

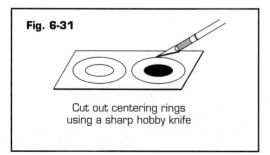

Fig. 6-31

Cut out centering rings
using a sharp hobby knife

they are flat. To make a centering ring, accurately measure the inside diameter of the large tube and the outside diameter of the small tube. Take a drawing compass and create two concentric circles of the diameters you just measured (remember to divide the diameter by 2, because you will be using it to set the radius on the compass). Make two identical rings and cut them out using a hobby knife (Fig. 6-31).

Glue the rings to the engine tube as shown in Figures 6-30 or 6-32. You may need to make a notch for the engine hook if the rings are near the ends of the tube. If you don't have a ring to hold the engine hook down, it can be adequately secured by wrapping several layers of masking tape around the middle of the hook.

If you have a tube coupler that will fit into the larger tube, you can glue your centering rings to it. This will make it easier to slide the rings into the larger tube (Fig. 6--32).

You can also make your own adapter rings. Cut long thin strips of paper about 6.35 mm (¼") wide. Apply glue to one side and carefully wrap it around the smaller tube until you achieve the right thickness to slide it in the larger tube (Fig. 6-33). Position the strip of paper properly, because you won't be able to slide it after the glue is dry. You may have to use multiple strips of paper to achieve the proper thickness.

If the difference between the two tube diameters is greater than 12.7 mm (½"), it is probably easier to make a flat disk centering ring than

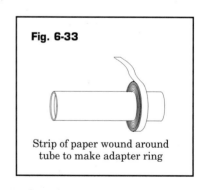

Fig. 6-32

Cut notch for
engine hook

Masking tape

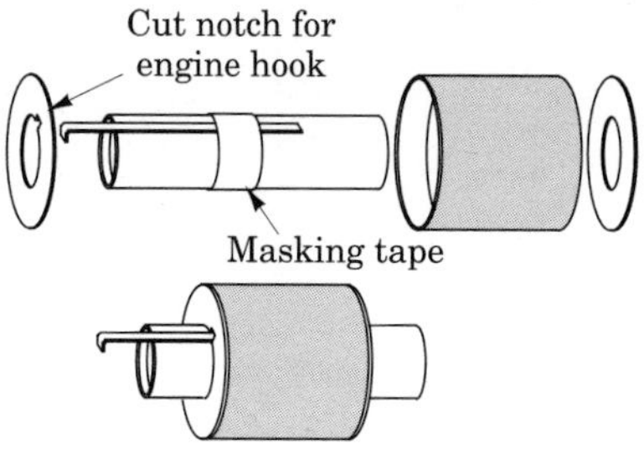

Gluing the centering rings
to a tube coupler allows easier
installation of engine mount.

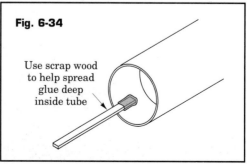

Fig. 6-33

Strip of paper wound around
tube to make adapter ring

Fig. 6-34

Use scrap wood
to help spread
glue deep
inside tube

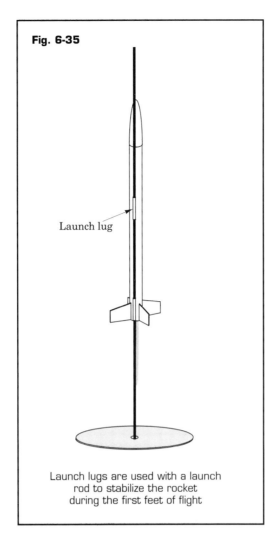

Fig. 6-35

Launch lug

Launch lugs are used with a launch
rod to stabilize the rocket
during the first feet of flight

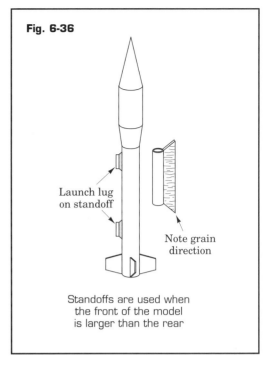

Fig. 6-36

Launch lug
on standoff

Note grain
direction

Standoffs are used when
the front of the model
is larger than the rear

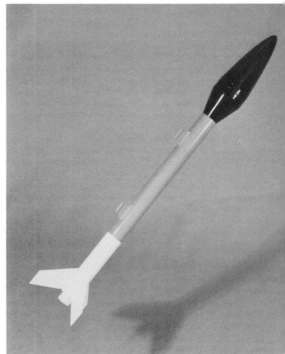

Launch lug stand-offs are often used with
rockets that have large diameter nose
cones. (photo by Steven A. Bachmeyer)

an adapter ring. A centering ring will
also weigh less than an adapter ring.

After the engine mount is done, glue it
into the body tube (Fig. 6-34). Use a
scrap piece of balsa wood to get glue
down into the tube. Make sure the
engine mount is securely glued—you
don't want it coming loose in flight.

Launch Lugs

A launch lug is a small round, hollow
tube attached to the side of the rocket. It
slips over the launch rod to guide the
model during the first few feet of flight
until stabilizing velocity is reached. Soda
straws or coffee stirring straws make
excellent launch lugs for small rockets up
to a D engine.

On small rockets a single lug
approximately 51 mm (2") long can be
glued directly to the model. Position it so
it spans the model's center of gravity and
is perfectly aligned with the model's
centerline.

On longer and heavier models more
than 31.75 cm (12.5") and 25 grams, split
the lug into two shorter lengths and glue
half to each end of the body tube. Make
sure the two lugs line up straight. Check
this by running the launch rod through
the tubes before the glue hardens.

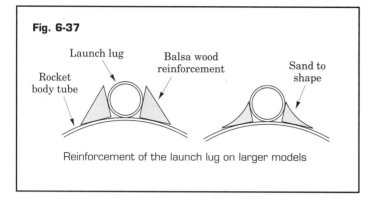

Fig. 6-37

Launch lug

Rocket body tube

Balsa wood reinforcement

Sand to shape

Reinforcement of the launch lug on larger models

1. Start by making a drawing of your proposed nose cone. You will need to know the exact dimensions of the nose and the size of the tube it will fit into. The shoulder of the nose cone must fit into the tube properly. As a rule of thumb, the outside diameter of the shoulder should be 0.152 mm (0.006") smaller than the inside diameter of the tube. Don't worry about being exact—as you can adjust the fit later.

On some designs the nose of the rocket may interfere with the installation of launch rod. In these cases mount the lugs on short pylons so the launch rod will clear the nose (Fig. 6-36). To prevent the pylons from splitting in half, make sure the grain of the wood runs perpendicular to the centerline of the model.

With bigger rockets you will need larger launch lugs and a larger diameter launch rod. Generally, for models using D or E engines, a rod of 4.7 mm (³⁄₁₆") can be used. Taller models, greater than 1.06 m (3.5 feet), or rockets using larger engines (F or G) should use 6.4 mm (¼") diameter launch rods with a length greater than 1.22 m (48") long. This will prevent excessive swaying in a breeze.

To increase the bonding strength, glue strips of balsa wood on each side of the lug. After the glue has hardened, sand the balsa to create a large fillet (Fig. 6-37).

For easier attachment of the igniter clips when the rocket is sitting on the pad, put the lugs on the same side of the rocket as the engine hook.

Launch Lug Sizes

3.18 mm (⅛"): Small models, up to a C engine
4.76 mm (³⁄₁₆"): D or E engine models
6.36 mm (¼"): Models taller than 48" using an F or G engine

Designing and Making Nose Cones

The nose cone, as the name implies, is the foremost part of the rocket. It is generally tapered to reduce drag. You can choose any size or shape you want for your model, but sometimes you may want one that is not currently available. Here are instructions for making your own balsa nose cones.

2. Select a block of hard balsa wood at least 3.2 mm (⅛") larger in cross section and 6.4 mm (¼") longer than the length of the proposed nose cone (Fig. 6-39). Cut the block down to this size if it is much larger. If you can't find a block, make your own by laminating several smaller planks together with wood glue.

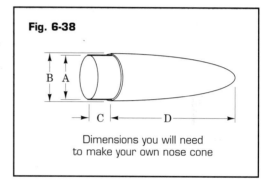

Fig. 6-38

Dimensions you will need to make your own nose cone

3. Locate the center of the end of the block by drawing diagonal lines across the corners (Fig. 6-40). You are going to drill a hole into the block to accept a wood dowel. Try to find a hardwood dowel approximately 6.4 mm (¼") in diameter. Drill the hole down approximately ½ the length of the block. Make sure it is straight and concentric with the centerline of the block (Fig. 6-41).

4. Glue the hardwood dowel into the hole and let it set. Cut the excess length sticking out to 5 to 7 cm (2" to 3") long.

5. To speed the process of turning the nose cone, you can roughly shape the wood by carving it with a hobby knife (Fig. 6-42). Be sure to leave some excess material for the next step.

6. Turn the nose cone on a lathe, drill press, or in a hand-held electric drill firmly mounted in a bench vise. Mount the dowel in the chuck so that the face of the block is as close as possible to the chuck on the machine. Set the rotation speed of the motor moderately fast. Using coarse sandpaper or a wood file, shape the wood into the desired nose

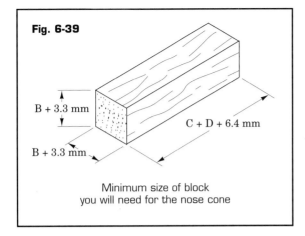

Fig. 6-39

$B + 3.3$ mm

$B + 3.3$ mm

$C + D + 6.4$ mm

Minimum size of block
you will need for the nose cone

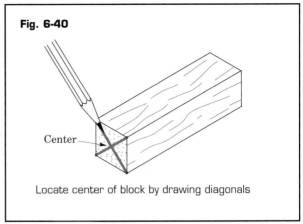

Fig. 6-40

Center

Locate center of block by drawing diagonals

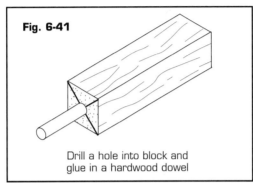

Fig. 6-41

Drill a hole into block and
glue in a hardwood dowel

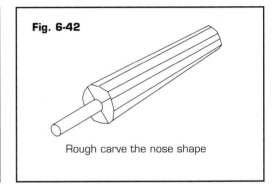

Fig. 6-42

Rough carve the nose shape

cone shape (Fig. 6-43). Do not use too much pressure, as you might snap off the wood dowel. Check the dimension often to avoid taking off too much. When the dimensions are close, switch to finer grades of sandpaper. For the shoulder, you might find that a jeweler's file or an emery board will give you the sharpest

edge. Test-fit the shoulder into the body tube often to achieve a proper fit.

7. When the nose cone is done, cut off the dowel extending from the end (Fig. 6-44). You can sand the bottom of the nose cone base to make it flat.

Carve and sand nose cones with odd dimensions to achieve the desired shape. Canopies and cockpits can be easily made this way too.

Fitting Nose Cones: Always check the fit of the nose cone into the body tube even if you purchased the nose cone or shoulder from a kit manufacturer. If the fit is too loose the nose might come off too early in flight. If this happens it usually

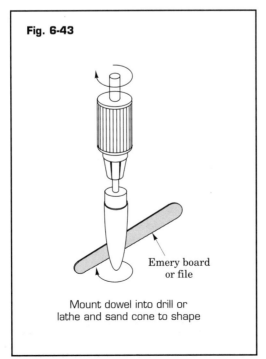

Fig. 6-43

Emery board
or file

Mount dowel into drill or
lathe and sand cone to shape

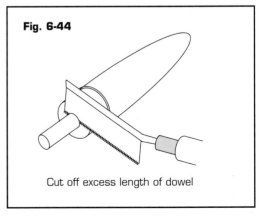

Fig. 6-44

Cut off excess length of dowel

shreds the recovery device and damages the model. If the fit is too tight the nose cone might not come off when the ejection charge goes off, causing the rocket to land nose first at high speed.

Be sure to test the fit. The nose cone should not fall off if the model is inverted but should start to come out if it is wiggled slightly. You can loosen the fit by sanding the outside of the shoulder, or tighten it by adding strips of masking tape around the perimeter of the shoulder.

Shock Cords & Mounts

To keep the nose cone from separating from the rest of the rocket and being lost on every flight, attach a shock cord from the nose cone to the body of the rocket. The type and size of cord depends on the size of the model.

Small diameter braided fishing line works well on small models. Since it doesn't stretch to absorb the forces of the ejection charge, how it is attached is important. Methods of attachment are described below. The cord should be approximately 45.7 cm (18") long for small models (at least twice the length of the body tube).

Medium-sized models or those using regular-size engines should use longer and stronger shock cords. Rubber cord covered with fabric works well for these models. You can find it at fabric stores, in a variety of sizes. The ribbon type is the most common, but you can also find it as a round cord. Try to use the cord that is covered with cotton fabric instead of polyester. Polyester sometimes melts from the heat of the ejection charge and could cause you to lose your rocket. Cotton doesn't melt and can take much higher temperatures before it starts to char.

The length of cord for medium-sized models should be at least 61 cm (24"), and if you have room in your rocket, make it longer. But beyond 122 cm (48"), you are adding too much weight.

Large models, like those powered with E or F engines need larger chords. Elastic ribbon of at least 6 mm (¼") wide by 1.22 m (48") long is a good starting point for these large models. On G engines, the cord should be at least 1.82 m (72") long.

If you want to use a more exotic material like Kevlar, be careful how you mount it. Kevlar doesn't burn or melt, so it can be attached close to the engine without fear of separation due to the heat. But this cord is so strong and abrasive that it can cut through the sides of body tubes. If you plan to use it, keep it short so it doesn't extend out of the body tube. You will need a second cord tied to the Kevlar cord as shown in Figure 6-45.

Attaching the shock cord to the nose is as simple as tying it on. Plastic nose cones are usually molded with a loop designed for attaching the shock cord. On balsa nose cones, you will have to insert a metal screw eye, available at most hardware stores in a variety of sizes. Once you've inserted the screw eye and it glued to the nose cone you can tie the shock cord to it (Fig. 6-46).

On small models there is typically nothing inside the body tube to tie the shock cord to. In these cases you can create a simple shock cord mount from a sheet of paper cut into the shape shown in Figure 6-47. Spread wood glue over

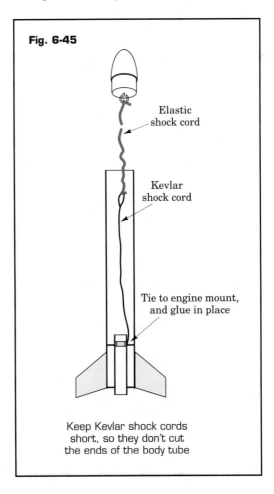

Fig. 6-45

Elastic shock cord

Kevlar shock cord

Tie to engine mount, and glue in place

Keep Kevlar shock cords short, so they don't cut the ends of the body tube

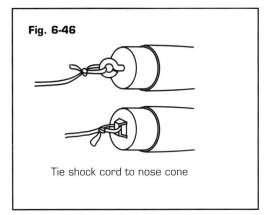

Fig. 6-46

Tie shock cord to nose cone

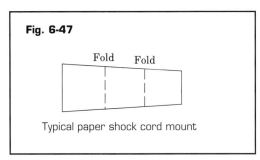

Fig. 6-47

Fold   Fold

Typical paper shock cord mount

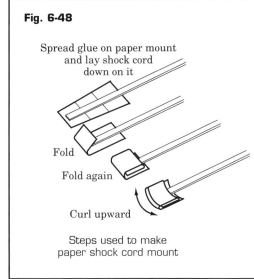

Fig. 6-48

Spread glue on paper mount
and lay shock cord
down on it

Fold

Fold again

Curl upward

Steps used to make
paper shock cord mount

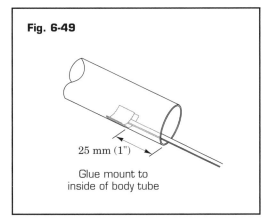

Fig. 6-49

25 mm (1")

Glue mount to
inside of body tube

one side of the paper and position one end of the shock cord at a slight diagonal across the length of the paper. Fold the paper twice at the fold lines indicated on the pattern (Fig. 6-48). Squeeze it between your fingers, and at the same time curl the edges up slightly to match the inside curvature of the body tube.

When the glue has set, glue the assembly into the body tube. Be sure to position it far enough into the tube so the nose cone shoulder can also be inserted into the tube (Fig. 6-49).

On larger and higher-powered rockets you can make a shock cord mount by tying the shock cord around a tube coupler inserted deep inside the model (Fig. 6-50). You can also build an integral shock cord mount inside the rocket. See Chapter 7 on higher-powered rockets for a drawing showing this type of mount.

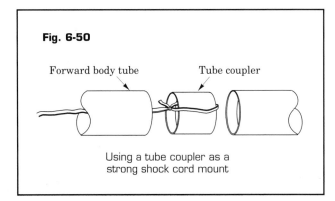

Fig. 6-50

Forward body tube   Tube coupler

Using a tube coupler as a
strong shock cord mount

Attaching the Parachute

Attaching the parachute to the model can be as simple as tying the shroud lines directly to the screw eye or plastic loop on the base of the nose cone. Because most parachutes are made with both ends of the shroud line attached to the canopy, you can attach it to the nose cone for easy removal.

Gather all the lines together and thread them through the loop on the base of the nose cone. Split the lines apart to create loops, gather up the crown of the parachute, and pass it completely through the shroud line loop. Pull on the lines until they are tight. The parachute is now securely attached (Fig. 6-51). To remove it, do the steps in reverse order. Another method is to attach it first to a fisherman's swivel hook (Fig. 6-52).

Constructing Transition Sections

Creating a smooth transition between body tubes of different diameters is essential to keeping the drag low. Transitions have special names depending on their orientation (Fig. 6-53). If the smaller tube is toward the front of the model the adapter is called a shoulder; if the smaller tube is to the rear a transition is called a boattail or reducer.

Many manufacturers sell ready-made transition sections. Either plastic or balsa, they are designed to fit selected size body tubes. If you need a different size you can make one by turning it from a block of balsa as described in the nose cone design section or from thin cardboard. Balsa and plastic boattails can be made from nose cones as shown in Figure 3-13 on page 25. Transition sections of thin cardboard are sometimes called shrouds.

You will need the following equations and drawings 6-54 through 6-56 to make your own cardboard transition shrouds. The same equations can be used to make paper cones, too. To make a cone, set the diameter of the smaller tube to zero.

$$D = \frac{(A-B)}{2} \qquad E = \sqrt{C^2 + D^2}$$

$$r_1 = \frac{E \times B}{(A-B)} \qquad r_2 = \frac{E \times A}{(A-B)} \qquad \theta° = \frac{180 \times A}{r_2}$$

Explanation of Symbols for Figures 6-54 through 6-56

A = Large tube diameter
B = Smaller tube diameter
C = Length of transition
D = ½ the difference between tube diameters
E = Taper length on the transition
θ = Angle to draw transition
r_1 = Radius of inner edge of transition
r_2 = Radius of outer edge of transition

When drawing your transition section, be sure to add a small tab on one edge to glue it together as shown in Figure 6-55.

To align the tubes concentrically, build your transition as shown in Figure 6-56. You can make centering rings out of cardboard. Instructions for this are in the section on engine mount design on page 43. Position and align the tubes together before installing the shroud. Then install the preglued shroud by

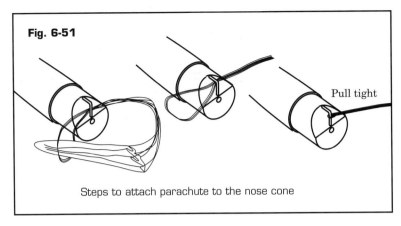

Fig. 6-51

Pull tight

Steps to attach parachute to the nose cone

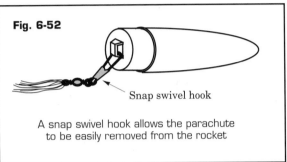

Fig. 6-52

Snap swivel hook

A snap swivel hook allows the parachute to be easily removed from the rocket

sliding it over the small tube before mating it to the large tube and gluing it into place.

Large transition sections made this way may feel soft or squishy. Although this may not cause a problem, they can be stiffened two ways. First, you can laminate another shroud over the top of the first to increase the thickness of the material (Fig. 6-57). This is better than trying to make one out of thicker cardboard, because it won't wrap easily without creasing.

The second way is to add internal braces or stiffeners under the cardboard before it is installed (Fig. 6-58).

Your design may require that the body tube separate at the transition section. This is more complicated, but it can be done. Figures 6-59 and

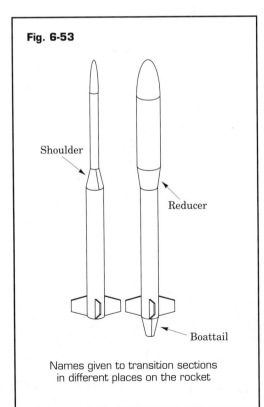

Fig. 6-53

Shoulder

Reducer

Boattail

Names given to transition sections in different places on the rocket

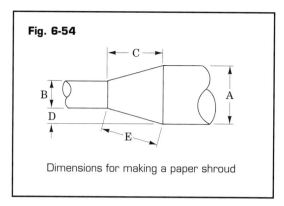

Fig. 6-54

Dimensions for making a paper shroud

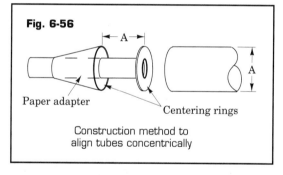

Fig. 6-55

Glue Tab

r_1

r_2

q

Before gluing the shroud in place, join the two tubes together. Notice that the shock cord can be attached to the lower tube. (photo by Steven A. Bachmeyer)

Fig. 6-56

A

A

Paper adapter

Centering rings

Construction method to align tubes concentrically

6-60 illustrate such a transition. The heavy braided cord is a loop firmly glued to the inside small body tube. It extends outward of the shoulder of the transition and can be used to anchor the shock cord or as a loop for attaching a parachute.

Constructing Odd-Size Tube Couplers

Often you will need a tube coupler and either don't have one or the tubes being joined are a nonstandard size. You can

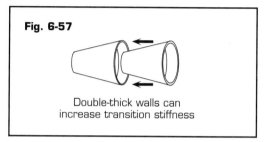

Fig. 6-57

Double-thick walls can increase transition stiffness

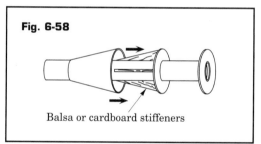

Fig. 6-58

Balsa or cardboard stiffeners

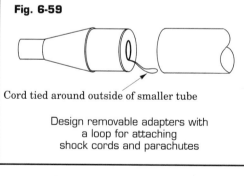

Fig. 6-59

Cord tied around outside of smaller tube

Design removable adapters with a loop for attaching shock cords and parachutes

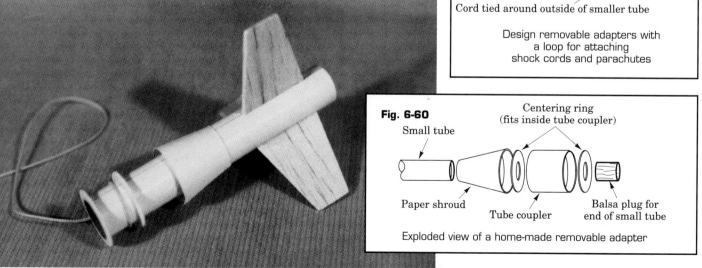

Fig. 6-60

Small tube

Centering ring (fits inside tube coupler)

Paper shroud

Tube coupler

Balsa plug for end of small tube

Exploded view of a home-made removable adapter

make your own tube coupler if you have an extra length of body tube of the size being joined or larger.

First, cut the tube to the proper length. In general, it should be cut to approximately 1.5 times the diameter of the tubes being joined. So if you are joining a two tubes of 25.4 mm (1") diameter, make the length 38.1 mm (1.5"). Next, cut the tube down one side—make a straight cut (Fig. 6-61). Now roll the tube and temporarily insert it into one body tube. With a pencil, mark the amount of overlap on the coupler (Fig. 6-62).

Pull the coupler out of the tube and cut the overlap off. Don't discard the excess, as you will use it to reinforce the tube coupler. Now glue the tube coupler into the tube so that half extends out. Take the excess that you cut off previously and glue it on the inside of the tube coupler along the joint where the two edges come together. Finally, glue the other body tube onto the protruding tube coupler and allow this to fully dry.

To make sure the tubes are perfectly aligned, lay them in a 90-degree channel (the one you use for making straight lines along the length of body tubes) until the glue has dried.

Creating Custom Parts

A custom part is anything you can't buy or otherwise easily obtain. Many custom parts were described in the previous sections. These include odd-size nose cones, transition sections, cockpits, and shock cord mounts. Usually the part you need is some type of external detail. These are the hardest to find, but you can produce substitutes. Here is a list of methods or ideas you can use to create that special piece.

1. Carve it from a block of balsa wood or Styrofoam
2. Build it up from sheets of paper, styrene, or balsa
3. Modify some other available part
4. Vacuumform it
5. Make a plastic resin casting

The last two items on the list are techniques used by experienced modelers. These methods are complex and require special equipment and materials. If you would like additional information on those topics, talk to your hobby dealer, check out books in your local library, or look for ads in plastic modeling magazines for manufacturers who sell these specialized products.

This model was made by gluing sheets of balsa together to make a large block. It was then carved to shape and hollowed out to reduce weight. Finally, the fins were attached. (photo by Steven A. Bachmeyer)

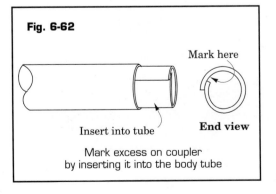

Fig. 6-61

Cut

Dia.

1.5 x Dia.

Cut lengthwise

Making a custom size tube coupler begins by cutting off a length of body tube and slicing it down one side

Fig. 6-62

Mark here

Insert into tube

End view

Mark excess on coupler by inserting it into the body tube

7
Building Higher-Power Rockets

Building rockets to withstand the forces of flight is pretty easy when you are powering them with a D engine or smaller. Above this size, the forces and the rockets become larger. These larger models are termed higher-powered rockets. Outwardly they similar except for their size, but inside the tube they are quite different.

The main difference is that higher-powered models are built to withstand larger forces. There are many similarities between the small rockets and their larger brothers, and most of the techniques you learned for those models are valid for the big ones. This is especially true if you followed the advice on how to make an item stronger.

One key philosophy of aeronautics remains true no regardless of the size of the vehicle: build strong but keep the mass low! I can't tell you how many times I've seen rocketeers build models as tall as a full-grown person and weighing more than 10 pounds (4.54 kg). Do not be confused—weight does not equal strength. Strength depends on choosing the correct materials and, more importantly, how the model is designed and constructed. The techniques described in Chapter 6 will provide more than adequate strength for almost any model rocket you build. Keep the weight of your rockets low because low weight means increased performance as well as added safety. A lighter rocket does not have the same potential of doing damage or being damaged as a heavier one.

The design of these high-powered models must take into account the added forces. The largest forces occur at the back end of the model, so this is where you should concentrate your efforts. Try

(photo by Marc Lavigne)

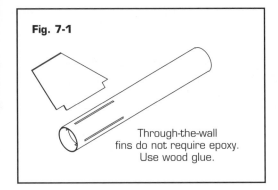

Fig. 7-1

Through-the-wall fins do not require epoxy. Use wood glue.

to design the pieces so they interlock with each other, so no forces are transferred to the glue joints. This will minimize the amount of glue and help keep the mass low. For example, the body tube should have slots cut into it to accept tabs on the fins (Fig. 7-1). This through-the-wall fin attachment is strong yet requires little glue. Here are some other tips and techniques uniquely suited to high-powered rockets.

Adhesives

Because you are going to design your rockets to limit the forces experienced by glue joints, you should not have to change to different types of adhesives. Use the correct adhesive corresponding to the materials being bonded.

One of the big reasons for excess weight in a model is the use of epoxy as the primary bonding agent. Epoxy is strong, but if you are bonding paper to paper or paper to wood, wood glue is stronger because it penetrates into the pieces. You'll need three times as much epoxy to get the same strength. Use epoxy only where you are transferring a shearing force through the joint. For example, if your fins were butt joined to the body tube instead of attached through-the-wall, I suggest epoxy. Otherwise regular wood glue is sufficient.

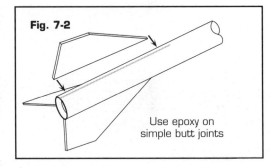

Fig. 7-2

Use epoxy on simple butt joints

Body Tubes

Most large body tubes have sufficient strength to handle the flight loads of high-powered rockets. Problems usually start with rockets of unusually long lengths. If the length exceeds 20 times the diameter of the tube you might consider strengthening the tube. There are two ways to do this.

First, find a tube with a greater wall thickness. This works, but it is very heavy. The second way is to add stiffeners along the length of the model. Since the greatest stress location will be just forward of the fins, start strengthening the tube there.

Make the stiffeners out of wood strips—preferably spruce, but thick balsa will also work. When you apply them to the outside of the tube they also add decoration to the rocket (Fig. 7-3). If you are going for a low-drag model, then you can add them on the inside (Fig. 7-4).

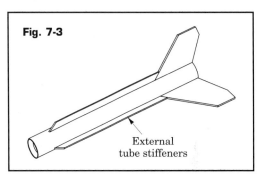

Fig. 7-3

External tube stiffeners

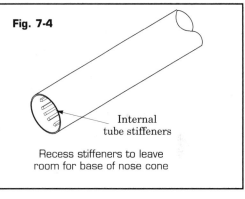

Fig. 7-4

Internal tube stiffeners

Recess stiffeners to leave room for base of nose cone

Sometimes the tube is cut by the shock cord. This is termed the zipper effect. Don't blame the body tube for this—the engine is the culprit. The problem occurs when the recovery system is not deployed at the apogee of the flight, or when the model weathercocks into the wind and never really slows down at apogee. In other words, the model is still moving forward at high speed when the parachute is deployed, and the shock cord is stretched back along the tube, cutting it down one side.

To prevent this, choose the correct engine for the model, with the appropriate delay time. If the model

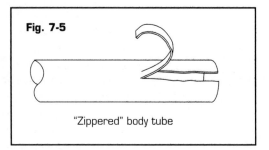

Fig. 7-5

"Zippered" body tube

has a tendency to weathercock, aim it with the wind, not into it, and select an engine with a shorter delay. This will cause a more vertical launch and a slower velocity at apogee. Final solutions might be to have the rocket come down in two pieces, separate in the middle of the model, or to use rear deployment (Fig. 7-6)

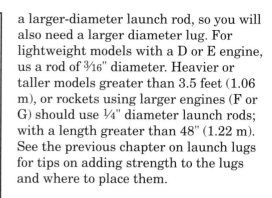

Fig. 7-6

Mid-body separation

Preventing Zippered Tubes

1. Choose the correct rocket engine delay time
2. Prevent weathercocking—launch straight up on calm days and with the wind on breezy days
3. Lengthen shock cord
4. Use rear or mid-body deployment

Launch Lugs

As the rocket gets larger you will need a stiffer launch rod to keep it stable while it sits on the pad. This typically requires

a larger-diameter launch rod, so you will also need a larger diameter lug. For lightweight models with a D or E engine, us a rod of 3/16" diameter. Heavier or taller models greater than 3.5 feet (1.06 m), or rockets using larger engines (F or G) should use 1/4" diameter launch rods; with a length greater than 48" (1.22 m). See the previous chapter on launch lugs for tips on adding strength to the lugs and where to place them.

Shock Cords

Shock cords take a tremendous beating during flight. On bigger rockets you'll want a stronger and longer cord. On models powered with E, F or G engines, use at least 1/4"-wide elastic. It can be purchased at fabric or craft stores. Try to find the kind covered with cotton thread, since it can take more heat than polyester-covered ribbon. The length of the cord should be a minimum of 48" (122 cm) on an E engine model, and at least 72" (183 cm) on G-powered models. The longer the better.

Some modelers are switching to Kevlar shock cords, since they are virtually fireproof and incredibly strong. This works, but be careful if you choose this method because Kevlar can zipper-cut body tubes. Kevlar cuts any non-Kevlar cords, too. If possible, don't mix Kevlar with non-Kevlar lines on heavy rockets.

Shock Cord Mounts: Bigger rockets also mean higher separation forces, which will put more stress on the shock cord mount. Above the D engine the typical paper shock cord mount is no longer acceptable. You must integrate the mount into the design. There are several ways to do this, including tying the shock cord to an internal brace (Fig. 7-7), slipping the shock cord around a tube coupler (Fig 7-8), and tying it to a

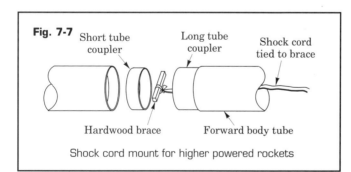

Fig. 7-7 Short tube coupler   Long tube coupler   Shock cord tied to brace

Hardwood brace   Forward body tube

Shock cord mount for higher powered rockets

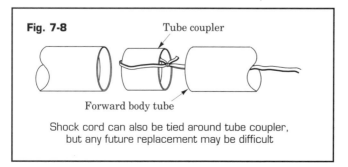

Fig. 7-8   Tube coupler

Forward body tube

Shock cord can also be tied around tube coupler, but any future replacement may be difficult

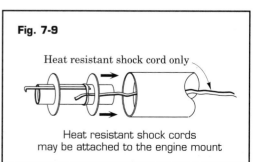

Fig. 7-9

Heat resistant shock cord only

Heat resistant shock cords may be attached to the engine mount ejection baffle (Fig. 7-18), or to a steel or Kevlar cable attached to the engine mount (Figs. 6-45 and 7-9).

Since shock cords often get burned, check the integrity of the cord by pulling hard on it prior to each flight. It is better to replace it now than to be picking up a thousand pieces of rocket after it crashes. When preforming your preflight test, also give a tug on the end attached to the nose cone. If you have a heavy wood nose cone, make sure the screw eye is large and strong enough to handle the additional forces so it doesn't get ripped out at ejection.

Pressure Relief Holes

High-flying models see a dramatic change in atmospheric pressure over the course of their flight. On the ground the pressure is higher than at the apogee of the trajectory. During flight the pressure inside the rocket remains high, equal to the atmospheric pressure of the rocket just prior to launch. Because of this, the air inside will try to escape. If there is no pressure relief hole, the pressure will tend to push the nose off the rocket. If this happens while the rocket is still traveling at high speed, the model will fail in some way.

The pressure relief hole should be at least 3/16" (5 mm) in diameter and positioned just below the nose cone so air can vent through the hole.

Engine Mounts

The strength of the engine mount is determined by the centering rings holding it in place. If they are sufficiently strong the mount will not fail. After the rings, the most important factor is how the engine is held in place. It must be restrained from moving forward or backward.

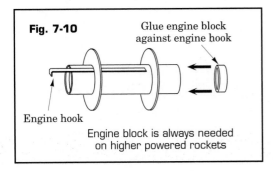

Fig. 7-10

Glue engine block against engine hook

Engine hook

Engine block is always needed on higher powered rockets

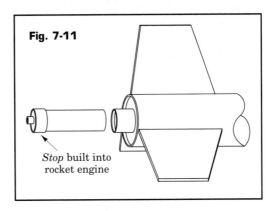

Fig. 7-11

Stop built into rocket engine

Fig. 7-12 Drill and tap hardwood blocks for engine retaining screws

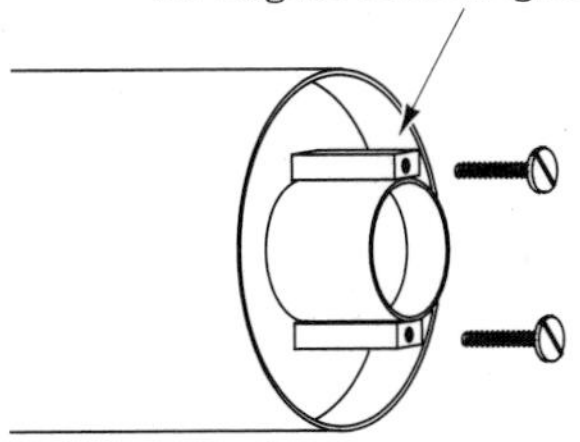

Method of restraining high powered rocket engines

To prevent the engine from possibly moving forward, an engine block is usually glued into the body tube directly ahead of the engine (Fig. 7-10). Some of the newer composite rocket motors have the engine block built directly into the motor, so you may not need a block at all if you plan on installing them into your rocket (Fig. 7-11).

Restraining the engine from sliding backward out of the rocket is just as important as keeping it from sliding forward. This is usually done with an engine hook. Another way is by gluing blind nuts on the forward side of the aft centering ring or by gluing hardwood blocks to the side of the motor tube as shown in Figure (Fig. 7-12). Drill and tap holes in the block to accept screws with large heads. The motor is then held in place by twisting the screws into the blocks after the engine is installed, with the head of the screw over the aft end of the motor.

One method you should never use on high-powered rockets is friction fitting or taping them into place. The high heat of the engine will soften or melt the glue on the tape. Use some type of mechanical fastener to hold the engine in place.

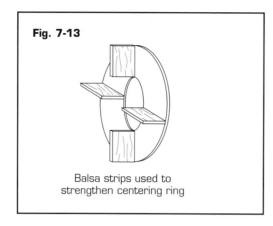

Fig. 7-13

Balsa strips used to
strengthen centering ring

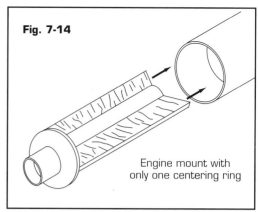

Fig. 7-14

Engine mount with
only one centering ring

Centering Rings

On model rockets using D engines or smaller, cardboard rings have sufficient strength to handle the loads imposed by the rocket engine. Above this level of power, however, you will want to make the rings stronger. You might want to build the rings from plywood, which has greater strength. If you decide to do this, try to find a low-density plywood that goes under the name "Lite-Ply" or "Wop-Pop," in order to keep the weight down.

But you don't necessarily have to change to heavier materials when it is so easy to strengthen lightweight cardboard ones. Simply gluing strips of balsa wood onto the rings between the two tubes adds a great deal of strength to the rings. The direction of the wood grain is critical, though, so be sure that it runs perpendicular to the longitudinal axis of the rocket (Figs. 7-13 and 7-14). Note that if you use through-the-wall fins you are already strengthening the centering rings (Fig. 7-15).

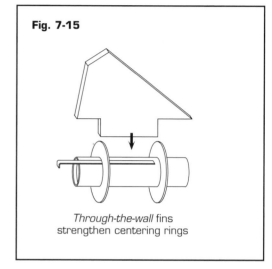

Fig. 7-15

Through-the-wall fins
strengthen centering rings

Stuffer Tubes

Larger diameter rockets have a correspondingly larger internal volume. When the ejection charge of the engine ignites it may not be strong enough to pressurize this internal volume sufficiently to push the nose cone and parachute out of the rocket. To decrease the volume to be pressurized, a smaller tube inside the outer body tube carries the ejection charge gases from the engine to the parachute compartment. It is called a stuffer tube.

All large-diameter rockets should use a stuffer tube. An added benefit is that the stuffer tube increases the strength of long tubes, so other reinforcement may not be needed.

Ejection Charge Baffles

An ejection charge baffle is a mechanical device used as a substitute for recovery wadding. It works by slowing down the gases of the ejection charge, thus giving the gas time to cool

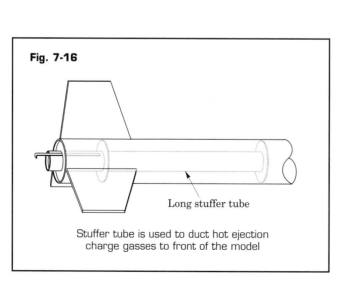

Fig. 7-16

Long stuffer tube

Stuffer tube is used to duct hot ejection
charge gasses to front of the model

before reaching the parachute. These devices also trap burning particles that might burn the parachute. Figure 7-17 depicts a simple baffle system.

Inspect and clean baffles frequently to prevent them from clogging, because they are trapping particles as they work. You may wish to design your baffle to be removable for inspection and cleaning.

Problems sometimes caused by a baffle are failure to eject the parachute or kicking the engine out of the rocket. This is because the air pressure is lower in front of the baffle than behind it (closer to the engine). Low pressure in front means there is less force to eject the parachute, while higher pressure behind means more pressure trying to kick the engine out of the rocket. Always check the baffle and make sure it is not obstructed, and also check the strength and integrity of the engine mount and the retaining device holding the engine in the rocket.

One easy alternative to ejection charge baffles on large-diameter rockets is a parachute compartment. Think of it as a cup or bucket centered inside the larger tube. The hot ejection charge gases are allowed to pass around the compartment so the parachute is completely protected. The nose cone will simply pull the chute out of the compartment because the chute is attached to its base. Figure 7-18 illustrates the design of a simple parachute compartment.

Recovery Systems

On large rockets you will probably use a parachute as the recovery device. For large rockets, use a cloth parachute instead of a plastic one. Most kit manufacturers sell nylon parachutes, which work great on these big rockets, although they are a bit more expensive. Types of fabric that also work well are cotton, silk, "rip-stop Nylon," Tyvek kite cloth, and Nomex. Just make sure the shroud lines are sewn on properly so they can handle the larger opening forces.

Proper size chute for the rocket will be discussed in Chapter 10, "Rocket Recovery Systems." If you don't have a large parachute of the proper size, you can use two or more parachutes in a cluster as shown in Figure 7-19.

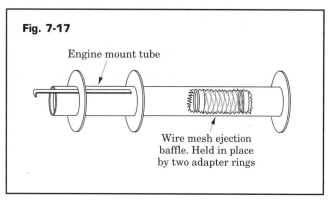

Fig. 7-17

Engine mount tube

Wire mesh ejection baffle. Held in place by two adapter rings

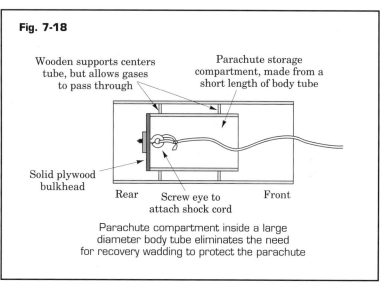

Fig. 7-18

Wooden supports centers tube, but allows gases to pass through

Parachute storage compartment, made from a short length of body tube

Solid plywood bulkhead

Rear

Screw eye to attach shock cord

Front

Parachute compartment inside a large diameter body tube eliminates the need for recovery wadding to protect the parachute

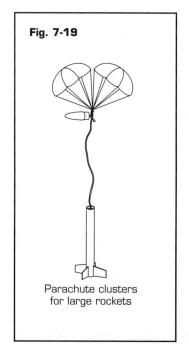

Fig. 7-19

Parachute clusters for large rockets

8

Painting and Decorating

There is more to decorating a rocket than applying paint and decals. The process of creating a smooth and attractive appearance on a rocket is called finishing. If done properly, a good finish will result in a sleek, smooth surface that not only becomes the envy of your friends, but enhances the performance of the model because it decreases drag.

A good finish does not come from the paint—it comes from careful construction. Here are some tips to help you construct your model to make it ready to paint. These steps will result in a nearly perfect finish if you follow them exactly; the level of quality is up to you.

The most unattractive parts of many models built by average rocketeers are rough, unfilled balsa fins and balsa nose cones. Balsa wood acts like a paint sponge, and if it is not suitably filled and sealed, the paint magnifies the grain and roughness of the wood. If it is not filled, you will never achieve a gloss appearance on balsa wood.

To seal balsa wood, start by sanding withlowh grit sandpaper, such as 400 grit. Apply sanding sealer with a paint brush and allow to dry. Sanding sealer, or balsa filler coat as it is sometimes called, can be found in hobby stores. You can make your own by adding talcum powder to aircraft dope. When the sealer is dry, sand it smooth. Repeat this procedure until all the pores and wood grain are invisible. If you seal the fins before attaching them to the rocket, sand off any sealer on the root edge so the glue will bond better to the fin.

Sand the entire rocket when construction is completed. Examine it closely for gaps or voids. If there are defects, fill the voids with filler paste. Use the filler paste sparingly, as the more you apply, the more you'll have to sand off. Allow it to harden completely and sand it smooth. Feather the edges of the filler with 400 grit sandpaper to blend it perfectly with the surrounding area. Pay particular attention to fillets around fins. The blend of the fillets should be very smooth if you want a perfect finish.

To help you hold the rocket while spray painting, roll a piece of heavy paper into a cone and insert it into the engine mount. Before painting, always read the safety instructions on the paint can and make sure you wear safety goggles to protect your eyes. It is best to paint outside so you don't breathe any fumes. Choose an area away from buildings and cars, and paint with your back toward the oncoming wind so you don't get overspray on your clothes.

Paint the entire model with a paint primer. Use a primer that can be easily sanded. This will help you when it dries because you will find areas that have gaps or voids. Sand them and fill the

Fig. 8-1

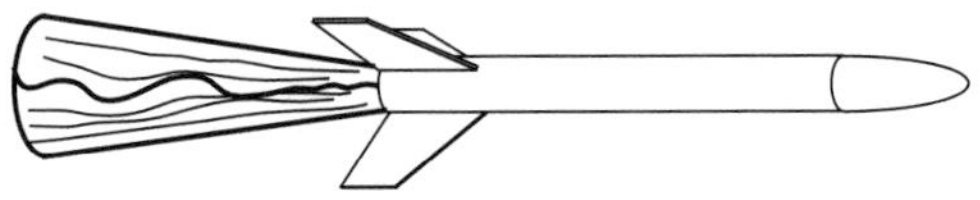

Rolled paper, used to
hold rocket while painting

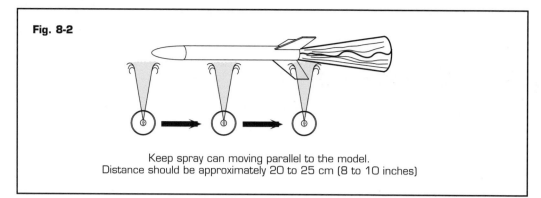

Fig. 8-2

Keep spray can moving parallel to the model.
Distance should be approximately 20 to 25 cm (8 to 10 inches)

cracks or blemishes with filler paste. If
they are very small, sometimes simply
sanding the primer will get rid of them.
Repeat this procedure until all blemishes
and paint runs are gone. Give the rocket
one last final light coat of primer and
allow it to dry for a minimum of 24
hours—or follow the instructions on the
paint can.

Now you are ready to paint. If you
used a dark color primer and are
painting your model a bright color like
yellow, red, or orange, give the model a
light undercoat of white paint first. This
will make the color even brighter. Allow
this undercoat to dry before painting on
it. Apply paint in several light coats
instead of one heavy one to prevent
running. Take your time here. You
spent a lot of time designing and building your rocket—don't ruin it now by
being in a hurry.

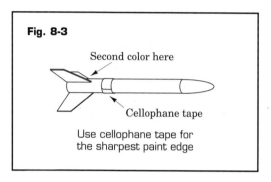

Fig. 8-3

Second color here

Cellophane tape

Use cellophane tape for
the sharpest paint edge

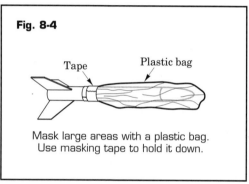

Fig. 8-4

Tape   Plastic bag

Mask large areas with a plastic bag.
Use masking tape to hold it down.

Multicolor Painting: Adding colors to
the rocket will enhance its good looks.
The key to getting a good multicolored
rocket is to let the underlying paint dry
and harden completely. Wait for a
minimum of 24 hours before even
touching the model. If you want to find
out if the paint is dry, don't touch the
rocket, touch the paper cone you inserted
into it to hold it while painting. To tell if
the paint has hardened, try to make an
impression into the paint with your
fingernail. Again, don't do this on the
rocket itself, as you could easily mar
the surface.

Before you do anything else, make
sure the paints are compatible with each
other. Sometimes spraying the second
color over the first will cause the lower
paint to dissolve, crack, and bubble. This
is called "crazing." Make a test by first
painting something you will be throwing

away later, like a spare body tube. Paint
it with the first color and allow it to dry
completely. Then spray it with the second
color. If the test is good, you are ready to
continue working on your model.

When the first paint color has
completely hardened, you are ready to
start masking the areas where you don't
want the additional color. For the
sharpest line between colors use clear
cellophane tape. To make it easier to
remove later, press the sticky surface
against your forehead. This will allow
the tape to pick up just the right amount
of skin oil so it can be pulled up easily.
Mask larger areas by taping down plastic
garbage can liners in place. Don't use
paper, as the paint could soak through
the fibers to the model. Press the tape
down firmly so there are no gaps. Paint
the model and let it completely dry
before removing the plastic or tape.

Applying Decals: The final step in finishing is applying decals. Before you start, make another check of the rocket to be sure the paint has completely dried.

Apply water transfer decals by first soaking them in warm water to dissolve the glue on the backing paper. The decal will slide easily off the paper onto the surface of the rocket. Once you have it positioned, gently blot the excess water away with a soft cotton cloth or paper towel. Bubbles under the decal can be worked out by pressing the bubble toward an edge.

If you are applying water transfer decals over paint with a dull finish you will first need to give the rocket a coat of clear gloss paint (sometimes called glosscote). It allows decals to stick better and prevents a fog from appearing under them. Allow this to dry before applying decals. After the decals are dry, and if you want the model to have a dull finish again, spray the rocket with a clear dull paint (sometimes called dullcote). Before you spray the entire rocket, test the compatibility of the paint with the decals on a test sample. It is better to ruin a test sample than your entire rocket.

Pressure-sensitive decals will stick to almost any surface, and you don't have to apply clear gloss paint. However, pressure-sensitive decals have a gloss finish, so if you want them dull you'll have to spray the model with dullcote after the decals are applied.

After cutting around the perimeter, apply the pressure-sensitive decals individually by peeling off the backing paper and laying them into place on the model. Place the middle of the decal down first and press toward the edges, working out any trapped air. If you have bubbles, cut a small slit in the decal with a hobby knife and press the air out through it.

Large pressure-sensitive decals can be hard to position. First mark the rocket with a pencil where the edge of the decal should be placed. Then peel only that edge of the decal off the backing paper. It should now be easier to position the decal correctly. When the edge is positioned, remove only small portions of the backing paper at a time while pressing the exposed sticky side down against the rocket. When the entire decal has been applied, erase the pencil line.

You might also find it easier to apply large pressure-sensitive decals if you first soak them in soapy water (one drop of dishwashing detergent to a bowl of water). The water and soap will act a as lubricant, so you can slide the decal around on the rocket. When it is in the correct position, press down firmly to remove the water underneath it. Remove any remaining water or air bubbles by slitting the decal with a sharp hobby knife.

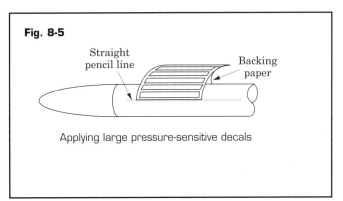

Fig. 8-5

Straight pencil line

Backing paper

Applying large pressure-sensitive decals

9

Repair Techniques

Eventually, all models suffer damage. Most of the time it is relatively minor, such as scuffed paint. Other times it can be slightly more serious, like a broken fin or a bent tube. Depending on how bad it is, most models can be repaired to fly again. The repair techniques presented here will help you restore a new appearance to your models without a lot of extra hassle.

Summary of Repair Techniques

1. Collect all pieces together
2. Examine model closely for any hidden damage or hairline cracks
3. Remove decals in the damaged area
4. Repair structural damage
5. Repair or replace any cosmetic parts or assemblies
6. Fill and seal all exposed wood grain
7. Prime and paint rocket
8. Replace decals that were removed or damaged

Scuffed Paint: Rockets commonly land on hard ground and are dragged along by the parachute, causing scratches in the paint. Your first step is to examine the rocket for structural damage, such as a cracked fin or a crushed tube. Those repair techniques are listed below, and you should fix this damage before attempting to repair the finish. If there are any decals in the area of the damage, remove them now.

If the scuff damage is limited to one area and you don't feel it is necessary to paint the entire model, mask the perimeter of the damaged area with masking tape (Fig. 9-1). Next, sand it until you get down to the primer under the paint. If the damage is on a fin,

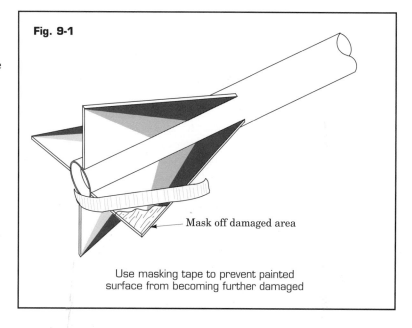

Fig. 9-1

Mask off damaged area

Use masking tape to prevent painted surface from becoming further damaged

examine it for exposed wood grain. This grain needs to be filled and sealed. If the voids or gaps are deep, use a paste-type filler. After filling or sealing the wood grain, sand the surface smooth, starting with 350 grit sandpaper and working up to a fine grain, such as 400 grit paper.

Next, paint the damaged area with paint primer. Cover the entire rocket with a plastic garbage bag, exposing only the area to be painted. Inspect when masking to see that all gaps are sealed. Use a sandable primer, and after it is dry, sand smooth any flawed areas. Repeat the primer application until no more flaws are visible or until you are satisfied with the appearance.

After the final application of primer has dried, remove the tape. This will expose the edges of the primer. You will notice a sharp raised area at the dividing line between the primer and the other painted surface. For a perfectly smooth finish, sand the edges of the primer with moistened "wet/dry" sandpaper. Use a very fine grit, such as 600. Work slowly and carefully. Clean the area after sanding with a damp cloth and allow it to dry thoroughly.

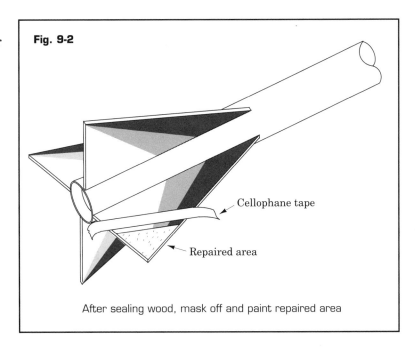

Fig. 9-2

Cellophane tape

Repaired area

After sealing wood, mask off and paint repaired area

Remask the area, this time with cellophane tape, and position it slightly farther back from the primer area. By using cellophane tape you will create a sharp paint line. Reposition the plastic garbage bag to protect the rest of the rocket from overspray and paint the area with the correct color. You may need to paint with white first so the top color is brighter. This is especially true if the top color is light, such as yellow, orange, or red.

Let the paint dry at least 24 hours before removing the plastic and tape. The area should match the rest of the rocket. You may notice a raised line around the perimeter of the painted area. If you want to remove it, try buffing it with a polishing compound—ordinary toothpaste on a rag works well. You may also want to spray the entire model with a clear coat, such as glosscote or dullcote. This will also help hide blemishes.

Repairing Damaged Balsa Fins: A damaged fin is the second most common repair needed on a model rockets. The damage can take several different forms: a dent, a crack, a chip, or complete obliteration.

Dents are indentations in the fins where no loss of wood fiber has occurred. If the wood is exposed, try adding a drop of water over the dent. This sometimes causes the fibers to swell and may remove the dent. If not, fill the indentation with a paste-type filler, allow to dry, and sand the area smooth.

Cracks occur in two places, along the joint holding the fin to the model or somewhere parallel to the wood grain.

Either way, the repair technique is similar: get glue into the split line and allow it to dry. A good glue to use in this situation is water-thin instant glue. It penetrates deep into the grain of the wood. After the glue has dried, fill voids with the paste-type filler and seal the exposed wood with a sealer. If the crack occurred at the body tube, make a new fillet out of glue or epoxy.

Chipped fins are those from which a piece has broken off. It helps if you can find the piece and simply glue it back into place. Apply glue to the edges before you reinsert it into position. This will allow the glue to penetrate deeply into the fibers of the wood.

If the broken piece is lost you can make a new piece. First, cut away the damaged area and cut a piece of wood to match (Figs. 9-4 and 9-5). Cut it slightly large so it can be sanded to a perfect match later. Glue it into place and allow the glue to harden completely. If there are any gaps along the glue line, fill them with a paste-type filler.

After the filler has dried, sand the fin into shape. This includes sanding the airfoil into the fin, if it had one. Seal the new exposed wood with a wood sealer and prepare the area for painting.

When a fin has been damaged severely, replace it completely. This also goes for plywood fins, since they shatter when they break. Remove the old fin from the rocket. If the glue joint along the body tube is very strong, don't try to snap the fin off—it could damage the body tube. You can cut the fin off with a hobby knife or a razor saw. Try to make the cut as close to the tube as possible without damaging it.

Using coarse sandpaper, remove the rest of the fin from the body tube. Sand the old fillet away, too. When you've finished, the paper of the body tube should be exposed, so the joint of the new fin can be as strong as the first joint.

Make a new fin by tracing around one of the remaining fins on the rocket. Sand and seal the surfaces before attaching the new fin into the location of the old. Then apply a new fillet to match the remaining ones on the rocket. Now the model is ready to be painted.

Damaged plastic fins are harder to

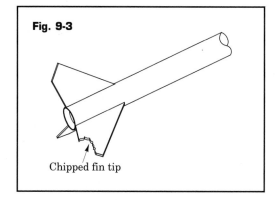

Fig. 9-3

Chipped fin tip

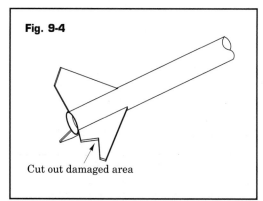

Fig. 9-4

Cut out damaged area

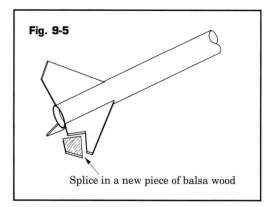

Fig. 9-5

Splice in a new piece of balsa wood

repair. If necessary, replace them entirely. Follow the steps above to remove and replace a broken fin.

Nose Cone Repair: Since there are two basic materials for nose cones, there are different repair strategies. Balsa nose cones are treated much like balsa fins. If the nose is just dented and all the wood fibers are intact, place a drop of water on the dented area. With luck, the fibers will swell, and the dent will pop out. If this fails, fill the area with filler paste. After it has hardened, sand it into shape. Seal any exposed grain and prepare the surface for painting.

Plastic nose cones are slightly harder to repair. Small plastic nose cones are usually made of styrene, which is easy to glue back together. Plastic model cements work well on this material. Use a liquid plastic cement to glue the damaged area back together. This works well on cracks, since the liquid will penetrate and bond the edges together.

On large nose cones you may need to determine what the part is made of. Bigger parts are sometimes made of polyethylene or polypropylene, two types of plastic that do not readily accept glue. If the nose is styrene, you can use plastic model cement; otherwise, you'll have to apply a doubler to the inside of the part with epoxy. This involves cutting a hole in the back of the nose to gain access to the inside. The doubler can be anything that gives rigidity to the damaged area. Fiberglass cloth applied with epoxy works well because you can be shape it easily before the epoxy cures and hardens.

After completing the repair, you may have to reinforce the inside of the rocket around the plastic loop so it can still hold the nose cone to the rocket. To prevent the rocket from being damaged if the loop should fail, tie the parachute to the shock cord rather than to the loop on the nose cone. When damage to the plastic nose is extensive, it may be easier and wiser to simply replace it.

Repairing Body Tubes: Body tubes most commonly suffer three types of damage. The first is crushing around the top. This can occur when the rocket lands on the ground front end first, or it can be the result of nose cone snap-back. Nose

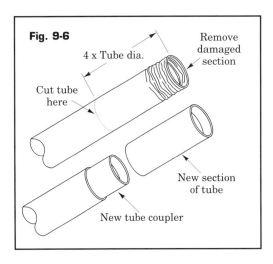

Fig. 9-6

4 x Tube dia.

Cut tube here

Remove damaged section

New section of tube

New tube coupler

cone snap-back is caused at ejection when the nose extends all the way out on the shock cord and recoils back into the top of the body tube, causing crushing (Fig. 9-6).

The way to prevent snap-back is to make the shock cord longer or make it of some material that doesn't store energy. But if the damage has already occurred you must determine your next course of action. If the damage is slight, such as delamination of a paper layer or minor flaring of the tube, you can do a quick repair. Wetting the fibers of the paper tube with water-thin instant glue. You'll have to work quickly because the glue will set up fast. While the glue is still liquid, reshape the tube with your fingertips. To prevent your skin from sticking to the tube, wear plastic gloves or cover your hand with a plastic sandwich bag.

The other two common types of damage are zippered tubes and the buckling of long tubes, both of which require replacement of the damaged sections. Zippered tubes occur when the recovery device is deployed while the rocket is at high speed. The nose cone and shock cord immediately slow down while the rest of the rocket keeps traveling forward. The body tube is often cut down the side by the shock cord when this happens. See page 53 for an illustration of a zippered tube. Buckling occurs on longer body tubes. It is a kink that results when the tube tries to bend

beyond its capability to resist bending.

Begin repairs by removing the damaged part. In Chapter 6 I described a way to make a straight cut around the tube. It called for wrapping a straight piece of paper around the tube next to the cut line (Fig. 6-1). This is the recommended method for cutting tubes with fins already attached. If the damaged area is near the top of the tube, I recommend that you cut it down at least four tube diameters, so you will have room to insert the nose cone after replacing the section.

Clean out the inside of the remaining body tube with a damp cloth to remove any residue from the ejection charge, since the glue will not bond the tube if it is dirty. Now you can join a new tube coupler and a new section of tube to the model. Use wood glue for bonding paper tubes, since it will give a stronger bond. Fill the seam between the two body tubes with paste-type putty. Fill the spiral seams this way, as well, to make the model smooth.

Removing Old Decals: You'll have to replace old decals, since it is impossible to salvage them. You can remove water transfer decals easily by laying a sticky piece of tape over them and quickly peeling it away. It may take several attempts to remove the entire decal.

Peel up pressure-sensitive decals carefully. Use your fingernail or hobby knife to grab a corner to start peeling. These decals tear easily, so take your time. Remove the entire decal. Many times it leaves a glue residue behind on the surface. The best solvent to remove this is rubber cement thinner. Other solvents, such as lacquer thinner or acetone, don't work well on the adhesive and may dissolve the paint. Always test the solvent on a small area, so you don't ruin the entire surface of the model.

New decals can be ordered from the manufacturer. If they are out of stock, you may have to change the decor of the model. Techniques for applying new decals are listed in Chapter 8, "Painting and Decorating."

10

Rocket Recovery Systems

(photo by Marc Lavigne)

Streamer Design

Use streamers on any small rocket with a mass less than about 30 grams (1.05 ounce) or on rockets that fly extremely high. Rockets that fly to high altitudes would otherwise drift out of sight with the wind and you would probably lose them.

Use almost any type of thin, soft, flexible material to make a streamer. Such materials include thin plastic sheet, crepe paper, and fabrics like cotton, silk, nylon, and polyester. The color is up to you, but consider those that show up against the sky as well as on the ground. Red and orange are good colors. If you don't like the color of your streamer, you may be able to color it with a permanent marker.

The area of the streamer depends on the weight of the rocket. Have at least 8.5 cm2 (1.3 in^2) of single side surface area per gram of returned model mass (the mass of the rocket plus the mass of an expended rocket engine case). In general, make the length of the streamer at least 10 times its width. This will give the most amount of drag for the area of the streamer.

Example: Find the minimum size streamer to safely recover a 16 gram model with an empty mini-engine casing that has a mass of 4.12 grams

$$Area\ of\ Streamer = \left(\frac{8.5\ cm^2}{g}\right) \times (16 + 4.12\ g)$$
$$Area\ of\ Streamer = 171\ cm^2$$
$$Width = W$$
$$Length = L = 10 \times W$$
$$Area = W \times L$$
$$Area = W \times (10 \times W)$$
$$Area = 10 \times W^2$$
$$W = \sqrt{\frac{Area}{10}}$$
$$Width = 4.14\ cm$$
$$Length = 41.4\ cm$$

You can attach your streamer to your rocket the same way you attach a parachute (see p. 48).

Parachute Design

Parachutes can be used on almost any size rocket. A parachute can control the model's descent speed more accurately and bring the model down more slowly than any other recovery method. The best materials are any strong, thin, soft, flexible material. For small models, thin plastic sheets work very well because they can be folded up tightly to fit into small-diameter body tubes. Some sources for parachute canopies include Mylar, plastic drop cloths, dry-cleaning bags, trash bags, and gift-wrapping plastic. Use care when selecting a plastic material for a parachute. Test it by trying to tear it in both directions— sometimes the material is strong in one direction but weak in another. Use only plastic that is strong in both directions.

For rockets with a descent mass greater than 300 grams (10.5 ounces), use a cloth material like cotton, silk, polyester, or nylon. These materials can withstand the larger opening forces that bigger models can create.

Heat-resistant parachutes can be made from certain types of plastic and cloth. For a plastic chute, you can try oven-roasting bags. They are used to cook large turkeys and other game birds. For a heat resistant cloth, Nomex works very well. It is often used to make flight suits for pilots and jackets for firefighters. Some model rocket manufacturers sell Nomex parachutes.

If you want the rocket to come down slightly faster and without drifting far in windy conditions, cut a *spill hole* in the top of the canopy. This allows air to flow through, increasing the descent rate. The larger the spill hole the faster the model will fall. Again, try to find a material with a high-visibility color, both in the sky and on the ground.

Parachute Size

As a general rule of thumb, design the chute so the descent velocity of your rocket should be 3.5 to 4.5 meters per second (11.5 to 14.8 feet per second). You can determine the area of the parachute from the following equation:

$$S = \left(\frac{2 \times g \times m}{\rho \times C_d \times V^2} \right)$$

where S is the area of the parachute, g is the acceleration due to gravity, which has a value of 9.81 m/s at sea level, m is the mass of the rocket (with empty engine)

as measured in grams, ρ is the density of air (1225 g/m³) at sea level, C_d is the coefficient of drag and is estimated at 0.75 for a round canopy, and V is the descent velocity you choose. If you want a round canopy, the diameter is found by the formula:

$$D = \left(\frac{4 \times S}{\pi} \right)$$

where D is the diameter of the parachute and π has a value 3.14.

The chart shown is a quick reference for typical sizes of parachutes versus their descent mass, based on a round canopy.

Rocket Mass	Parachute Diameter
20 g	22 cm (8.5")
40 g	31 cm (12")
80 g	43 cm (17")
100 g	48 cm (19")
150 g	59 cm (23")
200 g	69 cm (27")
300 g	84 cm (33")

If you are using a canopy of another shape you can easily find the area from the following formula valid for regular polygons:

$$Area = \frac{n}{4} \times D^2 \times tan\left(\frac{180°}{n} \right)$$

where n is the number of sides, and D is the distance as measured across the polygon's flats. Below are listed the areas of four common parachute shapes— circles, squares, hexagons, and octagons.

Parachute Shape	Area Formula
Square	D^2
Hexagon	$0.866 \times D^2$
Octagon	$0.828 \times D^2$
Circle	$\frac{1}{4} \times \pi \times D^2$

Shroud Lines: Shroud lines can be made from a variety of materials, as most strings or thin cords will work well. Try to find a heat-resistant material to withstand the heat of the ejection charge. Cotton string works better than synthetic materials such as nylon or polyester (if they have the same thickness). Kevlar also has high heat resistance and makes an excellent shroud line material.

The length of each shroud line is usually 1.0 to 1.5 times the diameter of the canopy. Additional length does not

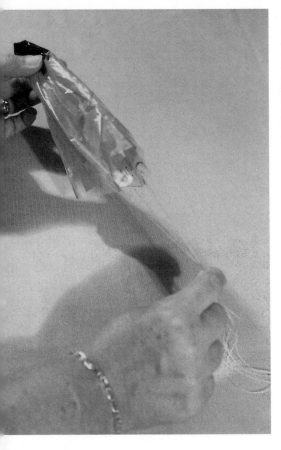

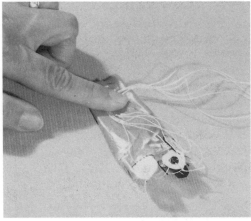

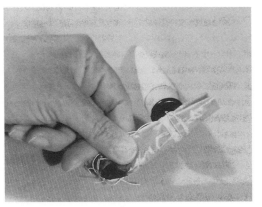

increase the parachute's effectiveness and only makes it easier for the lines to tangle. If the ends of the shroud lines are each attached to the canopy, be sure to double the length of each before you cut them.

Attaching Shroud Lines: Plastic parachutes have to be reinforced where the shroud lines are attached. This can be done using self-adhesive notebook reinforcement rings. Punch a hole through the plastic in the middle of the reinforcement ring, and tie the string to the chute.

For additional strength on larger parachutes, loop the shroud lines over the top of the canopy and secure them with tape to the canopy. This will protect the plastic from overexpanding and possibly tearing.

If you plan to use a cloth parachute, the only currently acceptable method for attaching the shroud lines is to sew them to the canopy material.

Proper Parachute Folding Techniques: The technique you use to fold the parachute for insertion into the body tube can affect its chances of opening. This is especially true on rockets with small-diameter body tubes using plastic parachutes.

To fold a parachute, begin by grabbing the it at the apex of the canopy and pulling outward to form a spike. Fold this spike in half. On plastic parachutes, do not fold lengthwise any more than you have already. Take the shroud lines and gently fold them backwards so they lay on top of the folded parachute. Now fold the sides of the parachute inward so you cover the shroud lines. Gently roll the parachute into a something that resembles a long cigar. There may be some extra shroud line hanging out of the chute. Wrap them loosely around the outside of the rolled chute.

Insert the parachute into the body tube last, after you have put in the recovery wadding and shock cord line. This will protect it from the heat of the ejection charge. The parachute should fit loosely inside the tube. If you think it is too tight, it probably is. Re-pack the chute until it is loose within the tube. You can check the tightness by blowing into the back end of the rocket. If the parachute moves, it will probably blow out of the tube by the force of the ejection charge.

Dusting with talcum powder just prior to flight helps keep the parachute loose and will aid the opening forces. Don't prep the parachute until you are ready to launch, because plastic sometimes sets and becomes stiff, which may cause it to fail to open fully. This risk is particularly great during cold weather.

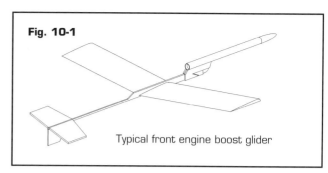

Fig. 10-1

Typical front engine boost glider

Glider Design

Gliders accomplish more than typical sport rockets and give extra excitement to a rocket flight. Moreover, the added complexity of these models creates additional challenges to rocketeers who want to expand their skills into other areas of aeronautics.

Designing gliders boosted by rockets takes additional thought because the vehicle has to withstand the forces of launch that can approach 100 mph (161 km/hr). Additionally, the glider has two phases of flight, *boost* and *glide,* and it must be aerodynamically stable in both phases. During the flight, the CG must switch from being forward of the CP during the boost phase to being in the same location as the CP for a stable glide. Shifting the CG is the key to successful glider operation

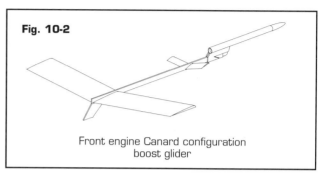

Fig. 10-2

Front engine Canard configuration
boost glider

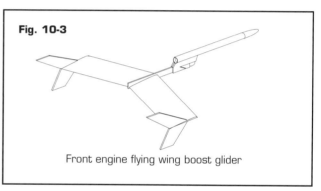

Fig. 10-3

Front engine flying wing boost glider

(Fig. 10-4). Before designing any glider, read this entire chapter to get a feel for how one operates.

Types of Gliders: Gliders used in rocketry are classified into two categories. Boosted gliders, known as *boost gliders* (BG), are simple gliders. After a rocket motor lofts the model into the air and the propellant

is completely burned up, the rocket motor falls away from the glider. *Rocket gliders* (RG) are usually more complex than boost gliders because the empty rocket engine casing does not separate from the glider. These models comes down in one piece with no separation of parts.

Subcategories of each of these are characterized by the location of the rocket motor and the location of the wing. If the wing is forward of the horizontal tail the model has a *conventional* configuration. If the horizontal tail is ahead of the main wing the model is a *canard* configuration. Finally, if the glider has no horizontal tail it is called a *flying wing*.

Rocket Motor Position on Gliders: Rocket motor placement is up to you, but typical locations are either at the front or the rear of the model. Placement is critical for proper operation. It will have

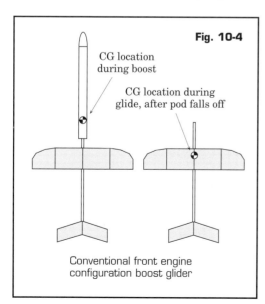

Fig. 10-4

CG location during boost

CG location during glide, after pod falls off

Conventional front engine configuration boost glider

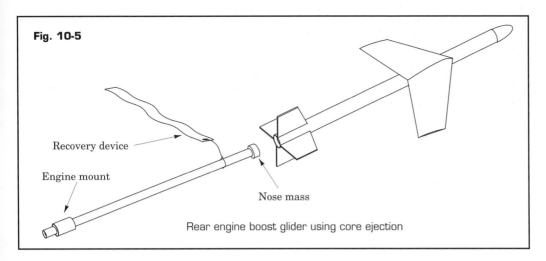

Fig. 10-5

Recovery device

Engine mount

Nose mass

Rear engine boost glider using core ejection

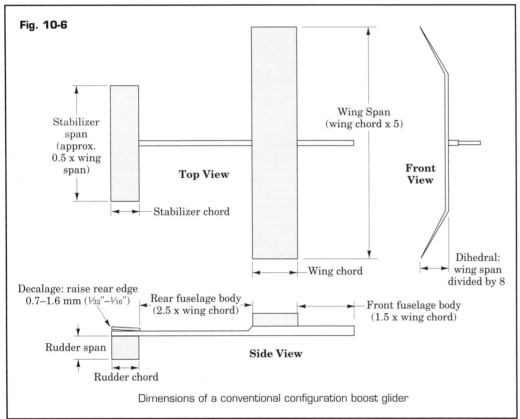

Fig. 10-6

Stabilizer span (approx. 0.5 x wing span)

Top View

Stabilizer chord

Wing Span (wing chord x 5)

Front View

Wing chord

Dihedral: wing span divided by 8

Decalage: raise rear edge 0.7–1.6 mm ($\frac{1}{32}$"–$\frac{1}{16}$")

Rear fuselage body (2.5 x wing chord)

Front fuselage body (1.5 x wing chord)

Rudder span

Side View

Rudder chord

Dimensions of a conventional configuration boost glider

a direct effect on aerodynamic stability since the CG must be ahead of the CP for a stable boost phase. In gliders this is usually accomplished by locating the rocket motor near the front of the glider. The relatively heavy engine pod will shift the CG forward of the CP. The farther forward the CG, the more stable the rocket will be during boost. To give extra stability, make the engine pod longer so it extends farther forward, or add nose mass to it (Figs. 10-5 and 2-7).

The CP of a conventional glider is located approximately ¼ to ½ the length of the wing *chord* behind the *leading*

edge of the wing. When the engine burns out, the CG of the model must move back to coincide with the CP for the model to maintain a stable glide. In boost gliders you can attain this shift in CG by dropping the engine pod off the glider. In rocket gliders, since you keep everything attached to the glider, you have two options—move the CG rearward or move the CP forward. We'll discuss this later.

Placement of the motor at the rear of the model causes a conflict with the boost stability. This can be overcome by moving a control surface on the model after engine burnout to change the location of

Size Chart for Gliders Using Differing Engine Sizes

		Engine Power			
		1/2A	A	B	C
Wing	Chord	2"	2.5"	3"	4"
	Span	10"	12.5"	15"	20"
	Area	20 in²	31.25 in²	45 in²	60 in²
Stab	Chord	1.2"	1.5"	1.8"	2.4"
	Span	5"	6.75"	7.5"	10"
	Area	6 in²	10.13 in²	13.5 in²	24 in²
Rudder	Chord	1.2"	1.5"	1.8"	2"
	Span	1.0"	1.3"	1.5"	1.8"
	Area	1.2 in²	1.95 in²	2.7 in²	3.6 in²
Fuselage Body	Rear	5"	6.25"	7.5"	9.0"
	Front	2.5"	3.13"	3.75"	5.0"

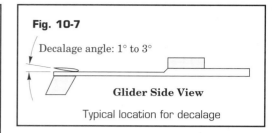

Fig. 10-7

Decalage angle: 1° to 3°

Glider Side View

Typical location for decalage

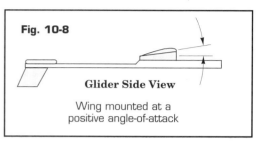

Fig. 10-8

Glider Side View

Wing mounted at a positive angle-of-attack

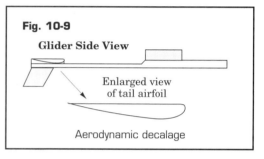

Fig. 10-9

Glider Side View

Enlarged view of tail airfoil

Aerodynamic decalage

the CP, or by dropping some mass out of the model to move the CG back over the proper wing location. The latter is usually called *core ejection*, because the entire engine and some nose weight is ejected out of the rear. Figure 10-5 shows how to accomplish this change in CG.

Sometimes the CG and the CP are both shifted. This is usually a combination of ejecting the engine and moving a control surface. The effect combines the advantages of a lower glider mass and increased efficiency by moving a control surface.

Design of Conventional Configuration Gliders: Gliders using the conventional configuration, where the wing is ahead of the tail, are usually the easiest to build and fly successfully. Construction starts with determining the size of the aerodynamic surfaces. The table above shows typical proportions of a conventional glider expressed in inches. These sizes were developed by Dr. Gerald M. Gregorek at Ohio State University in 1970. Figure 10-6 shows

how to use these dimensions in the construction of your models.

Determine the thickness of the wood for the different parts of the glider from the table below.

Construction methods of gliders do not differ greatly from those of other model rockets. If you want long glide times, remember to keep the mass of the glider low. Do this by eliminating any paint. Sand the balsa surfaces and seal them with aircraft dope. Some aircraft dopes have color pigments in their mixtures, but if they don't you can color your models by using permanent felt-tip markers. For gliders, choose a dark color for the bottom of the glider and a bright color for the top. This will help you find it both in the air and on the ground.

One key construction tip is unique to gliders. Add negative *decalage* to the horizontal tail. Decalage is defined as the relative angle between the wing's *angle-of-attack* and the horizontal stabilizer's *angle-of-attack*. This

Wood Type and Thicknesses for the Different Glider Parts

Engine Power	Wing	Tail Surfaces	Fuselage Boom
1/2A	1/16" light balsa	1/32" med hard balsa	1/8" hard balsa
A	1/16–3/32" light balsa	1/32" med hard balsa	1/8" hard balsa
B	3/32–1/8" light balsa	1/16" light balsa	1/8" spruce
C	1/8" hard balsa	3/32" light balsa	1/8" spruce

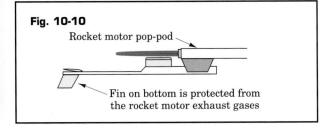

Fig. 10-10

Rocket motor pop-pod

Fin on bottom is protected from the rocket motor exhaust gases

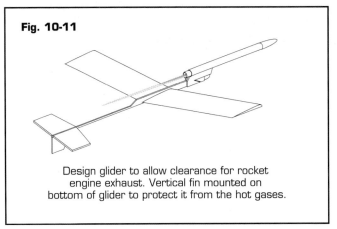

Fig. 10-11

Design glider to allow clearance for rocket engine exhaust. Vertical fin mounted on bottom of glider to protect it from the hot gases.

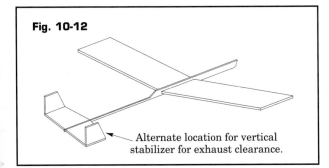

Fig. 10-12

Alternate location for vertical stabilizer for exhaust clearance.

difference in angle allows the glider to pull out of a dive. This angle is usually very small, between 1 and 3 degrees.

There are a few ways to add decalage. The most common is to install the tail at a negative angle-of-attack so the trailing edge is higher than the leading edge (Fig. 10-7). Another way is to add the decalage to the wing by installing it to the boom (the body of the glider) at a positive angle-of-attack (Fig. 10-8). The final method is to mount both the wing and tail at the same angle-of-attack, but sand the horizontal tail into a cambered airfoil shape and mount it upside down, with the convex side downward (Fig. 10-9). This is aerodynamic decalage and is actually the most efficient method for gliders with fixed horizontal stabilizers.

Something else you may have noticed in the illustrations is that the *vertical tail* is mounted on the bottom of front engine gliders. The reason for placement this is simple. The rocket engine is mounted on the top of the fuselage boom, and the exhaust might otherwise burn the tail. It really doesn't matter if the vertical tail is on the top or bottom—place it where it won't be damaged (Figs. 10-10 and 10-11). Another option is to place the vertical stabilizer on the tips of the horizontal stabilizer. In this case, the rudder can be mounted on the top or the bottom (Fig. 10-12).

Engine Pods for Boost Gliders: The way to shift the CG in boost gliders is to eject the engine pod. The engine pod

(sometimes called a *glider pop-pod*), is a typical model rocket without any fins, but with a means of attaching the body tube to the boom of the glider. Inside, it contains a recovery system for bringing it safely to the ground. Since this is so similar to a typical rocket, I'll just concentrate on the methods used to attach the body tube to the glider.

Most pods are held to the glider boom by a simple friction fit. This is what prevents them from falling backward off the glider while the model is sitting on the pad prior to launch. To keep the pod from coming off during the thrust phase of the flight, the pod has a hook that engages some type of catch on the boom of the glider. Side plates on either the boom or the pod prevent the pod from releasing laterally.

Figures 10-13 through 10-15 show methods you could use in your own boost glider designs. You may not want your model to rely on friction to hold the pod to the glider. Figure 10-16 shows a pod that is prevented from falling backward by the interaction between the launch rod and the hook-and-catch mechanisms.

The pop-pod should fit snugly onto the boom but side rearward easily. The pod falls off the glider when the streamer is ejected from the model and the drag on the streamer pulls the pod rearward, releasing it. A test to determine the snugness of the pod can be performed as follows: place the pod on the glider—it should stay attached to the boom without falling off or otherwise moving. Hold the glider by the boom in the launch position, ie., vertically, but just behind the wing. Give the glider a slight downward snap with your wrist—the pop-pod should fall

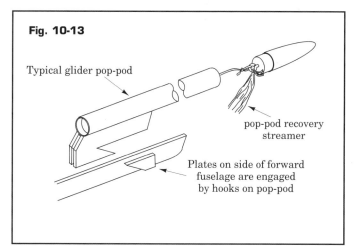

Fig. 10-13

Typical glider pop-pod

pop-pod recovery streamer

Plates on side of forward fuselage are engaged by hooks on pop-pod

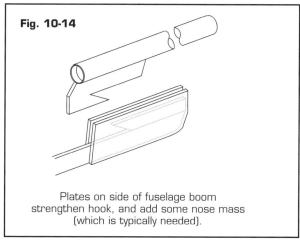

Fig. 10-14

Plates on side of fuselage boom strengthen hook, and add some nose mass (which is typically needed).

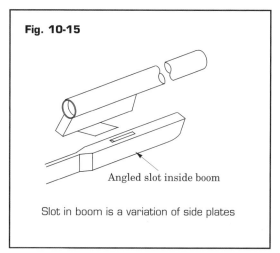

Fig. 10-15

Angled slot inside boom

Slot in boom is a variation of side plates

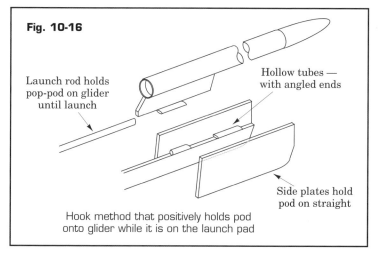

Fig. 10-16

Launch rod holds pop-pod on glider until launch

Hollow tubes — with angled ends

Side plates hold pod on straight

Hook method that positively holds pod onto glider while it is on the launch pad

off easily. Sand the sides if the boom of the pod is too tight, or add small strips of adhesive tape to their sides if the pod is too loose.

The recovery device for the pod should be as small as possible, yet allow a safe recovery for the rocket engine and pod. Use a streamer instead of a parachute, since there is less chance of the glider getting tangled in a streamer when the pod is jettisoned.

The length of the pod plays an important role in the stability of the rocket during the boost phase. The design conflict you must solve is this: the pod should be long for a stable boost, but this will add excess mass to the entire vehicle. I recommend that you start with a long pod and gradually reduce the length until you feel comfortable that you have minimized the weight while still keeping the rocket stable.

One thing all front-engine boost and rocket gliders must have is exhaust clearance. Placing the pod on a short pylon so the exhaust does not impinge on the wing or tail of the glider (Fig. 10-10). Typical values of clearance are from ½" to ¾" (12.7 to 19 mm) above the fuselage boom. If it is much higher than this the rocket could loop in the air by pitching downward as it clears the launch rod. When construction is complete it is time to trim the model for flight. See page 80 for this last step.

Canard Glider Design

Canard gliders are characterized by a small horizontal stabilizer in front of the main wing. The advantage of this design is that they have less tendency to stall compared with conventional gliders. Additionally, the horizontal tail helps create positive lift instead of negative lift, which is typical of conventional designs. Although canard gliders are fun to design and build, don't expect them to outperform conventional gliders. They haven't been proven to outglide other types even with the extra lift provided by the canard wing.

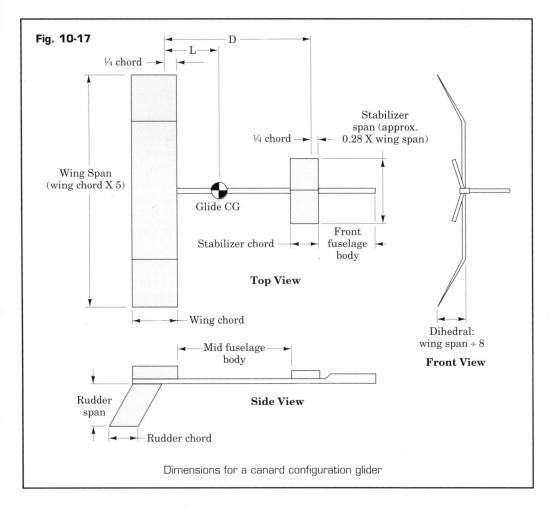

Fig. 10-17

Top View

Wing Span
(wing chord X 5)

¼ chord

D

L

Glide CG

Stabilizer
span (approx.
0.28 X wing span)

¼ chord

Stabilizer chord

Front
fuselage
body

Wing chord

Dihedral:
wing span ÷ 8

Front View

Mid fuselage
body

Rudder
span

Side View

Rudder chord

Dimensions for a canard configuration glider

There haven't been many designs of canard boost gliders, so it is harder to generate firm design rules. You will have to experiment more with your designs to get them to fly properly. A good place to start is by sizing your glider. The table and Figure 10-17 on this page show some general sizes for canard aircraft.

The thickness of wood is the same as for conventional gliders of the same engine power. Use the table on page 70 to determine the type and thickness of balsa wood you'll need.

Several qualities are unique to canard configuration airplanes. First, the canard must have a higher *coefficient of lift* than the main wing. You can do this by giving the larger aft wing a symmetrical airfoil section, while the forward canard should have a cambered airfoil, mounted at a positive angle-of-attack (Fig. 10-18). Also, give both the canard and main wing some dihedral. Dihedral is defined as raising the wing tip higher than the root edge, where it attaches to the fuselage boom. Without this, the glider will not be stable along the roll axis.

Give the rudder on a canard aircraft a lot of backsweep for maximum lateral stability (Fig. 10-17).

Finally, the location of the CG is more difficult to determine, since it is not at the ¼ chord location on the main wing. It is forward of this location. Assuming

Dimensions of Canard Type Gliders with Different Engine Sizes

		Engine Size		
		½A	A	B
Wing	Chord	2	2.5	3
	Span	10	12.5	15
	Area	20	31.25	45
Stab	Chord	1.2	1.5	1.8
	Span	2.75	3.46	4.16
	Area	3.3	5.2	7.5
Rudder	Chord	1.2	1.5	1.8
	Span	1.85	2.31	2.77
	Area	2.22	3.47	5
Body	Front	1.93	2.83	3.73
	Middle	3.86	5.66	7.46
	Total	9	12.5	16

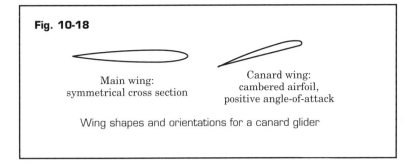

Fig. 10-18

Main wing:
symmetrical cross section

Canard wing:
cambered airfoil,
positive angle-of-attack

Wing shapes and orientations for a canard glider

that the lift coefficients are the same for both wings, the ratio of the wing areas leads to the CG location. The equation below and Figure 10-17 will give you a good starting point for determining this location:

$$L = \frac{A_c}{A_w} \times D$$

Where L is the location of the CG measured forward from the ¼ chord line of the main wing, A_c is the surface area of the canard, A_w is the surface area of the larger main wing, and D is the distance between the ¼ chord lines of the wing and the canard. The location of the CG will probably be slightly ahead of this point because of the difference in the lift coefficients of the two lifting surfaces. You can determine the exact location later by actual hand tossing.

The location of the CG for the boost portion of the flight should be between the quarter and half chord lines on the canard wing. You will have to adjust this CG by the proper position and size of the engine pod.

Flying Wing Design

Flying wings are stable airplanes without horizontal tails. Not only do flying wings look neat, they are very efficient gliders. By stripping the glider down to the bare bones, and when only the wing remains, you've eliminated a lot of drag. This drastic reduction in drag is what allows the flying wing to fly fast and efficiently.

As you may realize, a wing by itself will not fly straight and level—it is unstable. Yet flying wings do fly straight and level. They are simple looking, but in reality they are quite complex.

Stability in a flying wing can come from using a stable airfoil section, by geometric means, or a combination of both. The most common stable airfoil section is a simple cambered one where the trailing edge has been bent upward, called a *reflexed airfoil (Fig. 10-19)*. With this simple airfoil, and by properly positioning the CG of the wing, your flying wing will fly straight and level. The CG is usually in front of the wing, and this requires a short fuselage. This simple glider is called a *flying plank (Fig. 10-21)*. Another type of flying wing that uses a reflexed airfoil is the delta wing

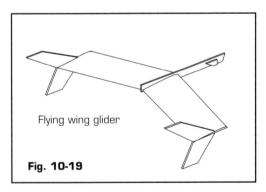

Flying wing glider

Fig. 10-19

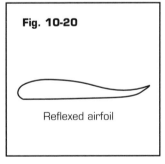

Fig. 10-20

Reflexed airfoil

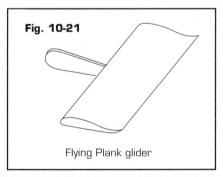

Fig. 10-21

Flying Plank glider

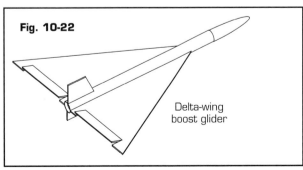

Fig. 10-22

Delta-wing
boost glider

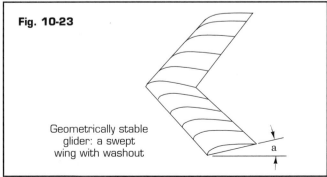

Fig. 10-23

Geometrically stable
glider: a swept
wing with washout

a

configuration. On this long airfoil the trailing edge or the elevons are bent slightly upward to provide stability.

Geometric stability is accomplished by sweeping the wing backward and adding *washout (Fig. 10-23)* to the tips. This is a permanent warp of the wings to decrease the angle-of-attack of the wingtips. Warping the tips of balsa wings can be done, but it is difficult. A simpler way is to cut the tips of the wings at a slight diagonal with respect to the centerline of the glider and bend them down as shown in the photo below. This is called a *diffuser tip wing*.

The sweep allows you to manipulate the CG of the wing. The CG must be ahead of the CP for the wing to be stable, and sweeping the wing moves the CP rearward, as Figure 10-24 shows.

Finding the location of the CP is somewhat complicated, but it can be done if you follow these steps and refer to Figure 10-25. First, draw the outline of the wing to scale. Now extend the *root edge* of the wing upward and downward by the length of the *tip chord*. Do the same thing to the tip edge, but this time the length to extend is the *root chord* length. Next, draw two diagonal lines from the ends of the two lines you just extended. The intersection of these diagonal lines is the average chord of the wing. You can find the length of this chord by drawing a vertical line through the intersection of the two diagonal lines to the leading and trailing edges.

Now measure and mark the root edge a distance of ¼ the length of the *root edge* length. Repeat this on the tip edge

using a distance of ¼ of the *tip edge* length. Connect the two points you just marked—this line becomes the ¼ chord line. The CP of the half wing is at the intersection of the ¼ chord line and the average chord line. You can draw a horizontal line from this point to the root edge of the wing. This point is the CP of the entire glider.

When you balance the glider, make sure that when you start the CG is slightly ahead of the CP. You may need to add a short fuselage to move the CG far enough forward (Figs. 10-20 and 10-21).

One problem with flying wings is they are not very stable in yaw. To increase stability, add a vertical tail. Put it as far back as possible and sweep it backward.

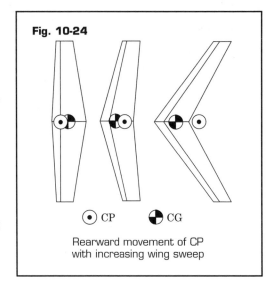

Fig. 10-24

⊙ CP   ◑ CG

Rearward movement of CP with increasing wing sweep

Photo below: a simple diffuser-tip flying wing. (photo by Steven A. Bachmeyer)

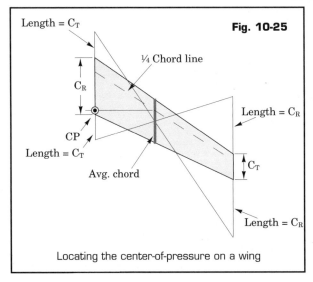

Fig. 10-25

Length = C_T

¼ Chord line

C_R

Length = C_R

CP

Length = C_T

Avg. chord

C_T

Length = C_R

Locating the center-of-pressure on a wing

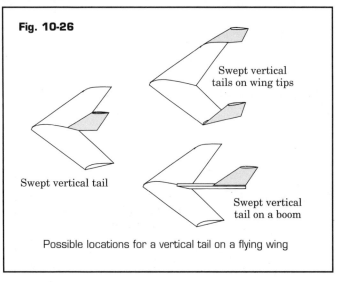

Fig. 10-26

Swept vertical tails on wing tips

Swept vertical tail

Swept vertical tail on a boom

Possible locations for a vertical tail on a flying wing

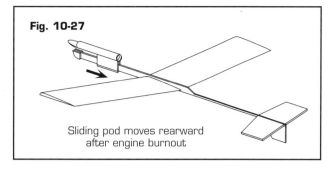

Fig. 10-27

Sliding pod moves rearward
after engine burnout

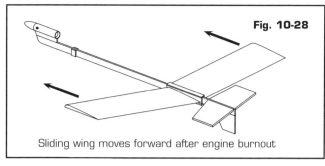

Fig. 10-28

Sliding wing moves forward after engine burnout

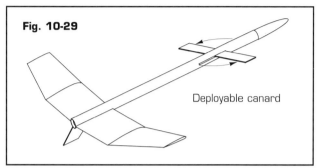

Fig. 10-29

Deployable canard

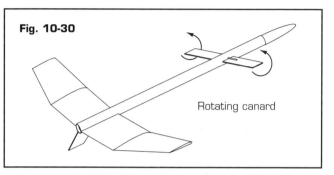

Fig. 10-30

Rotating canard

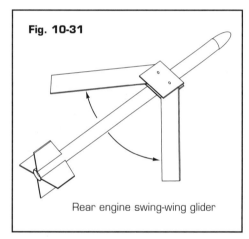

Fig. 10-31

Rear engine swing-wing glider

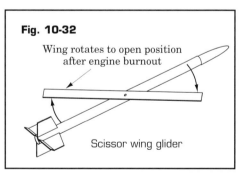

Fig. 10-32

Wing rotates to open position
after engine burnout

Scissor wing glider

If you have a swept wing you could install two smaller tails on the tips of the wings. A boom could also extend rearward of the wing on which a tail could be placed (Fig. 10-26). Also remember to give the wing a couple of degrees of dihedral. This will help the model be stable in the roll direction. Use the sizes of the wing listed above in the section on designing canard configuration gliders. This will give you a good starting point for a flying wing with the right proportions.

Trimming the glider for flight (which I'll describe later) is similar to trimming a normal glider. If the glider nose-dives, though, you will have to reflex the wing more to get a level glide.

Rocket Glider Design

Rocket gliders do not drop any parts from the vehicle during any part of the flight. This presents a problem because the CP

and/or the CG of the model must shift in order for it to become stable in glide. The solution is to find a mechanism which allows you to shift one or both of these parameters.

It is impossible to list every way to make the transition from boost to glide, but here are a few proven methods. They are illustrated in Figures 10-27 through 10-35.

1. Sliding pod or sliding mass
2. Sliding wing
3. Deployable canard
4. Movable, or rotating canard
5. Swing or "scissor" wings
6. Flop wings
7. Movable elevator
8. Deployment of flexible wings

The design criteria usually call for some simple device to actuate the mechanism, but this is sometimes harder than it looks. Most of the devices listed above rely on stored energy, which is usually supplied by a stretched rubber band or spring. When the tension on the rubber band is released, the mechanism, such as raising the elevator, is set into motion. The hard part is holding the rubber band in a stretched position.

Many rocketeers have found that one of the easiest ways to hold tension on a rubber band is with a thin thread. This thread is tied in a loop, and part of this loop passes in front of the rocket motor. When the ejection charge on the motor ignites, it sends hot gases forward. These gases burn through the thread and release the tension on the rubber band (Fig. 10-36).

Another way to change configuration is to use the exhaust gases to push something. For example, if you put a sliding plug inside the engine mount tube (called a piston), it would be pushed forward by the ejection charge gases. The movement of the piston could affect the configuration of the glider somewhere else. Even the engine itself could be a piston, and by sliding backward, it might change the configuration.

Finally, two other actuating methods are available. These are electronic devices and mechanical timers. They are much more complex to design, but you can easily visualize them. For example,

you could install a radio control servo system inside the glider, and not only trim it for a steady descent, but actually control its flight and bring it down where you want it to land.

One change you can make to rocket gliders as compared to conventional boost gliders is to increase the size of wing and control surfaces. Since the vehicle will then be carrying more mass in its glide configuration, you'll want to make some changes to bring it down to the ground more slowly. In general, increase the size of the glider by 10 to 15 percent.

Additional Design Ideas

Glider designs always present a challenge. My challenge to you is to

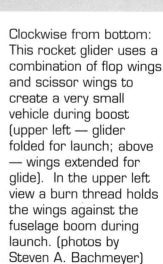

Clockwise from bottom: This rocket glider uses a combination of flop wings and scissor wings to create a very small vehicle during boost (upper left — glider folded for launch; above — wings extended for glide). In the upper left view a burn thread holds the wings against the fuselage boom during launch. (photos by Steven A. Bachmeyer)

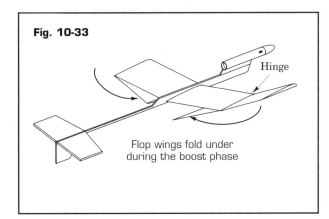

Fig. 10-33

Hinge

Flop wings fold under
during the boost phase

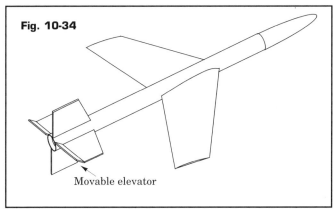

Fig. 10-34

Movable elevator

make yours unique. By making something new you will experience the thrill of a new invention. Here are two suggestions that might spark an idea.

Flexible fabric wings could really improve the performance of your gliders. (Fabric is anything that can be rolled up and stored inside a body tube. Thin plastic sheet is a flexible fabric.) You can probably already see the advantage of storing the wing inside the tube: you can get high altitudes because the frontal area of the rocket is reduced, and the glide time will be much longer because of the additional height. Figure 10-35 shows a flexible fabric boost glider.

In the discussion of boost gliders I said the glider was the major part of the design. This is not always the case.

When the pod is the major part and the glider is just an add-on, it is called a *parasite glider*. A parasite glider is carried aloft on a very stable and much larger rocket booster (Fig. 10-38). An advantage of this arrangement is that one part of the complex design process is eliminated: making sure the rocket is stable during boost. This can allow you to concentrate on getting the glider to fly in a stable manner or to increase its gliding efficiency.

Construction Tips

Like any model rocket, a glider must be both strong and lightweight. Low mass increases performance, allowing it to boost to higher altitudes and glide for

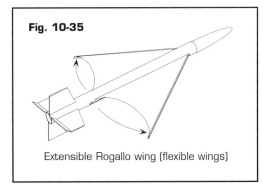

Fig. 10-35

Extensible Rogallo wing (flexible wings)

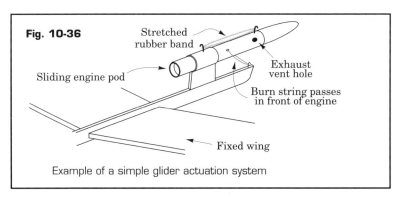

Fig. 10-36

Stretched
rubber band

Sliding engine pod

Exhaust
vent hole

Burn string passes
in front of engine

Fixed wing

Example of a simple glider actuation system

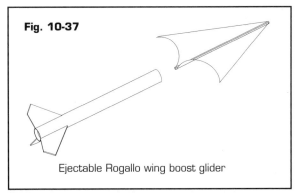

Fig. 10-37

Ejectable Rogallo wing boost glider

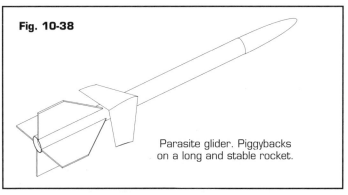

Fig. 10-38

Parasite glider. Piggybacks
on a long and stable rocket.

longer periods. At the same time, it must withstand forces generated by traveling at speeds approaching 100 miles per hour (161 km/hr), so you must pay close attention to the quality of your construction.

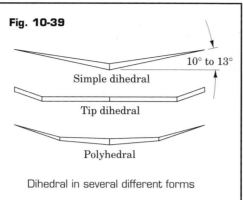

Fig. 10-39

Simple dihedral

10° to 13°

Tip dihedral

Polyhedral

Dihedral in several different forms

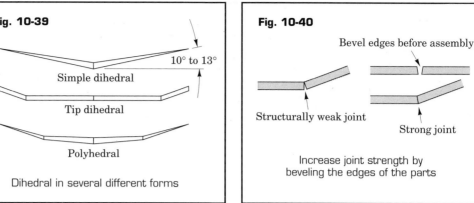

Fig. 10-40

Bevel edges before assembly

Structurally weak joint

Strong joint

Increase joint strength by beveling the edges of the parts

The big factor in the forces trying to tear your glider apart is excess drag. Build the model to minimize this force. The methods for doing this include proper airfoiling of the wings and the horizontal and vertical stabilizers. Round the edges of the fuselage boom and apply good clean fillets between all adjoining parts. Shape and sand all the components individually before you assemble them. Inspect the parts before putting them together. Check and make sure the airfoil you sanded on the left wing matches the one on the right, or your model will not fly straight—it could do loops, rolls, and unplanned turns. Make sure there are no voids or gaps between mating parts. They could signal a weak joint in the structure.

For the model to be stable in roll, and to pull out of downward spiraling turns, you will have to add dihedral to all your gliders. As I noted previously, dihedral is raising the wing tip higher than the root edge, where it attaches to the fuselage boom. Adding dihedral gives the glider a tendency to fly upright and to keep it in this position. Typically, the tips are raised to give an angle of 10 to 13

degrees (Fig. 10-39). To increase the efficiency of the wing, dihedral can be added in small increments along the span of the wing. This is called *polyhedral*.

Before cutting the wing to form dihedral, sand the entire wing and shape it to the correct airfoil. This can be done with a small wood plane or sandpaper. When the wing is cut to add dihedral, bevel the edge to form an angled joint (Fig. 10-40). This ensures maximum gluing area for the strongest joint. Fillet the joint with a small bead of glue for extra strength. On larger models I recommend that you reinforce all wing joints with lightweight fiberglass cloth soaked with epoxy.

Since the fuselage boom takes a lot of stress from hard landings, it should be constructed out of straight, hard balsa wood. For larger models powered by C

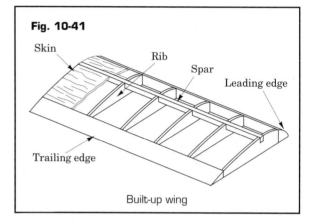

Fig. 10-41

Skin

Rib

Spar

Leading edge

Trailing edge

Built-up wing

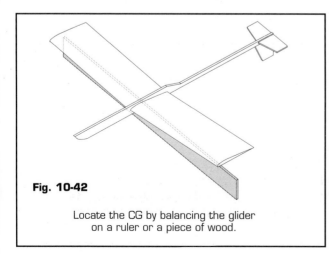

Fig. 10-42

Locate the CG by balancing the glider on a ruler or a piece of wood.

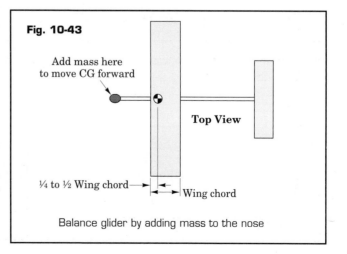

Fig. 10-43

Add mass here to move CG forward

Top View

¼ to ½ Wing chord

Wing chord

Balance glider by adding mass to the nose

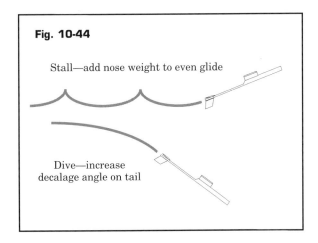

Fig. 10-44

Stall—add nose weight to even glide

Dive—increase decalage angle on tail

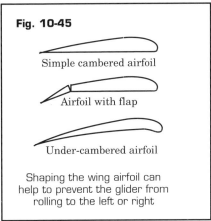

Fig. 10-45

Simple cambered airfoil

Airfoil with flap

Under-cambered airfoil

Shaping the wing airfoil can help to prevent the glider from rolling to the left or right

engines or greater, use a hardwood such as spruce or birch.

Lightweight wings can be made by using the built-up method (Fig. 10-41). This is more laborious, as it requires cutting out a series of accurately shaped ribs and spars, but the result is an extremely lightweight wing. The skins on built-up wings can be covered with tissue paper and aircraft dope, thin balsa wood sheeting, or the thin heat-shrinkable plastic sheet called as *Monocote*.

Add strength to solid balsa wood wings by covering them with a skin made from tissue paper affixed to the wood with aircraft dope. This dope not only attaches the paper to the wood, it shrinks the paper slightly as it dries and adds strength to the tissue.

Trimming: The Art of Making it Fly Straight

The final act prior to launching is to adjust the vehicle's aerodynamic control surface and to properly position the CG to achieve a straight, stable glide. This is called trimming the glider.

The first step is to determine where CG is currently located by balancing the model on your fingertip. For conventional gliders you want the CG at about ¼ the length of the chord measured from the leading edge as shown in Figure 10-42. If the model is tail-heavy, add a bit of modeling clay to the nose to move the balance point forward until it is at the right location (Fig. 10-43). Check the sections on canard configuration or flying wings for the proper starting location for the CG on these models.

If the model is nose-heavy, remove some clay or trim a little bit of wood off

the nose of the fuselage boom. If you can't do either, continue on with the next step, as sometimes this shortcoming can be fixed.

Give the model a soft hand toss. Find a grassy area to lessen the chances that the model will be damaged by a hard landing. Use a light toss on the first throw to see if it is about to do something drastic like pitching upward into a stall or rolling over on its back and diving straight into the ground. Usually it will pitch up. If this happens, add clay to the nose and repeat until the pitching tendency goes away.

If the glider dives toward the ground without a gentle glide, either you have too much nose weight or you need to increase the decalage angle of the tail. Increasing the decalage angle will help balance a nose-heavy glider.

Next, it's time to toss the glider harder. Add or remove some clay mass to the nose to straighten out the glide. If it wants to bank to one side, one wing is producing more lift than the other, so if the glider rolls to the right, the right wing isn't producing as much lift as the left. Another cause may be that one wing is heavier than the other. Either way, you'll have to change the airfoil shape by sanding the wing that is dipping (Fig. 10-45). This not only removes excess mass, it increases the lift produced by that wing. If reshaping the wing does not fix the problem, add a bit of clay to the tip of the other wing. Do this only as a last resort to fix a tendency to roll.

If the glider is flying straight on each toss, throw it straight up to see if it will pull out of a dive. The ability to pull out of a dive is controlled by the decalage angle. The larger this angle, the faster it will pull out. Too much decalage angle and you have to add extra nose weight to achieve a gentle glide. Moistening the trailing edge of the horizontal stabilizer will soften the fibers in the wood. After doing this, gently bend the trailing edge of the horizontal stabilizer upward

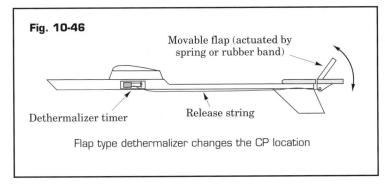

Fig. 10-46

Movable flap (actuated by spring or rubber band)

Dethermalizer timer

Release string

Flap type dethermalizer changes the CP location

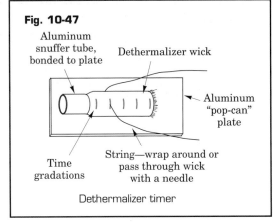

Fig. 10-47

Aluminum snuffer tube, bonded to plate

Dethermalizer wick

Aluminum "pop-can" plate

Time gradations

String—wrap around or pass through wick with a needle

Dethermalizer timer

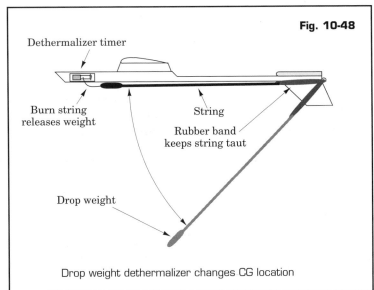

Fig. 10-48

Dethermalizer timer

Burn string releases weight

String

Rubber band keeps string taut

Drop weight

Drop weight dethermalizer changes CG location

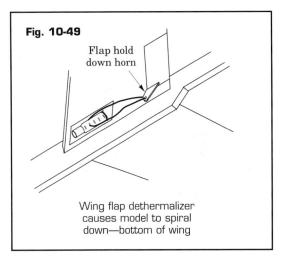

Fig. 10-49

Flap hold down horn

Wing flap dethermalizer causes model to spiral down—bottom of wing

slightly to add decalage to an already-constructed glider.

Experience helps when it comes to building and flying gliders. The more you build the greater your knowledge will become of aerodynamics, and you will see that quality construction pays off. Not only will the gliders go together faster, they will require fewer tosses to trim them out for a level glide and their performance will be phenomenal. Your models will become progressively lighter and stronger. You will begin to change control surfaces instead of adding or removing weight. In short, you will have more fun and gain greater confidence in your abilities and designs.

Dethermalizers

After you gain experience building and launching several gliders, a really nice glider will fly away, never to be seen again. At this point you may consider adding a dethermalizer to future high-efficiency gliders. A *dethermalizer* is a device that triggers (at a certain time) a

retrimming of the glider to bring it to the ground faster.

The heart of any dethermalizer system is the timer. A few types of timers are commonly used; the dethermalizer wick is the most common. The special wick, which looks like a cotton cord, is ignited with a match just prior to launch. The cord smolders at a predetermined rate, and when the wick burns through a string, it releases the mechanism for bringing the model down faster. As you might expect, a burning cord can become a fire hazard, so you should also add a *snuffer tube* as a means of extinguishing the cord after it burns through the string. A snuffer tube is a short length of aluminum tube with a diameter slightly smaller than the dethermalizer wick, which is

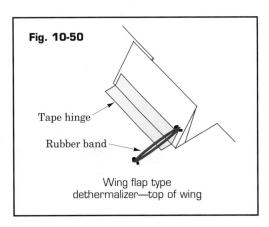

Fig. 10-50

Tape hinge

Rubber band

Wing flap type dethermalizer—top of wing

The typical RC rocket glider is significantly larger than other gliders because it must carry radio gear (photo by Ed LaCroix)

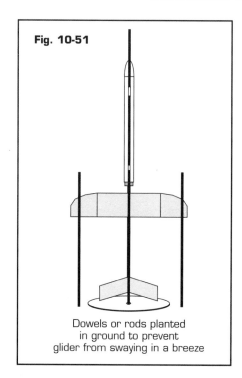

Fig. 10-51

Dowels or rods planted in ground to prevent glider from swaying in a breeze

squeezed tightly into it. When the wick burns inside the tube it is extinguished by a lack of oxygen. To keep the wood from burning, glue a thin metal sheet to it as shown in Figure 10-47. Aluminum from a soft drink can works great.

Other timers that don't present a fire hazard are becoming more common. These include wind-up timers and *silly putty* timers. They can be complex and are beyond the scope of this book.

Besides the timer, the system needs some way of changing the trim of the glider. This can be done by changing the location of either the CG or the CP. Figures 10-46 through 10-50 illustrate several ways to do this.

Engine Selection and Launching Tips

Selecting the proper rocket motor for your glider is just as important as good design and quality

construction. Gliders with large wings that project far out from the centerline of the vehicle create large forces on lift-off that try to rip the wings off the vehicle. It is important to select a rocket motor with low average thrust for your glider to keep the velocity, and hence the forces, low. For example, use an A3 engine instead of an A10 rocket engine. Also, because gliders do not boost as high as typical model rockets, choose a fairly short delay time in the motor: use an A3-2 instead of an A3-4 engine.

The launch rod is another area where your rocket can be damaged or where problems can occur that prevent successful operation. The igniter leads are one of the greatest concerns, especially on front engine boost or rocket gliders. Tape the leads, near the clips, to the launch rod. This will prevent them from falling on the wings or tail and possibly snagging the rocket at liftoff. The same thing can be accomplished by adding an *umbilical mast* next to the launch pad and taping the wires to it.

Gliders have a tendency to sway in the wind as they sit on the launch pad. You can modify your pad to provide support to the wings while it sits there prior to launch. An example is shown in Figure 10-51 where two dowels pushed into the ground prevent the glider from rotating while it sits on the launch pad.

Radio Controlled Rocket Gliders

Radio controlled rocket gliders offer both the excitement of model rocketry and the controllability of model aircraft. This special category of model rockets has only now become popular because radio systems have become smaller and more reliable, and rocket engines capable of lifting heavier weights have become available. These were the last two things preventing the crossover between model rocketry and RC model airplanes.

Designing radio controlled rocket gliders is similar to designing the smaller boost and rocket gliders. The models is bigger, probably by a factor of five or more, because they will have to carry a weighty radio system. Typically, the micro radio systems have a mass of around 113 grams (4 ounces).

All the design criteria of the small

Troubleshooting Chart for Conventional Configuration GBs

Boost Phase

Problem	Causes	Solutions
Wings rip off model	Engine thrust too great	Use Lower thrust engine.
	Wing joints weak	Sand joint edges straighter and use larger fillets and let glue harden completely.
	Wings too long	Design wings with longer chord, shorter span.
Model fails to boost straight	Improper CP and CG location	Add nose weight to pop pod or increase its length to move CG forward.
		Move CP farther aft by increasing the area of the tail surfaces, or sweeping them aft.
	Wing or fin not mounted straight	Check alignment of all aerodynamic surfaces and reposition as necessary.
Model rolls on boost	One wing not creating enough lift	Check alignment of wings, or reshape wing airfoils to produce even lift.
Model turns left or right during boost	Rudder not aligned straight	Check alignment of rudder and reposition as necessary.
	Rudder too small	Increase size of rudder and sweep it aft.
Pod fails to separate	Too much friction between pod and fuselage boom	Sand sides of boom to reduce friction.
Pod falls off too soon	Not enough friction between pod and fuselage boom	Add tape to sides of fuselage boom to increase the friction.
Recovery device snags glider	Bad luck	Increase length of pop pod. Redesign pod to separate into two parts.

Glide Phase

Problem	Causes	Solutions
Glider pitches up and stalls	Not enough nose mass	Add nose mass to the airplane until the glide levels out.
	Decalage angle too great	Move horiz. tail or bend trailing edge down.
Glider nose dives	Too much nose weight	Remove nose mass until the glide levels.
	Decalage angle too small	Move horiz. tail or bend trailing edge up.
		Set wing at a higher angle-of-attack.
		Sand a cambered airfoil in horizontal tail, and mount it upside down, so convex side is down.
Model rolls left or right and spirals to the ground	One wing not creating enough lift	Check alignment of wings, or reshape wing airfoils to produce even lift.
		Cut an aileron into the wing that needs more lift, and deflect it downward.
		Add mass to the tip of the high wing.
Model turns left or right	Rudder not aligned straight	Check alignment of rudder and reposition as necessary.
	Rudder too small	Increase size of rudder and sweep it aft.
Model makes a rolling turn	Not enough dihedral	Increase the dihedral of the main wing.
Glider tossed about in wind	Glider too light	Add nose mass.

gliders also apply to the larger ones. Check the CG location for both boost and glide, and trim the model by hand tossing before boosting it with a rocket motor. Build the model strong, but keep its mass low.

Since larger engines are used (E, F, or G), the models must also be built stronger. They require construction techniques more closely matched with model airplanes, such as foam core or built-up wings.

Don't try to build and fly a radio controlled rocket glider until you have built and flown model airplanes. Rocket-powered gliders take off so fast that events happen in milliseconds. In under 4 seconds, your model will achieve speeds close to 100 mph (161 km/hr). You won't be able to learn to control it at those speeds in such a short time. Your model will probably crash, destroying itself and the onboard radio system. Learn to fly a slow-flying sailplane—they make good training aircraft.

By building and flying a sailplane you'll also learn how to mount the radio and the servos, and how to properly hook up the control systems. After you have mastered the skill necessary to build and pilot a model airplane, your first rocket powered glider should be a vehicle designed as a trainer. You'll be training yourself to fly a rocket!

The best trainers for radio controlled rocket gliders are vehicles having a conventional configuration. Avoid flying wings, canards, and other exotic-looking airplanes until you have a lot of skill flying less sensitive models. The boost is the part of the flight you should be most concerned about. Design your glider to boost as straight as possible without any control input from the radio system. The best way to do this is with a pop-pod, which was shown in the previous chapter on boost gliders.

The pop-pod on a radio controlled glider works the same way as on a smaller model. The difference is that it is much larger because of the bigger engines and the larger glider. When the pop-pod falls off the glider after engine burnout, it greatly reduces the glide mass of the model, making longer-duration flights possible.

Selection of an improper rocket engine can destroy your rocket. Bigger rocket

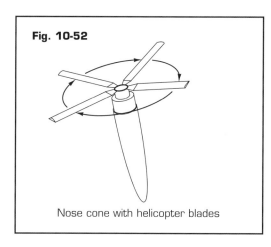

Fig. 10-52

Nose cone with helicopter blades

engines usually have high initial thrust levels. The high levels will rip the wings off almost any glider. You must choose engines with the lowest possible average thrust. For example, an E6 or E15 is a better choice than an E30. Because of the low thrust levels, the model's mass must be kept low or it could fall over after it clears the launch rod. Its an awful sight to see a model thrash itself to pieces on the ground with the engine still burning. The engines have a maximum recommended lift-off weight, which is supplied by the manufacturer—never exceed this mass!

You must also select the delay times of the engines carefully. If you are using a pop-pod, select an engine with a built-in ejection charge; a short delay motor is probably best, as gliders do not boost high because of their large frontal areas. Some models, however, are not designed to use hot ejection gases. They may mount the engine at the glide CG point, where the empty case doesn't have to move for proper glide trim, or they may rely on some type of R/C ejection-separation instead. In those cases, select a plugged engine. These engines have no ejection charges, but have a solid bulkhead on the front of the motor to prevent hot gases from shooting forward when the engine burns out.

Helicopter Design

Helicopter recovery is a method of returning the model, or part of it, to the ground by autorotation of vanes or blades. Technically these are autogyros, but most people call them helicopters because the model looks like a helicopter as it descends.

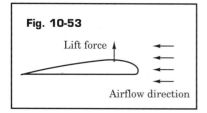

Fig. 10-53

Lift force

Airflow direction

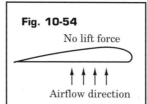

Fig. 10-54

No lift force

Airflow direction

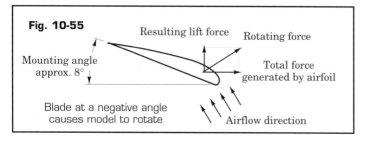

Fig. 10-55

Resulting lift force   Rotating force

Mounting angle approx. 8°

Total force generated by airfoil

Blade at a negative angle causes model to rotate

Airflow direction

Airfoil Shape and Blade Size: The shape of the airfoil will also determine how much lift is created. There hasn't been much research on what airfoil is best for a helicopter recovery model, but this shouldn't concern you unless you are trying to achieve maximum efficiency and the slowest possible descent rate. Almost any airfoil should give a descent rate slow enough to bring the model down safely. As an experiment, try different airfoils to see which improves the performance. Here are just a few you might try: a simple flat plate, a symmetrical airfoil, and a chambered airfoil with a flat bottom (Fig. 10-56).

You can make blades from a variety of materials. Balsa wood is an excellent choice, but lightweight plastic also works fine if properly used. The blades sometimes hit the ground hard when the model touches down, so they should be constructed to withstand these forces of flight and landing.

The size of the blades is up to you. Short, thin blades will cause faster rotation and higher descent velocities than long, wide blades. Generally, individual blades should be at *least* ¾ the length of the entire rocket, and approximately equal in width to the largest body tube diameter.

This method is complex to design and construct, ranking with rocket gliders in difficulty. However, it can also be the most rewarding when it works correctly.

The main components of the helicopter are its vanes or blades. In reality these are long high-aspect-ratio wings, mounted so air flowing over them creates lift. Unlike an airplane, the lift not only helps counteract the force of gravity, it also induces the model to rotate.

The rate of rotation is determined by the angle of the blade with respect to the oncoming airstream. In a helicopter, the oncoming air is from the model falling straight down. If the blade is perpendicular to the airstream, the airfoil will produce no lift and it will not rotate because no forces are produced to cause rotation (Fig. 10-54).

When the blade is angled downward air will flow over it, producing lift. You can divide this lift into two forces—one causing rotation, and one opposing the force of gravity (Fig. 10-55). So you must angle your blades slightly nose down with respect to the airflow. A good place to start is about 8 degrees.

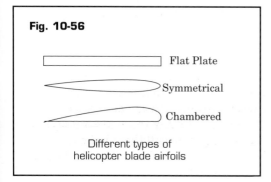

Fig. 10-56

Flat Plate

Symmetrical

Chambered

Different types of helicopter blade airfoils

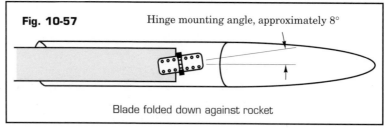

Fig. 10-57   Hinge mounting angle, approximately 8°

Blade folded down against rocket

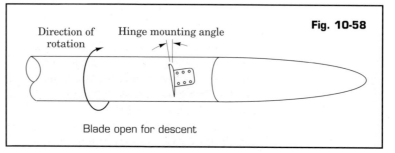

Direction of rotation   Hinge mounting angle   Fig. 10-58

Blade open for descent

One popular helicopter is this Rotaroc model, (photos below) with blades folded for launch, and extended. A burn string holds the blades down during the boost and coast phases of the flight. (photos by Steven A. Bachmeyer)

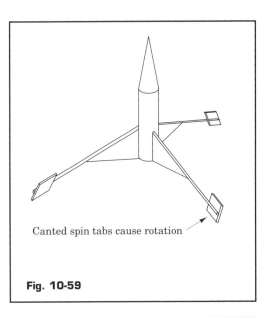

Canted spin tabs cause rotation

Fig. 10-59

Mounting the Rotor Blades: How you mount the rotor blades is up to you, but you must mount them on an angle so that when deployed they will be oriented properly to start the model rotating. To keep the blades parallel to the centerline of the model when they are folded in the boost configuration, mount the hinge on an angle. Figures 10-57 and 10-58 show one way to mount blades so they open at the correct angle.

The hinges that attach the blades to the model are very important. They must be rigid and strong so they don't break, and so they hold the blades at the proper angle while the model is spinning downward. For small models using up to a C engine, nylon airplane control surface hinges work fine. The one drawback to these hinges is that they are difficult to attach to smooth surfaces. The nylon plastic can't be penetrated by any glue, so nothing really grips it. If you use these hinges, try instant glues or epoxies. Try other hinges, too. It seems every other month someone invents a new hinge for model airplanes. Don't be afraid to try these new materials.

Don't limit your design to long slender blades that fold down against the side of the rocket's body. It may have blades that look like long fins. When the engine burns out, tabs on the fins cant over, causing the model to autorotate on the vertical descent.

You may have your design spin on ascent, too (Fig. 10-59). Keep these models light so they don't get damaged on landing—they usually fall slightly faster than those with long blades.

Where you attach the blades is also up to you. Some people like the blades near the top so the model has a favorable CG when the blades deploy. You need the CG below the deployed blades so the model stays stable. This is similar to a parachute, where the load is below the canopy for stability reasons. If you hinge the blades near the back of the model you must have sufficient nose mass to counteract the mass of the engine and tail.

Mechanisms For Deploying Rotor Blades: If your model will rely on deploying rotor blades or changing the deflection angle on a control surface, you will need some type of mechanism that

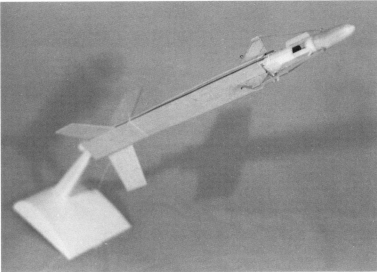

Right: Mounting the blades near the rear of the rocket is an option for the builder of helicopter models. This model uses a sliding nose section with tabs to hold the blades down during launch. **Below:** The same helicopter model with blades deployed. (photos by Steven A. Bachmeyer)

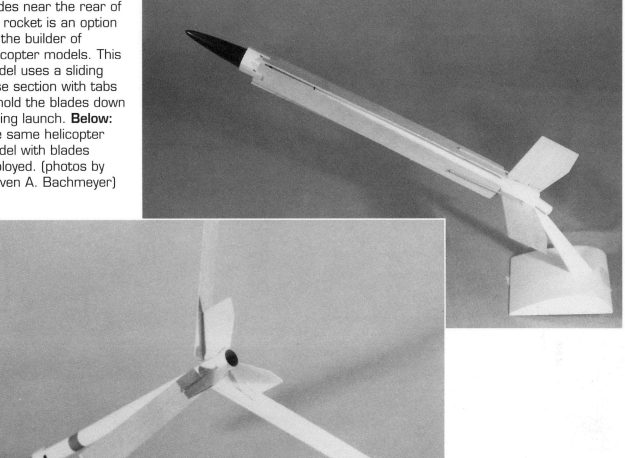

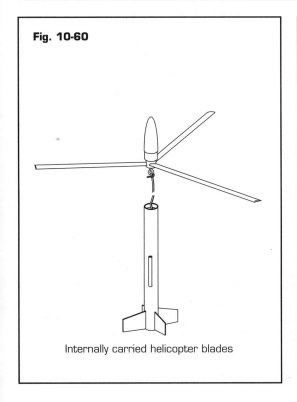

Fig. 10-60

Internally carried helicopter blades

Fig. 10-61

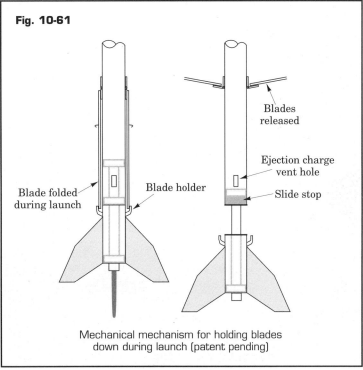

Blade folded during launch

Blade holder

Blades released

Ejection charge vent hole

Slide stop

Mechanical mechanism for holding blades down during launch (patent pending)

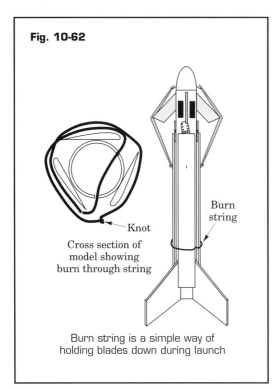

Fig. 10-62

Knot

Burn
string

Cross section of
model showing
burn through string

Burn string is a simple way of
holding blades down during launch

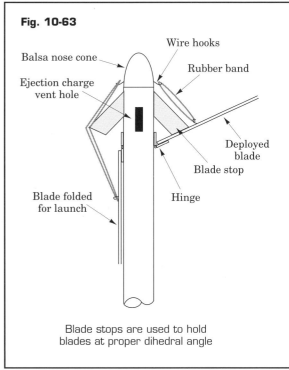

Fig. 10-63

Balsa nose cone

Ejection charge
vent hole

Blade folded
for launch

Wire hooks

Rubber band

Deployed
blade

Blade stop

Hinge

Blade stops are used to hold
blades at proper dihedral angle

performs this change. Deployment usually occurs when the ejection charge ignites, so methods of actuation use the gases from the engine to trigger something. This is similar to the methods used in rocket gliders.

The most common way to deploy the blades is by means of rubber bands. Springs work in a similar way. The blades are held by some type of latch or other mechanism, which is released when the ejection charge ignites. The blade is then pulled or pushed into the open position by the spring or rubber band. A loop of string wrapped around the outside of the blades and allowed to pass in front of the engine is one method of holding the blades down (Fig. 10-62). When the string is burned by the ejection gases, the blades are free to be deployed.

If the blades are carried inside the rocket, they might be deployed like a regular parachute—simply pushed out the top. Still another mechanism for holding the blades down is shown in Figure 10-61.

Movement of the rocket motor can also be the trigger to unlatch the mechanism holding the blades down. Even complex electronic or wind-up mechanical devices could be used to deploy them—the decision is yours.

Rocket Engine Selection: Most helicopter models are a lot like gliders—they have high drag and they may weigh more than typical models because of the rotors, the complicated hinges, and the deployment mechanisms. Because of this, these models don't coast as high, so they need shorter engine delay times. Unlike gliders, they are usually more streamlined and don't have large fins or wings projecting far out from the centerline of the model. Therefore, they can usually use any thrust level of rocket motor, while gliders need low thrust motors.

When you launch your rocket for the first time, follow the rules of the National Association of Rocketry. These rules require you to fly the unproved model apart from any spectators not associated with the actual launching of the model. Find a nice isolated area. After you have proved that your design works and is stable, tell the world! New helicopter designs that work are an accomplishment worth sharing with others.

11

Scale Models

Scale models are exact miniature replicas of actual rockets built by NASA, the military, or other science agencies. Some people build scale models to sharpen their building skills, others for competition events, and still others to show support for the purpose for which the real rockets were made. Mainly, they are built for fun and enjoyment.

Whatever the reason you build scale models, remember they are still model rockets. The only thing different is a higher grade of surface finish and extra external details. On the inside they look and operate the same as the models you are already familiar with. Knowing this, you should not have any apprehension about building a replica of a real rocket — just take your time putting on the finish.

The first step is to choose which rocket to model. If this is your first scale model, choose one with the classic model rocket shape, such as NASA's Asp, Apache, or Black Brant. A long rocket with big fins is a perfect start—one you can tell at a glance you will have no problem making stable. You may need to get space history books out of the library for pictures of real rockets.

One helpful book is **Rockets of the World** by Peter Alway. The address for ordering information is at the end of this book. **Rockets of the World** is a scale modeler's dream, with nearly all the most common scientific rockets ever flown. It has photos, dimensions, and a description of each.

You can also get dimensional data from photographs in space or military history books. If you live close to aviation or space museums, see if they have data

Marc Lavigne displays his replica of the 200th McDonnell Douglas Delta rocket. Marc took his measurements from the real rocket behind him (U.S. Air Force Photo).

Above: An Aerobee 1500 scale model built by Bob Koenn takes to the air under the power of a composite "E" rocket engine. (photo by Patrick McCarthy) Right: Using a dial caliper, Patrick McCarthy checks the accuracy of a scale model Russian Proton launch vehicle. (photo by Bob Koenn)

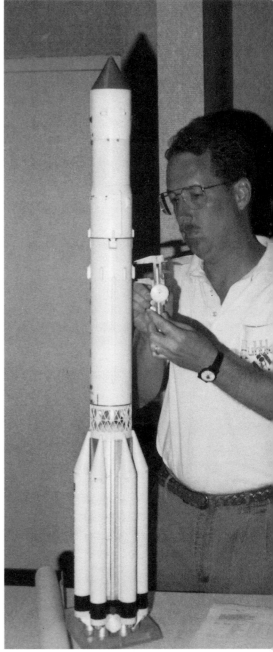

on the rocket you want to model. And finally, write to the National Association of Rocketry. Their address is listed at the end of this book. They are modelers, and many collect scale data. They may be able to help you obtain the data that you need.

Steps For Constructing a Scale Model Rocket

1. Select rocket.
2. Gather scale data and info on real rocket.
3. Select size of model, and convert actual rocket dimensions to your rocket size.
4. Sketch the model with all the scale dimensions listed.
5. Build and paint the model.

Once you choose a rocket you have to design your model. The scale you use will mainly depend on available body tube and nose cone sizes. For example, if you have a 25.4 mm (1.0") diameter tube, and the actual full size rocket is 81.28 cm (32") in diameter, then your model will be ⅟32 scale. The formula to determine your scale size is:

$$Scale = \frac{Model\ Size}{Full\ Size}$$

Using this formula, calculate the other dimensions of the rocket. If the length of the fin is 101.6 cm (40"), the length of that fin on your model will be 31.75 mm

(1.25"). This was obtained by multiplying the scale factor by the dimension on the full-size rocket. For those who like formulas, this is written as:

Model Size = Scale × Full Size

If you have a photograph of the actual rocket and you know one dimension, such as its diameter, you can find the others. First determine the scale of the picture. Take a ruler and measure the dimension you know. Then divide by the actual size of that dimension:

$$Photo\ Scale = \frac{Measured\ Dimension}{Actual\ Dimension}$$

For example, if you measured the diameter of the rocket at 22.35 mm (0.88") and you know the actual diameter is 81.28 cm (32"), then the photo scale is $^{0.88}/_{32}$, which equals .0275.

When determining other dimensions from the photograph, measure the length on the picture, and then determine its actual dimensional size by the following formula:

$$Actual\ Dimension = \frac{Measured\ Dimension}{Photo\ Scale}$$

So if you measured the fin span on the photo at 27.94 mm (1.1"), then the actual dimension is 27.94 mm divided .0275, which equals 1.016 m (40").

Once you have determined all the dimensions of your model, make a sketch of the rocket showing all these dimensions. After that, build it as you would any other rocket.

Depending on why you are making the model, you may want to build more than one. If you do, you can experiment with the first model, using different building methods, accurately determining the rocket's stability, and practicing painting techniques. The second model will be your perfect replica. In any case, have fun!

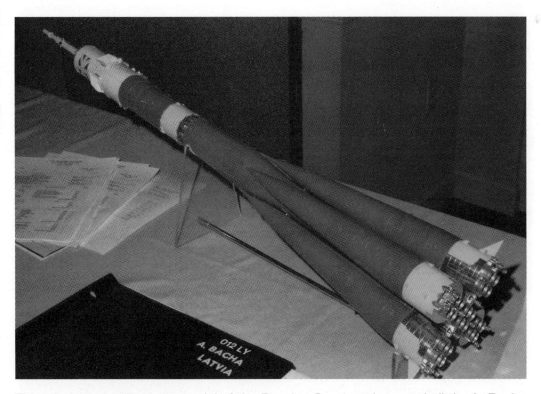

This museum quality scale model of the Russian Soyuz rocket was built by A. Bacha of Latvia. (photo by Patrick McCarthy)

12

Payload Rockets

Marc Lavigne built this rocket to hold a disc camera. The protrusion on the nose holds a mirror, allowing the camera to take multiple pictures looking downward (photo by Marc Lavigne).

A payload is the cargo carried by the model rocket. Developing a payload can be the challenge to keep your interest in rocketry after you think you have mastered everything else. Rockets are generally small and limited in how much mass they can launch, but this doesn't mean you can't design a payload that does something interesting. Payloads can be simple or complex. Simple ones can include things like a small glider or an action figure that comes down separately from the rest of the rocket. The level of complexity is entirely up to you.

What type of payloads can you launch? This is a tough question for the novice rocketeer to answer. Try to find out what NASA and other scientific organizations launch as experiments. Since model rocketry mimics real aeronautics, you can also mimic what these scientific organizations do for payloads.

NASA and other organizations usually classify payloads in any of several sciences. You may have heard talk about life sciences, materials sciences, or environmental sciences. These areas of concentration can be duplicated to one degree or another in model rocketry. Below is a short list of ideas for which you can develop payloads. They are categorized by scientific discipline.

Aeronautics
- Measure flight parameters of the rocket
- Measure the acceleration during the flight
- Measure acceleration coming off a piston launcher
- Measure the pitch, yaw, and roll rate of the model during flight

- Determine the rocket's velocity
- Determine altitude and range of the rocket
- Determine the drag of the model
- Measure the onboard vibrations inside the rocket
- Place wet paint drops on the rocket to see the streamlines
- Try thermographic paints to measure temperatures on the rocket
- Demonstrate the use of aeronautical tools like a pitot-static tube
- Determine the altitude of a rocket from an aerial photograph
- Use the rocket to drop models like gliders or even other rockets from high altitudes
- Try dropping objects that test new designs of parachutes or streamers
- Drop Ping-Pong balls to measure their drag coefficients

Mechanics
- Launch a simulated satellite that deploys antennas and panels
- Deploy a lander that self-assembles and lands upright

Electronics
- Launch a buzzer to help locate your rocket
- Launch a (legal) transmitter to study radio wave propagation
- Use a transmitter to make Doppler measurements
- Use the transmitter to downlink measurements (telemetry) made during the flight
- Create a satellite that uses solar energy to deploy lander legs
- Launch a strobe light as an optical location beacon

Chemical
- Study the growth of crystals during acceleration and during free fall
- Study how substances mix during free fall

Environment
- Take air samples at high altitudes, and study the results
- Demonstrate remote sensing using an onboard camera
- Study the geography of the launch site by photographic mapping
- Study the geology of the launch site
- Show how different wavelengths of light identify undetected things in

plants and minerals
- Study a lake or river life with aerial photography
- Measure water temperature in the middle of a lake from the air
- Chart currents in a lake or river with a rocket camera

Meteorology
- Measure temperature changes during flight
- Measure air pressure during flight
- Measure wind direction and velocity in various shear layers of the atmosphere during ascent and descent
- Measure humidity during the flight
- Measure the radiated heat of the earth

Biology
- Launch an egg to simulate launching astronauts (delicate objects)
- Study the effects of a launch on insects and small fish
- Study the effects of high acceleration on plants and single-cell organisms
- Try to attract birds to the rocket, and see how they relate to it in their territory

Acoustics
- Launch a payload that uses moving air to generate tones
- Measure the noise level inside a rocket during the entire flight
- Measure the noise spectrum inside a rocket
- Study the Doppler effect with sound waves and a moving rocket

Art
- Use colored chalk to "paint the sky"
- Take artistic aerial photographs
- Develop a payload that uses moving air to make tones that play a song

Rocket Stability and Control
- Develop the electronics to perform delayed rocket staging
- Develop a timer that delays the release of a parachute or some other dropped payload
- Develop a system that will control the rocket's path without human intervention
- Develop a dethermalizer for parachutes
- Create a momentum wheel system to prevent weathercocking

Payload Sections

Payloads are usually carried internally to protect them from the fast-moving airstream. If your payload is sensitive to heat, put it into its own compartment, called a payload section. By putting the cargo into a payload section, you can cushion it for more protection and retain it in the rocket body so it doesn't fall separately.

A payload section is usually placed on the top of the rocket and can be easily constructed using just a few parts. Figures 12-1 and 12-2 below show the basic payload section and a couple of simple variations.

Provide cushioning for very delicate payloads. For this you can use bathroom tissue, foam rubber, cotton batting, Styrofoam, or partially inflated balloons. Any lightweight and fluffy material will probably make a good cushion material.

If your payload has a lot of mass the rocket may be excessively stable. When this happens it will weathercock into the wind and may not achieve the altitude you desire. To prevent this you can decrease the fin area by 15 to 25 percent if the payload mass is about half of the rocket's empty mass. This will move the CP forward, making the rocket less likely to weathercock. Once you remove any fin area, never fly the model without the payload unless you fly it with ballast (inert mass) in place of the cargo.

Engine Selection for Payloads

Because of the extra mass of the payload the rocket will not coast as high after engine burnout. For this reason, select a shorter delay in the engine. If you make a mistake and use a long-burning engine, the model will probably arc over and head downward when the parachute is deployed. This can damage the parachute, because parachutes operate best when deployed at slow speeds.

You may also want to stage the model to get it to fly higher. This will expose your payload to different flight conditions, including a longer free fall, which it might be designed to exploit. In this case, choose an engine with a long delay before deployment of the recovery device. Engine selection is discussed in greater depth in Chapter 15.

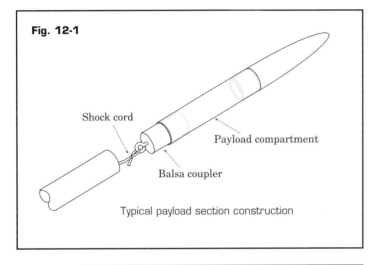

Fig. 12-1

Shock cord

Payload compartment

Balsa coupler

Typical payload section construction

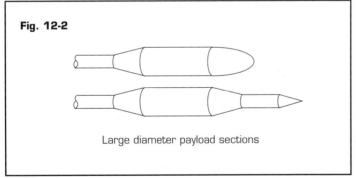

Fig. 12-2

Large diameter payload sections

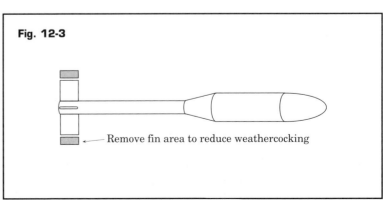

Fig. 12-3

Remove fin area to reduce weathercocking

13

Multi-Stage Rockets

A rocket having two or more engines stacked one on top of another and firing in succession is called a multi-stage. Normally each unit, or stage, is jettisoned after completing its firing. The reason rocketeers stage models is to enable the uppermost stage to attain a very high altitude. This is accomplished by dropping mass throughout the burn so the top stage can be very light and thus coast a long way upward.

For the sake of safety it is best to limit the number of stages to three or four. As the number increases, the liftoff mass of the model becomes so great that the lowest stage doesn't have enough thrust to get off the pad at a high speed. The model could clear the rod and then turn horizontal.

With a great number of upper stages it is also likely that the rocket will gradually weathercock into the wind, causing the upper stages to fire horizontally instead of straight up. Not only will you lose the model, you'll have a dangerous situation.

Engine Selection

As I said, the first criterion for selecting a rocket engine in a staged model is whether it can safely lift the rocket into the sky—including not only the upper stage engines, but the lower and intermediate stages, too. Check the recommended maximum lift-off mass of the engines. It should be included in the engine's package or the manufacturer's catalog.

If your model will rely on the lower engine igniting the upper engine, you'll have to select one specifically designed to

Ken Mizoi built this impressive three stage scale model of a NASA Black Brant X. (photo by Patrick McCarthy)

do this. These are called booster engines, and they are identified by an engine classification code ending with a zero (0). For example, the engine labeled with the classification code C6-0 is a booster engine. The zero means there is no ejection charge. The propellant burns through and expels hot gases forward out the engine (Fig. 13-1). There is no delay

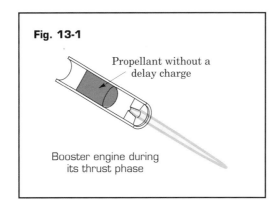

Fig. 13-1

Propellant without a delay charge

Booster engine during its thrust phase

charge built into the motor, which on a typical rocket would allow the model to coast before the recovery device deploys.

All stages below the uppermost should have a booster engine. The top stage is unique because it also needs a special motor, sometimes called a sustainer engine. The major difference in these motors is that they contain unusually long-burning delay charges. Since the top stage will have the highest velocity of the rocket's entire flight, it will have to coast a longer time to allow the rocket to slow down enough for the recovery device to be safely deployed. It will also coast to a very high altitude. The package these motors come in will clearly indicate that the motor is designed to be used as an upper stage engine.

Direct Staging

The most common method of igniting upper stage motors is direct staging. In this method the upper stage motor is ignited by the hot gases of the lower stage motor. It calls for no extra equipment or special techniques. The only requirement is that the upper stage motor be directly in line with the lower stage motor.

This method works because the special boosters have no delay charge. When the propellant is gone, hot gases inside the engine can escape out the top, igniting the upper stage motor (Fig. 13-2).

The reliability of successful staging is increased by having the engines as close together as possible. To help the process, tape the two engines together with cellophane tape. This prevents separation of the motors for a split second, allowing the gases enough time to ignite the upper stage motor. After the motor ignites, the tape melts away and the stages separate.

If the engines in your design are separated by a short distance, less than 12.7 cm (5"), you can still get reliable ignition of the upper stage motor if you allow some of the gases in front of the lower booster engine to vent to the outside air. If you don't, the stages will separate without ignition of the upper stage motor. This is because the hot air coming out the front of the booster engine pushes the cool air in front of it. If there is no place for the cool air to go, it prevents the hot air from getting into the nozzle of the upper stage engine.

The vent hole should be about 6.35 mm (0.25") in diameter, and even smaller if you use more than one hole. Place the hole as close to the bottom of the upper stage as possible. This will allow the hot gases to push all the cool air out of the inter-stage tube (Fig 13-3).

The direct staging technique does not work with composite motors. It only

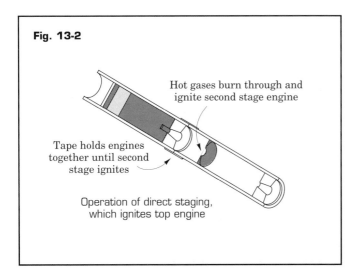

Fig. 13-2

Hot gases burn through and ignite second stage engine

Tape holds engines together until second stage ignites

Operation of direct staging, which ignites top engine

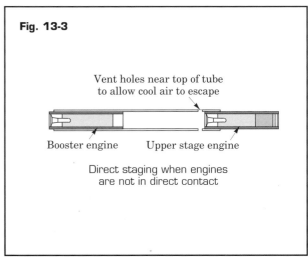

Fig. 13-3

Vent holes near top of tube to allow cool air to escape

Booster engine   Upper stage engine

Direct staging when engines are not in direct contact

works with black-powder engines as the upper stage motors. Composite engines are ignited from the top of the grain, not the bottom, like black-powder engines. Therefore, if you want to stage using composite motors you'll have to use an onboard ignition system. I'll discuss this briefly later in this chapter under "Indirect Staging."

Engine Mounts and Stage Coupling

The method you decide to use to join the stages together may affect the reliability and the stability of the model. Be sure to design your rockets so that the stages separate only in a straight line. This will help prevent tip-off, which is a sudden change in the direction of the upper stage directly attributed to the separation of the lower stage.

In minimum-diameter rockets the aft part of the upper stage engine can act as a tube coupler, keeping the stages together (Fig. 13-4). Tape the engines together when you use this method, so the lower stage doesn't separate prematurely. The upper stage will have to rely on a tape friction fit to hold it snugly in the upper stage of the rocket.

When the rocket diameter is much larger than the engine diameter, align the stages with a tube coupler. The engine tube of the lower stage should extend up through the stage so the engine of the upper stage is inserted into it or just touching it (Fig. 13-5). This will serve to guide the ejection charge gases from the booster engine to the sustainer engine.

One option is to insert the engine in the lower stage. You can tape the motors together, as is done in the minimum-diameter rockets, and insert the motor from the front of the stage. Or you can design your rocket so the engine is installed from the back (Figs. 13-4 and 13-5). If the engines are separated by more than 25.4 mm (1"), you'll have to modify the engine mount by installing the vent holes discussed above. Figure 13-6 shows you how to build this particular engine mount. In this engine mount, the rocket motor is installed from the rear of the rocket.

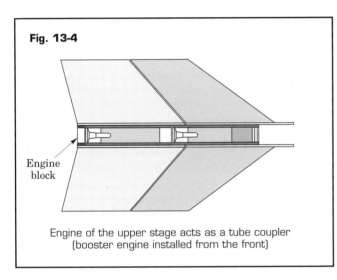

Fig. 13-4

Engine block

Engine of the upper stage acts as a tube coupler
(booster engine installed from the front)

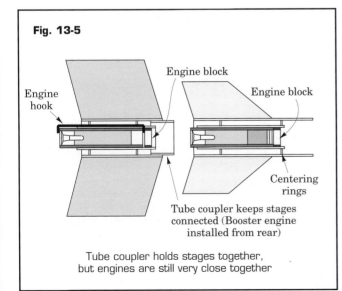

Fig. 13-5

Engine hook

Engine block

Engine block

Centering rings

Tube coupler keeps stages connected (Booster engine installed from rear)

Tube coupler holds stages together, but engines are still very close together

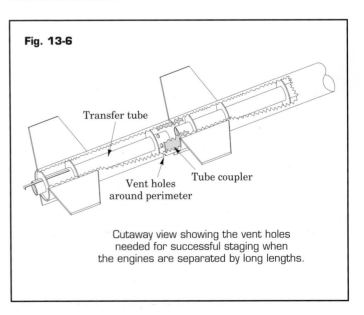

Fig. 13-6

Transfer tube

Vent holes around perimeter

Tube coupler

Cutaway view showing the vent holes needed for successful staging when the engines are separated by long lengths.

Fin Size

Staged models have a lot of mass toward the rear of the rocket because of the extra engines and fins. They can easily become unstable because the CG is located farther back on the rocket. Never exceed three or four stages because the models become extremely tail-heavy, and also too heavy in general for the engines to safely lift.

For stability, your staged model should have extra-large fins on each booster stage. This will move the CP rearward. You might also add some additional nose mass to move the CG forward. Perform stability checks on the rocket, including separate stability checks with each stage of the model installed (e.g., stages 1, 2, 3; stages 2 and 3; stage 3 alone).

Booster Stage Recovery

Short booster sections tend to be unstable and tumble end over end, allowing the booster section to be recovered after separation by tumble recovery. To help the tumbling process, design your boosters to be short. They should be approximately 3" to 4" (7.6 to 10.2 cm) long.

You can perform a simple stability check on your design prior to assembling the booster section. Take one of the fins and balance it on a pencil (Fig. 13-9). Make sure the pencil is perpendicular to the root edge of the fin. Mark the location on the fin. After assembling the booster, find its balance point with an expended engine installed (Fig. 13-10). If the fin balance point is at or forward of the booster balance point, the stage will

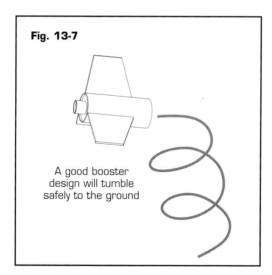

Fig. 13-7

A good booster design will tumble safely to the ground

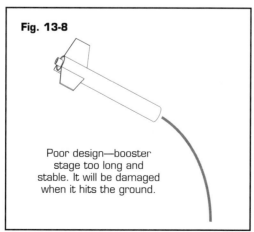

Fig. 13-8

Poor design—booster stage too long and stable. It will be damaged when it hits the ground.

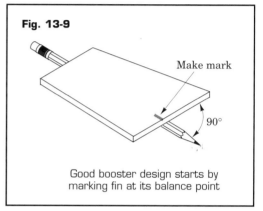

Fig. 13-9

Good booster design starts by marking fin at its balance point

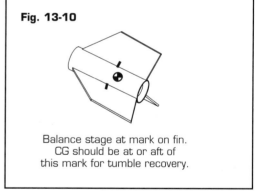

Fig. 13-10

Balance stage at mark on fin. CG should be at or aft of this mark for tumble recovery.

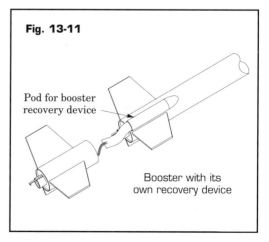

Fig. 13-11

Pod for booster recovery device

Booster with its own recovery device

be able to tumble safely to the ground. If not, the booster may become stable and fly straight into the ground. To prevent this, modify the booster section either by mounting the engine farther rearward or by installing another type of recovery device on the booster.

Since most booster sections are lightweight, you may need only a streamer to bring about a safe descent. In this case, a recovery pod attached to the base of the upper stage can store the streamer. Figure 13-11 shows how to install this recovery system.

Finally, sometimes booster sections are hard to find on the ground because of their small size. I recommend that you paint them a bright color for better visibility.

Variations of Direct Staging

CHAD Staging: CHeap-**A**nd-**D**irty (CHAD) staging is a form of direct staging in which the booster engine is not housed inside a finned stage (Fig. 13-12). It can only be used on models that are overly stable and can tolerate extra mass in the rear of the model. To use this staging technique, simply tape the booster engine directly to the engine in the upper stage. The engine just hangs off the back end of the rocket. At ejection, the motor separates and tumbles to the ground. Use care here, because the engine may fall to the ground quite fast. It is better to attach a streamer to it, inserted in a recovery pod mounted to the upper stage (Fig. 13-11). The streamer can also be taped and wrapped around the booster engine and held down with a thread attached to the upper stage (Fig. 13-13). When the upper stage ignites, it will not only burn the tape holding the engines together, it will also burn through the thread, releasing the streamer. Before flying a model with CHAD staging, remember to perform a check of the model's stability.

Gliding Boosters: The typical booster simply tumbles to the ground. A gliding booster is constructed so it will glide back to the ground like an airplane. If you use this recovery method, you must space the fins differently on the gliding stage. Figure 13-14 shows one way to do

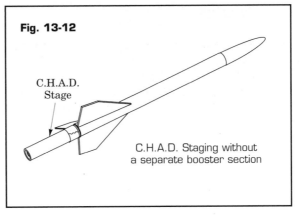

Fig. 13-12

C.H.A.D. Stage

C.H.A.D. Staging without a separate booster section

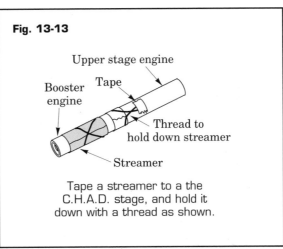

Fig. 13-13

Upper stage engine

Booster engine

Tape

Thread to hold down streamer

Streamer

Tape a streamer to a the C.H.A.D. stage, and hold it down with a thread as shown.

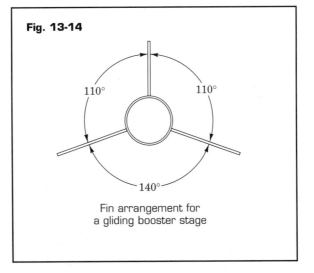

Fig. 13-14

110°   110°

140°

Fin arrangement for a gliding booster stage

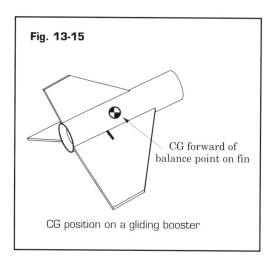

Fig. 13-15

CG forward of balance point on fin

CG position on a gliding booster

this. Prior to assembly, balance the fins the same way you would if this were a tumble recovery booster. When you balance the completed booster, you want the CG of the stage to be slightly forward of the fin balance point. When performing the balance test, make sure to install an expended engine in the stage.

The gliding booster is actually a variation of the flying wing glider, and the design rules are similar. Glide-test the booster section by giving it a hard toss. It may be necessary to trim the stage to achieve a proper glide. For tips on trimming, see Chapter Ten.

Indirect Staging: When your model design has a long distance between rocket engines, or has a composite rocket motor in the upper stage, you will have to use a different staging technique. Engine-to-engine direct staging will not be reliable, so the rocket will have to carry some type of launch system on board to ignite the upper stage. This is called indirect staging because the ignition of the upper stage engine is not started by the booster engine.

A simple technique is mercury switch staging. In this method the upper stage engine is ignited electrically by the same igniters you would use if the model were launched conventionally. The difference is that the launch system—the switch and the power supply—is carried in the rocket. The switch is usually a mercury switch mounted upside down in the rocket. The circuit is closed when the mercury flies to the top of the tube,

which happens when the first stage burns out and the rocket decelerates.

The power supply can be a small battery or a charged capacitor. One word of caution: make sure the model has some type of safety device interlock installed so it isn't accidentally ignited if you move it on the launch pad. Also, be sure to test the circuit on the ground and make sure it's working before you launch. Otherwise, the top stage may ignite and streamline into the ground.

Flying

Use caution when flying multi-stage rockets. Now that you have two or more stages, you have to consider twice as many details. Select a field at least as long and wide as the maximum altitude the rocket is expected to reach. These rockets can travel to incredible heights, so be sure there are no low clouds over the launch area to block your view of low-flying aircraft.

Fly staged models only on calm days because their large fin area makes them susceptible to weathercocking. This will cause the model to travel more horizontally than vertically. Also, because of the high altitudes, stage models drift farther with the wind. To limit this drift, use a streamer on the upper stage instead of a parachute. A streamer will allow the model to descend faster. Another option for heavier models is to use a parachute with a spill hole cut into its canopy. This will slow the model but still prevent excess drift.

Because of the weathercocking tendencies of these models, don't angle the rod into the wind. Always launch multi-stage models straight up or even angled slightly away from the wind.

You can install tracking powder in the upper stage to help you locate it more easily in the sky. Tracking powder is any nonflammable powder placed inside the rocket that is ejected at apogee into a large puff or cloud. The cloud can help you to locate your rocket at a very high altitude. Some powders that work well for this include tempera paint, chalk dust, and talcum powder. The colors that seem to work best are black for cloudy days and red when the sky is blue.

14

Clustered Engine Rockets

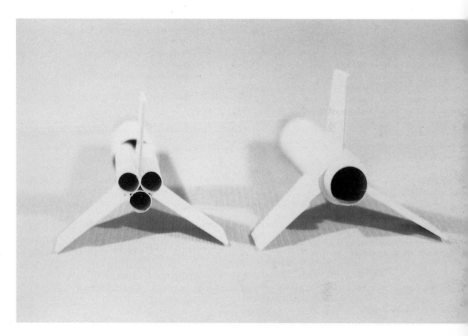

A cluster engine rocket next to a single engine rocket. (photo by Steven A. Bachmeyer)

The simultaneous ignition of two or more rocket engines designed to operate as a single unit to attain a higher liftoff thrust is called cluster ignition. Clustering is suitable when you need more thrust at liftoff to launch a larger or heavier rocket. It can also be done for fun—many modelers are impressed by a lot of fire and smoke accompanied by the loud thunder of the multiple engines. In fact, with the availability of larger and higher-thrust composite engines, clustering may be a technique that is done more for fun than for added power.

One advantage of clustering is the total liftoff thrust that can be generated. The total thrust and impulse of a cluster of engines is equal to the sum of thrust and impulse of the individual rocket engines. When launching two engines of the same type, the effect is equivalent to substituting one that is twice as powerful and burns in the same amount of time. For example, if you cluster two B6 motors together, they deliver the same amount of power as a C6 motor, but do it in half the time. So the equivalent engine is not be a C6, but a C12. Since C12s do not currently exist, you can use a cluster to achieve that combination (Fig. 14-1).

This added power also allows you to lift a rocket with twice as much mass. So if the maximum recommended liftoff mass of a B6 was 113.4 grams (4 ounces), then it can be doubled to 226.7 grams (8 ounces) if they are combined as a cluster. Thus, two B6s can lift twice as much as a single C6, which also has a maximum lofting capacity of 113.4 grams (4 ounces).

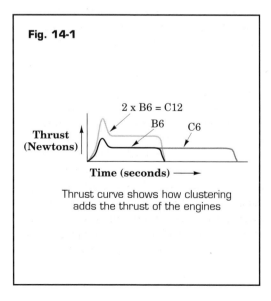

Fig. 14-1

2 x B6 = C12

B6   C6

Thrust (Newtons)

Time (seconds) ⟶

Thrust curve shows how clustering adds the thrust of the engines

Designing Clustered Engine Rockets

With all the extra power available, rockets that use cluster engines should be built extra-strong. They closely resemble higher-power rockets (see Chapter 7). The only significant difference is in the engine mounts, which need to be designed to hold the additional engines.

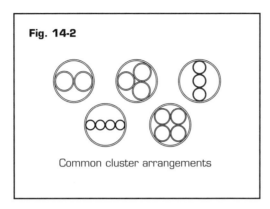

Fig. 14-2

Common cluster arrangements

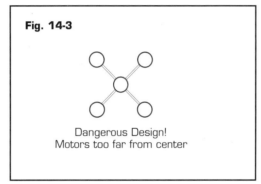

Fig. 14-3

Dangerous Design!
Motors too far from center

The first and most important consideration is that the thrust be evenly balanced around the centerline of the rocket. If there is more thrust on one side than the other, the model will veer off course and become unstable. Design the motor arrangements carefully so the motors are as close as possible to the centerline. If one motor fails to ignite, you want the remaining engines to lift the model off the pad without looping dangerously. Figures 14-2 and 14-3 illustrate several good designs and one bad design that should be avoided.

Select and arrange engines in the tube so they have similar delay times. For best reliability of parachute deployment, all the motors must fire the ejection charge at the same time. If one engine fires its ejection charge early, it could deploy the recovery device while the rocket is still traveling upward at a high rate of speed. This would probably shred the parachute or damage the rocket.

When building engine mounts, remember to build them light but keep them strong. Cluster rockets have a lot of mass near the aft end of the model. Keep this mass as low as possible. By the same token, make the engine mounts strong enough to withstand the higher thrust levels usually associated with multi-engine rockets.

Centering rings on cluster mounts can be more complex, and you may be tempted to skimp on them. Often the engine tubes, when combined, fit snugly inside the body tube of the rocket. The problem lies in the air gaps surrounding the tubes. You must fill these gaps (Fig. 14-4) or the ejection charge gases won't pressurize the body tube and push the parachute out. The model will streamline into the ground and destroy itself.

If the gaps are small, you can make some putty out of tissue paper and glue and plug them. Since it may take the glue a long time to dry, for larger gaps make a solid bulkhead out of cardboard or thin plywood.

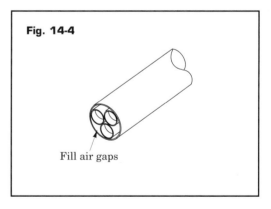

Fig. 14-4

Fill air gaps

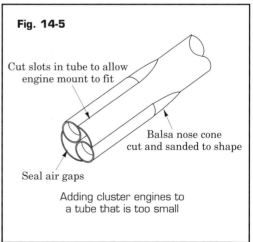

Fig. 14-5

Cut slots in tube to allow engine mount to fit

Balsa nose cone cut and sanded to shape

Seal air gaps

Adding cluster engines to a tube that is too small

If the body tube of the rocket is too small to fit the engine mounts, you may be able to cut some slots to give extra room. Figure 14-5 shows how to use a fairing to minimize drag in such cases. Make the transitions from a nose cone cut in half and carefully carved and sanded to fit the rocket. In this case too, remember to seal the air gaps that would allow the ejection gases to come out the rear of the rocket.

Fin Design

The only real concerns you will have with fin design are that they be strong enough to handle the extra loads imposed on them by the rocket engines, and that they be slightly larger. You will want to make them approximately 15 to 20 percent larger than fins on a similar-size model that doesn't have this extra mass in the rear.

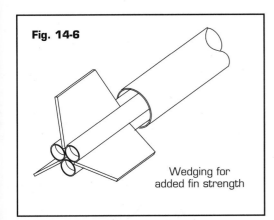

Fig. 14-6

Wedging for added fin strength

Some cluster engine mounts present an option for increasing the strength of the fins by wedging. You can do this by gluing the fins between the engine tubes on the model as shown in Figure 14-6. Other methods presented in Chapters 6 and 7 will also help you design fins to handle the higher loads.

Launching

The secret of launching cluster engine models reliably is to provide a lot of electrical current to all engines simultaneously. You can buy a commercially produced launch system or make your own. Whichever you use, make sure it is capable of delivering 10 amps of instantaneous electrical current to the igniters. Car batteries work great.

If your rocket has more than two motors you will need to make a clip-whip so all the igniters can be hooked up in a parallel circuit. A simple clip-whip is shown in Figure 14-7. Hook up the clip-whip to the igniters after you have paired the wires properly by twisting the leads of the igniters together as shown in Figure 14-8.

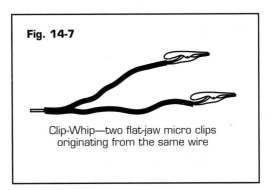

Fig. 14-7

Clip-Whip—two flat-jaw micro clips originating from the same wire

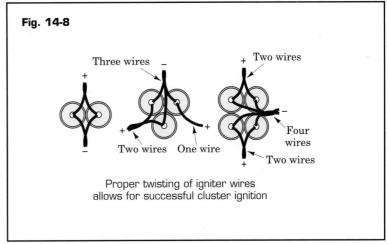

Fig. 14-8

Three wires

Two wires

One wire

Two wires

Four wires

Two wires

Proper twisting of igniter wires allows for successful cluster ignition

15

Rocket Engines

The rocket engine (or motor) is the device inserted into a model rocket to impart a thrust force, boosting it into the air. Model rocket engines are miniature solid fuel rocket motors that contain propellant, a delay element, and an ejection charge. Most rocket motors are designed to be used only once. They are usually manufactured with a paper or plastic case. A relatively new type of model rocket engine has been designed to be reused. These motors, called reloadable engines, are cost-effective only in the higher-power rockets, even though they are also available in smaller sizes.

Model rocket engines are classified by the amount of power they produce. The power rating is a product of the total thrust developed and the time in seconds for which the engine produces useful thrust. It is given the name total impulse. The following chart shows the rocket classification and the total impulse the engine produces.

Rocket Engine Total Impulse Classification System

Code	Newton Seconds
½A	.625–1.25
A	1.26–2.50
B	2.51–5.00
C	5.01–10.00
D	10.01–20.00
E	20.01–40.00
F	40.01–80.00
G	80.01–160.00
H	161.01–320.00
I	320.01–640.00

As you can see from this chart, the level of maximum total impulse doubles from one engine to the next. This chart can be extended as far as needed to classify even larger engines. You can convert to English units (pounds of thrust) by remembering that one pound equals 4.4 newtons.

Every model rocket engine has a designation code printed on it that gives you some specific information about how it operates. For example, the designation code on the engine of "C6-5" tells it apart from one that is labeled "B4-4."

The first letter in the designation code tells you the power level. This letter will help you choose an engine for your rocket by giving you a relative altitude between two engines. For example, a C engine will lift a model approximately twice as high as a B engine, and four times higher than an A engine. On the first flight of a rocket, use a relatively low-power engine to boost the design. This way you can get to know the flight characteristics of the model and, if necessary, make changes to improve performance.

The first number in the code tells you the average thrust produced by the engine. This level is expressed in newtons. In our example, the C6-5 engine produces an average of 6 newtons of thrust over its burn time. This number is very important when you select a rocket engine for your model. If your model is not built to withstand an average of 6 newtons of thrust, it may be ripped apart. For fragile models, you need to pay attention to this number. Many fragile rockets, like gliders or those with large thin fins, are damaged by an engine with too much thrust. Similarly, heavy rockets require a high average thrust to lift the model.

From this first number in the designation code you can also determine the approximate burn time. To do this, divide the total impulse at which the engine is rated by the average thrust level printed on the label. For example, a C6 engine has a maximum power of 10 N-s, (listed in the chart above) and has an average thrust of 6 newtons. Therefore, the burn time is 10 divided by 6, which equals 1.67 seconds.

Burn time and average thrust are important to modelers who want the rocket to fly to the highest altitudes. In Chapter 3 you discovered that the longer the burn time, the higher the model will travel. This is because a slow-speed rocket has less drag than a high-speed model, so it can coast longer.

The last number in the designation code is the time in seconds between propellant burnout and when the ejection charge fires. A C6-5 has a five-second delay before the ejection charge fires to push the parachute out of the rocket. Choose this delay time very carefully. The delay you pick depends on the mass of the model, how much drag it will produce, the angle at which it is launched, and how stable it is.

By intuition you know a heavy rocket will not travel as high as a lighter one. If you used a C6 in both a heavy rocket and a lighter one, which would have a longer coast time? The answer is, usually, the lighter one. So you need a longer delay time for a lighter model than a heavier one.

Drag has a similar effect on altitude as weight. A high-drag model will not travel as high as a low-drag model, so it will need a shorter delay time. High-drag models include most gliders and helicopters.

The angle at which you launch will also effect the altitude attained. You know that a model launched straight up will travel higher than one launched at an angle into the wind. The model will be at its slowest speed at the top of the trajectory arc, so the recovery device should be deployed at this point. If the rocket will reach the top of its arc sooner, as it will if it's launched at an angle, it should have a shorter delay time.

The stability of the model plays a role similar to the angle at which you launch the rocket. An overly stable model will weathercock into the wind, so it will have a trajectory similar to a model launched at an angle. Therefore, it needs a shorter delay. This is particularly true when you launch in windy conditions.

When you are just starting to design your own rockets, it is hard to know what delay times the model will need. The more experience you have in designing and building rockets, the easier it gets. You will probably make a few mistakes, but with luck the rocket will not be damaged. A few computer programs are available to help you choose the correct delay time for the motor. They calculate the altitude the model will attain and figure out how long it takes to get to that altitude. For these programs to be accurate, you need to know the coefficient of drag of the model and its empty mass. The coefficient of drag is hard to determine, especially for rockets with complex shapes. These computer programs are available from kit manufacturers, or you can find out about them from the National Association of Rocketry. Their address is at the end of this book.

To help you gain experience in selecting the proper rocket motor, I suggest you study the designs of other people. The easiest way to do this is with a catalog of a rocket manufacturer. You can look over their designs and find one that is similar to yours. Then you can use the same engines they use in theirs.

Types of Rocket Propellants

Two types of rocket propellants are used in model rocket engines. They are black-powder propellant and composite propellant. Black powder is common in small rockets, primarily because these engines are inexpensive to produce in large quantities. You will recognize a black-powder engine by its paper casing. The main ingredients of this type of propellant are potassium nitrate, sulfur, and carbon.

Black powder has several drawbacks, the main one being its low energy level per weight of material used. Another drawback is that it is sensitive to swings in temperature and humidity. If you store your rocket motors where the temperature and humidity constantly shift, the propellant may swell and contract. This changes the motor, and the chief effect is that it disintegrates when it is ignited. The lesson here is to store your motors where there is little or no variation in temperature or humidity.

Black-powder engines are also shock-sensitive. If you drop a motor on the ground, the propellant may develop a crack. This may also cause the motor to disintegrate when you launch it. Finally, the bigger the black-powder motor, the more susceptible it is to manufacturing flaws. This is why you don't see many black-powder engines larger than D or E.

A composite engine uses a chemically cured propellant formulation to achieve a higher total impulse-to-mass ratio. Typically, the energy per mass of propellant burned is at least twice that of black-powder engines. So the same mass of composite propellant has twice the total impulse of a black-powder engine. This is why a composite E engine can be made with the same physical dimensions as a black-powder D engine.

Physically, composite engines are mainly packaged in plastic casings. All reloadable engines use composite propellants that are assembled into a special aluminum case. The propellant grains, which have to be replaced between flights, are made inside a cardboard tube and sold separately from the special aluminum casing.

The main drawback of composite engines is that they are more expensive. But composite engines are much more stable than black powder, and they can handle swings in temperature and humidity. Composite propellant is often rubbery, and is not sensitive to shock damage when dropped.

Composite motors are usually ignited differently from black-powder motors, too. They must be ignited from the top of the motor, so nearly all have a hollow channel or through the center of the engine that allows the igniter to be inserted through the nozzle to the top of the motor. Sometimes there will be a noticeable delay between the time the igniter burns and when the engine actually starts burning. For this reason, composites are often considered harder to ignite. It's also why they should not be clustered with black-powder engines.

The chemicals used to make composite motors vary by manufacturer, the main difference being the oxidizer used. Some prefer ammonium perchlorate, and others potassium perchlorate. There are a variety of other differences too, and all these can affect how the rocket burns, the color of the flame, and the color of the smoke produced.

But no matter what propellant is used inside the rocket motor, all engines have the same type of designation code on the label. This is what you use to select the proper motor for your rocket.

Rocket Engine Charts

To help you choose the correct engine for your rocket, the next page carries engine selection charts from a variety of manufacturers. Pay particular attention to the column labeled "maximum lift-off mass with engine." Don't exceed this mass, as your rocket may never leave the launch pad—or it may take off horizontally once it does. Since manufacturers constantly add and delete engines, check the latest catalog from the manufacturer to see if a particular engine is in production.

Fig. 15-1

Forward bulkhead

High strength casing

Delay grain

Ejection charge

Composite propellant

Molded phenolic nozzle

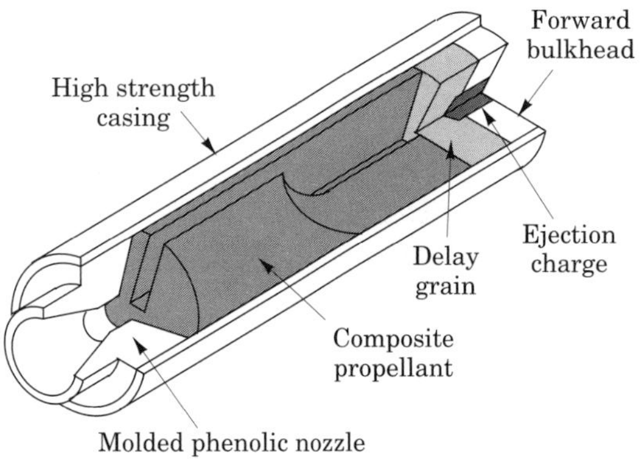

Typical composite engine construction

Engine Type	Total Impulse		Time Delay	Max Lift	Wt.	Max Thrust		Thrust Duration	Initial Weight		Propellant Weight	
	lb.-sec.	N-sec.		oz.	g	lb.	N		oz.	g	oz.	g
Single Stage Mini Engines												
1/2A3-2T	0.28	1.25	2 sec.	2	56.6	1.75	7.8	0.36 sec.	0.198	5.6	0.062	1.75
A3-4T	0.56	2.50	4 sec.	2	56.6	1.75	7.8	0.86 sec.	0.268	7.6	0.124	3.5
A10-3T	0.56	2.50	3 sec.	5	141.5	3.00	13.3	0.26 sec.	0.277	7.9	0.133	3.78
Upper Stage Mini Engines												
1/2A3-4T	0.28	1.25	4 sec.	1	28.3	1.75	7.8	0.36 sec.	0.212	6.0	0.062	1.75
Booster Stage Mini Engines												
A10-0T	0.56	2.50	none	5	141.5	3.00	13.3	0.26 sec.	0.235	6.7	0.133	3.70
Single Stage Regular Engines												
1/2A6-2	0.28	1.25	2 sec.	2.5	70.8	2.88	12.8	0.20 sec.	0.53	15.0	0.055	1.56
A8-3	0.56	2.50	3 sec.	4.0	113.2	3.00	13.3	0.32 sec.	0.57	16.2	0.110	3.12
B4-2	1.12	5.00	2 sec.	4.0	113.2	3.00	13.3	1.20 sec.	0.70	19.8	0.294	8.33
B4-4	1.12	5.00	4 sec.	3.5	99.1	3.00	13.3	1.20 sec.	0.74	21.0	0.294	8.33
B6-2	1.12	5.00	2 sec.	4.5	127.4	3.00	13.3	0.83 sec.	0.68	19.3	0.220	6.24
B6-4	1.12	5.00	4 sec.	4.0	113.2	3.00	13.3	0.83 sec.	0.71	20.1	0.220	6.24
B8-5	1.12	5.00	5 sec.	5.0	141.5	5.00	22.2	0.60 sec.	0.68	19.3	0.220	6.24
C5-3	2.25	10.00	3 sec.	8.0	226.4	5.00	22.2	2.10 sec.	0.90	25.5	0.450	12.70
C6-3	2.25	10.00	3 sec.	4.0	113.2	3.00	13.3	1.70 sec.	0.88	24.9	0.440	12.48
C6-5	2.25	10.00	5 sec.	4.0	113.2	3.00	13.3	1.70 sec.	0.91	25.8	0.440	12.48
Upper Stage Regular Engines												
A8-5	0.56	2.50	5 sec	2.0	56.6	3.00	13.3	0.32 sec.	0.62	17.6	0.110	3.12
B4-6	1.12	5.00	6 sec.	1.5	42.5	3.00	13.3	1.20 sec.	0.78	22.1	0.294	8.33
B6-6	1.12	5.00	6 sec.	2.0	56.6	3.00	13.3	0.83 sec.	0.78	22.1	0.220	6.24
C6-7	2.25	10.00	7 sec.	2.5	70.8	3.00	13.3	1.70 sec.	0.95	26.9	0.440	12.48
Booster Stage Regular Engines												
B6-0	1.12	5.00	none	4.0	113.2	3.00	13.3	0.80 sec.	0.58	16.4	0.220	6.24
C6-0	2.25	10.00	none	4.0	113.2	3.00	13.3	1.68 sec.	0.80	22.7	0.440	12.48
Single Stage D Engines [7.0 cm (2.75") long and 24 mm (0.945") in diameter]												
D12-3	4.48	20.00	3 sec.	14	396.2	6.4	28.5	1.70 sec.	1.49	42.2	0.879	24.93
D12-5	4.48	20.00	5 sec.	10	283.0	6.4	28.5	1.70 sec.	1.52	43.1	0.879	24.93
Upper Stage D Engines												
D12-7	4.48	20.00	7 sec.	8	226.4	6.4	28.5	1.70 sec.	1.55	44.0	0.879	24.93
Booster Stage D Engines												
D12-0	4.48	20.00	none	14	396.2	6.4	28.5	1.70 sec.	1.44	40.9	0.879	24.93
Plugged D Engines												
D11-P	4.48	20.00	plugged	16	453.1	6.2	27.6	1.82 sec.	1.55	44.0	0.879	24.93
Single Stage E Engines [8.9 cm (3.5") long and 24 mm (0.945") in diameter]												
E15-4	7.14	32.00	4 sec.	14	397.0	4.5	20.5	2.60 sec.	2.00	56.6	1.25	35.5
E15-6	7.14	32.00	6 sec.	11	312.0	4.5	20.5	2.60 sec.	2.02	57.3	1.25	35.5
E15-8	7.14	32.00	8 sec.	9	255.0	4.5	20.5	2.60 sec.	2.05	58.0	1.25	35.5
Plugged E Engines												
E15-P	7.59	34.00	plugged	15	425.0	4.5	20.5	2.60 sec.	2.12	60.0	1.31	37.2

16

Displaying Your Completed Model

After you have completed your rocket, you will want to display it proudly. Often a rocket won't stand upright on its own fins, so you may want to build a display stand for it. This can be very simple, and you can often use the same materials you used in building the rocket.

If you like, you can make your stand look like a real launch pad. If this type of stand is used to launch the rocket too, it is called a functional display launcher. If you are using it as a launcher, there are a few things to keep in mind when you design and build it. First, make sure there is some support method to guide the rocket during its first 3 feet (1 meter) of flight. This can either be a traditional launch rod, a tower that surrounds the model, or some other type of fixed guidance method.

Second, design and build the pad so it can easily handle the largest rocket you plan to place on the launcher. Make sure it has a wide, stable base so it won't tip over with the heavy rocket on it, even when the wind is blowing briskly.

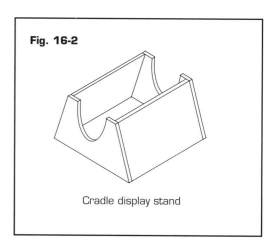

Fig. 16-2

Cradle display stand

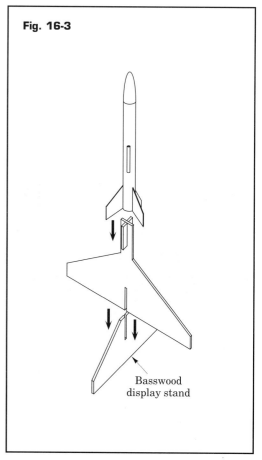

Fig. 16-3

Basswood display stand

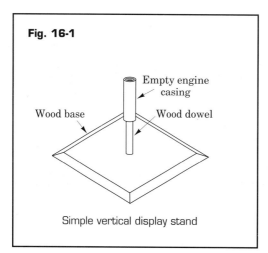

Fig. 16-1

Empty engine casing

Wood base

Wood dowel

Simple vertical display stand

Finally, I recommend that you build a blast deflector into the pad. This will protect it from the flame of the rocket engine, thereby making it more durable. You may also include some device to hold down the launch clips. This will prevent them from being thrown around by the exhaust gases of the rocket and possibly damaging the pad or the clips. Figures 16-3 through 16-3 illustrate some display stands which will give you some creative ideas for your own.

Marc McReynold built a functional display launcher for his scale model of NASA's Little Joe 1. (photo by Marc Lavigne)

APPENDIX
Other Design Resources

The National Association of Rocketry (NAR) is an organization within the United States that supports model rocketeers. They have an extensive collection of technical publications on model rockets available, and they also produce *Sport Rocketry* magazine. This magazine is produced monthly and often features rocket plans you can build. For information write to: National Association of Rocketry, P. O. Box 177, Altoona, WI 54720, U.S.A. (1-800-262-4872).

Rockets of the World. This book was mentioned in the chapter on scale rockets. It contains technical information and photographs of almost all of the world's scientific research rockets. For information on this book write to Peter Alway, P. O. Box 3709, Ann Arbor, MI 48106-3709, U.S.A.

For current information on rocket manufacturers I recommend that you get the latest issue of one of the model rocket magazines. *Sport Rocketry* and *High Power Rocketry* are both available at most hobby stores and major bookstores. They contain advertisements from manufacturers producing rocket kits, motors, parts, and accessories. If you can't find these magazines on the racks you can write to the publishers to get more information. The address for *Sport Rocketry* is listed above. You can get information on *High Power Rocketry* by writing the publisher at: High Power Rocketry, P. O. Box 96, Orem, UT 84059-0096 U.S.A.

Ablative materials. Special materials on the surface of a rocket that can be sacrificed (carried away, vaporized) by the heat produced by air friction flowing over a fast-moving rocket. Kinetic energy is dissipated and excessive heating of the main structure of the rocket is prevented.

Abort. Failure of an aerospace vehicle to accomplish its purposes for any reason. An abort may can be caused by human, technical, or meteorological errors, miscalculation, or malfunction.

Abrasive. Natural or artificial materials used for grinding or polishing. Natural abrasives include diamond, emery, sand, crushed garnet, and pumice. Artificial abrasives are made from natural materials and, in general, are either silicon carbide or aluminum oxide.

Absolute pressure. The sum of the gauge pressure plus the atmospheric pressure. The pressure used to determine the action of gases according to the gas laws.

Acceleration. The rate of change in velocity with time. Typical units of linear acceleration are meters per second per second (m/sec^2). Negative acceleration is commonly called "deceleration."

Acceleration due to gravity. Any acceleration due entirely to gravity, e.g., in a vacuum a freely falling body falls toward the earth's center at a velocity of 32.2 feet (9.81 m) the first second, with an increase in velocity of 32.2 feet (9.81 m) per second the next second. Velocity at the end of the second second is 64.4 feet (19.62 m) per second, etc. In air the rate of acceleration is modified by the force due to air resistance. A freely falling body will finally reach a speed at which the force of gravity and air resistance are equal and no greater speed is gained.

Accelerometer. An instrument that measures change in velocity, or measures the gravitational forces capable of imparting a change in velocity.

Acetate butyrate dope. A solution combining the fire-resistant qualities of acetate dope with the toughening properties of nitrate dope. See *Aircraft Dope.*

Acetate dope. Dope manufactured from cellulose and acetic acid.

Acetone. An inflammable liquid prepared by special fermentation of grain, forming butyl alcohol and acetone. A general solvent used as an ingredient for the thinning of dope, lacquer, and epoxy.

Acoustics. The science or study of sounds, including the generation, perception, measurement, reproduction, and control of material vibrations.

Acrobatics. Unnecessary flight evolutions voluntarily performed with an aircraft requiring or resulting in an abrupt change in its *attitude*, an abnormal attitude, or operations in excess of the aircraft's design level flight speed.

Acrylic resin or plastic. A thermoplastic resin resembling glass. Used in making transparent parts, such as lenses, windows, clear fins, etc.

Actuator. A mechanical, electrical, or pneumatic device that sets some mechanism into operation, throws a switch, or performs some other intermittent operation.

Adapter. The external part of the rocket that acts to smooth the transition between body tubes of different diameters. Adapters are made from a variety of materials, paper and balsa being the most common.

Additive. A substance added to a propellant to achieve some purpose, such as a more even rate of combustion.

Adhesive. Material applied between components to bond the components together structurally.

Advanced model rockets. Model rockets constructed of exotic materials, or capable of performing some function that differentiates them from traditional model rockets. *High-powered rockets* are not necessarily advanced model rockets.

Aerial photograph. Any photograph made from a vehicle in flight.

Aeroballistics. A term derived from aerodynamics and ballistics, dealing primarily with the motion of bodies, such as guided rockets, whose flight path is determined by applying the principles of both sciences to different portions of the path.

Aerodynamics. The science that deals with the motion of gases (especially air) and with the forces acting on solid bodies when they move through gases or when gases move against or around the solid bodies.

Aerodynamic center. A point located on the wing chord approximately one-quarter of the chord length back from the leading edge, about which the *moment coefficient* is practically constant for all angles of attack.

Aerodynamic drag. see *Drag.*

Aerodynamic heating. The rise in the skin temperature of a rocket due to the friction of the air at high speed.

Aerodynamic twist. See *Washin and washout.*

Aeronautics. A general term applied to everything associated with or used in any way in the study, design, construction, or operation of aircraft.

Aerosol. A mixture of fine liquid or solid particles and the gas or air in which they are suspended.

Aileron. Hinged flap or movable portion of an airplane wing, the primary function of which is to impart a rolling or banking motion to the airplane about the roll axis or longitudinal axis.

Air brakes. Any system on an airplane of air speed retarding devices that serve to increase the resistance of the airplane during a glide, landing, or maneuver.

Aircraft dope. The liquid material applied to the cloth, paper, or wooden surfaces of airplanes to increase strength, to produce tautness by shrinking, and to act as a filler for maintaining air and water tightness.

Air density. A measure of the number of molecules in relation to volume of air. Abbreviation: r.

Airflow. The relative flow of air past or around a body.

Airfoil. Any surface, such as a fin, wing, aileron, or rudder, etc., designed to obtain a useful reaction from the air through which it moves.

Airfoil section. The cross-sectional shape of an airfoil, parallel to the plane of symmetry or to a specified reference plane.

Air launch. See *Airstart.*

Air scoop. See *Scoop.*

Air speed. The rate or speed at which an aircraft is traveling through the atmosphere (air) entirely independent of any distance covered on the surface of the earth. Its symbol is V (velocity).

Airstart. An act or instance of starting a rocket engine while in flight, especially after a short delay following the burnout of a *booster engine.*

Alignment. The act of bringing into a straight line, usually referring to the fins being attached parallel to the longitudinal axis of the body tube.

Aliphatic resin. A type of carpenter's wood glue that penetrates into the pores of wood and paper. Once this glue has dried, it will not soften when exposed to water.

Altimeter. An instrument for measuring or indicating the elevation of an aircraft above a given datum line (such as sea level or ground level).

Altitude. The height above a given reference point, such as the earth's surface.

Anemometer. An instrument for indicating or measuring the speed of an airstream.

Angle-of-attack. The angle measured between the chord line (i.e., the straight line joining the centers of curvature of the leading and trailing edges) on an *airfoil* and the relative airflow, normally the immediate flight path of the rocket or aircraft. It is also called the "angle of incidence." As the angle-of-attack increases (the front of the wing becomes progressively higher than the rear), the amount of lift increases—up to the stall, at which point the wing produces zero lift.

Apogee. The peak altitude that a model rocket reaches in flight.

Aspect ratio. A ratio between the wingspan to the average wing chord length. Typically, the larger the aspect ratio, the lower the drag force is on a wing. It is found with the formula:

$$Aspect\ Ratio = \frac{(Wing\ Span^2)}{Avg.\ Chord\ Length}$$

Asymmetric fins. Lack of evenness or symmetry in size, shape, location, spacing or orientation of the fins on a model rocket.

Atmospheric pressure. The pressure at any point in the atmosphere due solely to the weight of the atmospheric gases above that point.

Attitude. The position or orientation of a rocket or glider, either in motion or at rest, as determined by the relationship between its axes and a reference line or plane (such as the horizon) or a fixed system of reference.

Attitude control system. A system within the flight control system that directs and maintains the desired attitude in the aerospace vehicle.

Autogyro. An aircraft or helicopter whose fall is retarded by drag created by a propeller whose axis is parallel to the ground. The propeller is driven only by the air forces and not by any mechanical or electrical means.

Axis (of an aircraft). Three fixed lines of reference, usually centroidal and mutually perpendicular. The first, the *longitudinal axis,* is parallel to the axis of the *thrust line.* The second, about which the plane rotates in *yawing,* is known as the *vertical axis;* and the third, the axis perpendicular to the other two, is called the *lateral axis.*

Ballast. An object used as a counterweight to maintain the balance of an airplane or rocket.

Ballistic missile. Any missile which does not rely on aerodynamic surfaces for lift and which utilizes reaction propulsion as a power source. Such a missile, normally guided by external means during the first portion of its flight, follows a ballistic trajectory determined by gravitational and atmosphere drag forces after launch power is cut off.

Ballistics. The science or art that deals with the motion, behavior, appearance, or modification of missiles or other vehicles acted upon by propellants, wind, gravity, temperature, or any other modifying substance, condition, or force; the art of designing missiles or other vehicles as to give them efficient motion and flight behavior within the limitations set up by their purpose. See also *Exterior ballistics*; *Interior ballistics*.

Ballistic trajectory. The path followed by a rocket being acted upon only by gravitational forces and the resistance of the air through which it passes. A rocket without lifting surfaces describes a ballistic trajectory after its propulsive unit stops operating.

Balsa wood. A tropical wood that is strong but low in density. It is used extensively in rocketry because it is easy to work with and because of its low mass.

Bank, to bank an airplane. To incline the airplane so the lateral axis makes an angle with the horizontal.

Base drag. That portion of pressure drag resulting from reduced air pressure aft of the rear end of a rocket. Base drag can be reduced by streamlining the rocket with a boattail, but this drag cannot be completely eliminated.

Baseline. The distance measured between a tracker and the launch pad for single-station tracking, or the distance between two trackers in dual-station tracking.

Basswood. A type of hardwood with very tight grain. Useful in making very smooth fins because the grain is easily filled.

Batten. A strip or bar secured to a wing or tail to prevent movement of the control surface. Used primarily on *Rogallo* wing gliders to prevent the fabric wing from fluttering.

Bay (body parts). Any specific compartment of the body of an aircraft or rocket, such as a payload bay.

Bay (wing). The structure included between two ribs on a wing or fin.

Beam; structural. A rigid body designed to transmit transverse loads in shear and/or bending to its point of support.

Bernoulli's Theorem. A theory of aerodynamics, which states that fluid pressure is inversely proportional to its velocity squared, i.e., increase the speed and decrease the pressure, or decrease the speed and increase the pressure. One common application of this important law is that the airflow over the upper surface of an airfoil causes a low-pressure area (suction) because the air stream has been speeded up, while the speed of the airflow over the lower surface of the airfoil remains constant; so the pressure is higher below the wing than above.

Biplane. an airplane with two wings placed one above the other.

Birch. A heavy, hard, strong, tough wood, often used to protect other woods.

Black-powder engines. A type of inexpensive model rocket engine that uses a pressed propellant composed mainly of potassium nitrate, sulfur, and carbon.

Blade twist, helicopter. Blade pitch-angle variation from root to tip.

Blast deflector. Any object used to divert the flame of a rocket fired from a vertical position. The object is usually made from metal or ceramic clay to withstand the intense heat so it can be used repeatedly.

Blister, paint. An air bubble formed under the skin of a paint. Causes may include oil residue on pre-painted surface or outgassing of solvent in paint from overexposure to high heat.

Blockhouse. A building, usually heavily reinforced to withstand blast and heat, that houses equipment for preparing and launching a rocket.

Blow down tunnel. A wind tunnel that operates by releasing stored air from a reservoir tank.

Blow through. A name describing the condition of a motor failure in which the propellant is ejected out the front end of a motor.

Boattail. The cylindrical section of a rocket's body that continually decreases in diameter. See also *Shoulder* and *Adapter*.

Body tube. A specially wound and treated cardboard or lightweight plastic cylinder used to make the fuselage (main body) of the rocket.

Booster. See *Boost Engine*.

Boost glider. A type of rocket-launched, free-flying glider that separates into two or more pieces after engine burnout. Parts may separate from the glider (usually by ejecting an engine pod) to change its mass distribution, creating stable glide. See also *Rocket glider*.

Boost engine. A special rocket engine without a delay element, used in staged models to ignite the top stage. The stage that contains the boost engine is commonly called a "booster."

Boost phase. The portion of flight when the engine burns, creating thrust.

Boundary layer. A layer of fluid (or air) close to the surface of a body part in a moving stream.

Buckle. A bend or kink in the surface of a structural member.

Buffeting. The repeated aerodynamic forces experienced by any part of an aircraft, caused by unsteady flow arising from a disturbance set up by any other part of the aircraft. See *flutter*.

Built-up fin. A strong and lightweight fin, created by making it hollow, with judicious placement within the structure of high-strength materials.

Bulkhead. A structural reinforcement around the inside perimeter of a fuselage or body tube in the form of a disk or tube. It may consist of a variety of materials, often paper or wood.

Bungee. A device or cord designed to limit forward movement of the nose cone at recovery device deployment. See *Shock cord*.

Burn. The chemical reaction that takes place inside a rocket engine which releases high-pressure gases at high temperatures.

Burnout. The point at which propellant is exhausted, ending combustion of fuel in the rocket engine.

Burnout velocity. The velocity of a rocket at the termination of thrust (i.e., at *burnout*).

Burn rate. The rate at which the burning surface of a solid-propellant grain recedes when the propellant is consumed within a combustion chamber.

Butt joint. The method of attaching the fin to the rocket by gluing the root edge directly on the outside of the body tube.

Caliber. The ratio of the body tube's diameter to its length. Most commonly used in determining stability: a rocket is stable if the *center-of-gravity* is one or more body tube diameters or one *Caliber*, ahead of the *center-of-pressure*.

Camber. The rise in the curvature of an airfoil from its chord, expressed as a percentage of the wing chord length.

Camouflage paint scheme. A paint pattern used to disguise or conceal a rocket from view.

Canard. A small horizontal stabilizer located forward of the main wing on a glider.

Canopy. See *Parachute canopy*.

Canted nozzle. A rocket nozzle whose center line does not lie on, or parallel with, the center line of the main body tube, but is tilted (canted) at some angle.

Cantilever beam. A projecting member with one end rigidly fixed and the other end projecting from the point of support, free to move vertically under the influence of vertical loads applied between the free end and the fixed end. A fin or a wing spar is an example of a cantilever beam.

Cap strips. The longitudinal members at the top and bottom of a beam, rib, or spar, which resist most of the bending loads.

Capsule. A small, sealed pressurized cabin with an acceptable environment, usually for containing a man or animal for extremely high-altitude flights.

Captive test. A test conducted while a rocket is secured to the launch stand, primarily to verify proper operation of the propulsion and flight control subsystems under full thrust conditions.

Case rupture. Splitting of the rocket engine caused by the failure of the case to hold the high pressures inside the engine.

Cast propellant. Solid propellant fabricated by pouring a soft propellant mixture into a mold and permitting it to solidify into the desired grain configuration.

CATO. Abbreviation for **ChATastrO**phic failure. Usually refers to a rocket engine that has exploded. See also; *Blow through* and *Case rupture*.

Centering ring. A bulkhead or structural reinforcement in a rocket that aligns and holds one body tube inside another.

Center-of-gravity. The balance point of the model, about which the model will always rotate. Abbreviation: CG.

Center-of-pressure. The point on the model where all the aerodynamic forces balance. Also called the *Aerodynamic Center*. Abbreviation: CP.

C.H.A.D. staging. (**CH**eap **A**nd **D**irty) A method of multi-staging for a single stage model in which a booster engine is taped to a sustainer engine. Rockets with C.H.A.D. staging do not have booster sections or fins on the lower engine.

Chord. The length of the line that joins the leading and trailing edges of a wing or fin.

Chuffing. The intermittent burning of a rocket engine accompanied by an irregular puffing noise. Usually caused by improper ignition technique or insufficient chamber pressure inside the motor.

Clean (design). An expression meaning that an aircraft or rocket is particularly free of external projections and is well *streamlined*, i.e., aerodynamically clean.

Clip whip. A short extension on the ends of launch controller wiring with multiple micro clips attached for clustering two or more rocket engines.

Cluster ignition. The simultaneous ignition of two or more rocket engines to operate as a single unit, attaining a higher liftoff thrust. The total thrust and impulse of a cluster configuration is equal to the sum of thrust and impulse of the individual rocket engines.

Coasting phase. The period immediately following propellant burnout and preceding the ignition of the ejection charge of the engine, during which the rocket coasts on its own momentum.

Coefficient of drag. A dimensionless number calculated by:

$$C_2 = \frac{Total\ Drag\ Force}{\frac{1}{2} \times Air\ density \times frontal\ surface\ area \times velocity^2}$$

It allows a direct comparison of the performance of two different models. Abbreviation: C_d

Combustion chamber. A cavity inside an engine where propellant is burned.

Competition model. Model rockets used in games or contests designed for a specific mission profile (i.e., maximum altitude for a given engine classification).

Component. Individual part of a mechanical assembly or system.

Composite engine. A model rocket engine using a chemically cured propellant to achieve a higher ratio of total impulse to mass ratio compared to black-powder engines, which have a lower ratio of total impulse to mass. The principal ingredient of a composite rocket propellant is the oxidizer, typically ammonium perchlorate (AP). The "glue" that holds the AP together and acts as the propellant fuel is a long carbon-chain molecule called hydroxyl-terminated polybutadiene (HTPB).

Composite material. A structural material made up of two or more separate materials, usually to create a new material of greater strength but lower mass. A fiberglass/epoxy sheet is one such material.

Concentric. Having a common center.

Cone. A geometric configuration having a circular bottom and sides tapering off to an apex.

Cone stability. The inherent stability, without the need of fins, of a model with the general shape of a cone. The CG must still be placed forward of the CP for stability.

Configuration. The arrangement of parts on a rocket or glider.

Contact cement. A flexible adhesive applied to both surfaces of the parts being joined together. Most useful on paper-to-paper bonds.

Continuity. The condition of a launch system having a complete electrical circuit to allow ignition.

Control surfaces. Flaps, tabs, or movable panels on wings, elevators, canards, or rudders used to set the glider to some predetermined *attitude*.

Conventional boost glider. The generic name given to a configuration of rocket-launched boost gliders where the engine is attached to the nose of the glider and the wing is in front of the horizontal tail.

Core ejection. Occurs in rear engine boost gliders when the engine mount tube is forced (or ejected) out the rear of the model, so the CG of the glider moves aft over the wing.

Countdown. The step-by-step process leading to a rocket launching. It is performed in accordance with a pre-designed time schedule, measured in terms of T-Time (T minus time prior to initiation of engine start and T plus time thereafter).

Coupler. A tube or cylinder used to connect two body tubes of the same diameter.

Covering, aircraft. The material covering the framework of an aircraft structure.

Craze. Cracking of paint into a rough surface texture caused by incompatibility of paint underlying paints or primer.

Cross section. The surface that would be exposed if a part were to be cut in half.

Cyanoacrylate. Chemical name given to a type of adhesive that hardens very rapidly. Sometimes called instant or super glue. Abbreviated: CA or CyA.

Decalage. The relative angle between the wing's *angle-of-attack* and the stabilizer's *angle-of-attack* on a glider. This difference in angle allows the glider to pull out of a dive.

Deceleration. The retarding or slowing down of an object, i.e., the decrease in the rate of change of velocity. Negative *acceleration*.

Deflection. The bending or displacement of the neutral axis of a structural member from the position it normally occupies, due to an external load.

Deflector. See *Blast deflector*.

Delay element. Slow-burning propellant that initiates the burning of the ejection charge after a predetermined time following termination of engine thrust.

Delay phase. See *Coast phase*.

Delta wing. A triangular wing having a low aspect ratio, tapered leading edge, and a straight trailing edge.

Density. The ratio of the mass of an object to its volume.

Deployment. That portion of a rocket's operation from the moment of ejection charge initiation to instant of inflation of the canopy for a parachute, or the complete extension of the rotor blades in a helicopter.

Design constraints. Factors that limit the size, shape, or configuration of a particular design.

Dethermalizer. A device on a glider that triggers (at a certain time) a retrimming of the glider to bring it to the ground at a faster rate.

Differential aileron linkage arrangement. Ailerons interconnected so that the upward displacement of one aileron is greater than the downward displacement of the other.

Diffusion tip wings. The wings on a type of *tailless airplane*. The wing tips are cut diagonally across the span and bent downward at the cut line, providing *washout* for the wing.

Dihedral. Raising of the wing tip upward relative to the wing root, thus giving the glider yaw and roll stability.

Directional stability. The tendency of an airplane to immediately return to its original direction of flight after being thrown off its flight course.

Direct staging. A method of multi-staging in which the lower engine ignites the upper stage engine without assistance from other devices.

Display launcher. A static base for holding a rocket that is not intended to be used for actual launching, although it looks as though it could.

Dive. Condition of a glider that noses down rapidly.

Dope. A liquid lacquer paint used on balsa wood to seal the pores of the wood grain.

Doppler effect. Apparent change in frequency of sound or light due to motion.

Downdraft. A downward moving body of air.

Downrange. In a direction away from the launch site, usually in direction of the relative wind in the area of the launch site.

Downwash. The air deflected perpendicular to the direction of motion of an airfoil, i.e., it is the bending down of the air column upon which the wing acts while in flight.

Drag. The resistance or friction force experienced by any moving object through air.

Drag recovery. A method of returning a model to the ground in which the large frontal area of the rocket provides sufficient resistance to bring the model down slowly.

Drogue parachute. A smaller canopy deployed to slow and stabilize the load, usually prior to main parachute canopy deployment.

Drone. A pilotless aircraft operated by remote control.

Dullcote. A brand name of clear paint that has a nonreflective finish when dry.

Egglofting. The launching of a raw hen's egg, the purpose of which is to return it to the ground without breaking the shell.

Ejection baffle. Any device or system forward of the rocket engine that slows and cools the ejection charge gases before they reach the parachute. It also deflects and traps any large particles resulting from the *ejection charge*.

Ejection charge. A chemical substance that produces a large volume of gas in a model rocket when ignited by the delay element. This gas pushes the recovery device out of the rocket or activates a deployment sequence of rotors, pistons, flaps, wings, etc.

Elevator. The movable control surface on the horizontal tail used to make the glider pitch upward (to pull out of a dive) or downward about the pitch axis.

Elevon. A horizontal aerodynamic *control surface* that combines the functions of an elevator and an aileron.

Empennage. The rear part of an airplane, usually consisting of a group of stabilizing planes (horizontal and vertical stabilizers). Sometimes this portion of the airplane is referred to as the airplane tail assembly, tail group, or tail unit.

Energy. The capacity for doing work.

Engine block. A hollow frame or *bulkhead* placed directly in front of a rocket engine to keep it from sliding forward into the rocket. See *Thrust ring*.

Engine hook. A bent piece of metal with a small angle at one end, which holds the engine securely in the engine mount.

Engine hook retainer ring. A ring of paper or plastic that holds the engine hook securely to the engine tube.

Engine mount. An apparatus that holds the engine firmly in place so it is aligned with the centerline of the model.

Engine tube. A body tube that is part of the engine mount into which the engine is inserted for flight.

Epoxy. A high-strength, two-part adhesive for bonding parts or for creating fillets.

Equipment pods. Capsules or compartments mounted on the outside of the vehicle in which equipment is stored for the flight.

Erosion, nozzle. A wearing away of the throat of a nozzle from the action of the hot exhaust gases of the rocket engine.

Escape velocity. The speed an object must reach to leave the pull of Earth's gravity.

Exhaust clearance. On front-engine boost gliders, the distance the engine must be placed upward so the gaseous plume does not impinge on other parts of the glider.

Exhaust velocity. The velocity of gases exiting through the nozzle of an engine.

Expansion ratio. The ratio of the section area of the nozzle exit to the section area of the nozzle throat.

Exterior ballistics. That branch of ballistics concerned with the behavior of a missile during flight, influenced by conditions of air density, temperatures, velocity, etc.

External force. Force applied to a structure or body from some outside source.

Fairing. Rigid material shaped to streamline a part to reduce drag.

Featherweight recovery. Rocket recovery system in which a very lightweight model falls slowly because it has low mass relative to its size. The drag force easily counteracts the force of gravity.

Fiberglass. A manmade material known for its strength and low mass.

Filler. A paste or liquid used for filling the pores of wood prior to applying paint.

Fillets. A fairing of glue or epoxy along the root edge of fins or wings (where they attach to the body tube) providing additional fin strength.

Fin- An aerodynamic surface projecting longitudinally from the rocket body to give it directional stability. Fins are the rocket's stabilizing and guiding unit.

Fineness ratio. The ratio of the length to the maximum diameter of a streamlined body. See *Caliber*.

Finishing. The art and practice of creating a smooth, attractive appearance on a model rocket.

Firewall. A fire-resistant bulkhead.

Flame bucket. An opening built into the launch pad into which the hot gases of the rocket pour. One of its sides turns inward to form the flame deflector; the opposite side is open. See also *Blast deflector*.

Flame deflector. See *Blast deflector*.

Flap. A movable control surface that deflects air. On the wing the flap is called an aileron, and on the horizontal stabilizer it is called an elevator. On the vertical stabilizer the flap is called a rudder. Flaps can also be used for brakes.

Flaperons. Missile control system, either differentially or integrally operated, which combines the attitude control of ailerons with the increased lift and braking effect of flaps.

Flat spin. A flight condition of rotation about the vertical axis while the longitudinal axis is inclined downward less than 45 degrees with the horizontal or level plane. Ailerons and tail surfaces are ineffective because the airplane is in a stalled condition; the downward path of

113

the airplane and the rotation carries the tail control group away from the slip stream.

Flat trajectory. The path described by a rocket flight that does not have a high arch.

Flex wing. A glider that uses thin, flexible plastic sheeting for a main lifting surface. This reduces the mass of the glider and allows the wings to be folded for launch so higher altitudes are reached. Flex wing gliders are sometimes called "flexies." See *Rogallo*.

Flight-critical item. A component that is absolutely necessary to the success of the vehicle's mission.

Flight path. The line connecting the continuous positions to be occupied by an aircraft or rocket as it moves through the air.

Flight path angle. The angle between the *flight path* of the aircraft and the horizontal.

Flight profile. A graphic portrayal of a rocket's flight as seen from the side, indicating the various altitudes along the route.

Flight test. A test of a component part of a flying vehicle to determine its suitability or reliability in terms of its intended function, done by making the component endure actual flight conditions.

Flight test vehicle. A test vehicle for the conduct of *flight tests*, either to test its own capabilities or to carry equipment requiring flight test.

Flightworthy. Of a aircraft or rocket, ready and sufficiently sound in all respects to meet and endure the stresses and strains of flight.

Flutter. An oscillation of definite period but unstable character set up in any part or an aircraft by a momentary disturbance, and maintained by a combination of aerodynamic, inertial, and elastic characteristics of the member itself. See also *Buffeting*.

Flying plank. A type of *tailless aircraft* that does not have a swept wing but uses a *reflexed airfoil* to achieve longitudinal stability.

Flying wing. A special shape of glider, designed and balanced for a stable glide, that has no horizontal tail or canards.

Foam core. A construction method for fins and wings in which a sheet of plastic foam is sandwiched between two skins made from stronger materials (balsa wood, fiberglass/epoxy, paper, or plywood).

Force. Any action changing the state of motion or position of a body. A force is a quantity and may be represented by a straight line, called a *vector*. A force has three characteristics, (1) magnitude, (2) direction, and (3) point of application.

Forced landing. Any landing of a aircraft or rocket due to structural failure or any other condition that makes continued flight either impossible or inadvisable.

Fore. Forward or in front of a designated position.

Form drag. The drag due to the vehicle's shape. For example, rounded and streamlined shapes have less drag than blunt shapes.

Former, or false wing rib. Any incomplete rib, frequently consisting only of a short section extending from the leading edge to the front spar, used to help maintain the form of the wing where its curvature is sharpest.

Framework. A structure used to create a strong yet hollow wing or fin.

Free fall. The fall of a body without being guided and without being retarded.

Free flight. Unconstrained or unassisted flight of a glider.

Friction. The resistance a body encounters in moving across the surface of another with which it is in contact.

Friction fit. A tight joining of two coaxial parts in which the inner part's outside diameter is equal to the outer part's internal diameter. The force of friction between the two surfaces in contact keeps the parts from moving.

Frontal area. The surface of the rocket that faces directly into the airstream.

Fulcrum. The pivot point about which a lever oscillates or turns.

Functional display launcher. A type of rocket pad with aesthetic qualities that give it an appearance of a real military or scientific launch pad.

Fuselage. The structure, of approximate streamline form, that houses the crew, passengers, or cargo.

Gantry. A crane rolling on rails, used for the erection and general servicing of large missiles. Sometimes also called a "Mobile Service Tower" (MST).

Gas. A fluid that tends to expand indefinitely.

Gimbaled motor. A rocket motor mounted on gimbal, which is a mechanical device for permitting an object to incline freely in any direction, so that it will remain level when its support is tipped.

Glide. The controlled descent by a heavier-than-air vehicle under little or no engine thrust, in which forward motion is maintained by gravity and vertical descent is controlled by lift forces.

Glide path. The flight of a glider in an *unpowered glide*, seen from the side. See also *Flight path*.

Glide phase. The portion of a glider's flight after engine burnout when the model glides like an airplane.

Glide ratio. The ratio of distance covered horizontally to height lost vertically.

Glide recovery. Rocket recovery system in which the engine's ejection charge causes it to convert into a glider and which creates lift as it flies through the air. See also *Boost glider*, *Rocket glider*, and *Flexies*.

Glider pop pod. See *Pop Pod*.

Gliding Booster. A lower stage of a multi-stage rocket that returns to the ground by using aerodynamic lift produced by the fins instead of other recovery methods.

Glosscote. A brand name of a type of paint that dries with a shiny and reflective finish.

Gore (parachute). The triangular portion of fabric between two adjacent meridian seams.

Grain (propellant). The propellant inside a solid fuel rocket. The grain is defined by its dimensions and surface shape.

Grain. See *Wood grain*.

Gravitation. Force of attraction that exists between all particles of matter everywhere in the universe. The law of gravitation is: Every particle of matter in the universe attracts every other particle with a force that varies directly as the product of their masses, and inversely as the square of the distance between them.

Gravity. The force that pulls down on any object near the surface of the earth.

Ground effect (floating or cushioning). An apparent increase in lift while flying an airplane close to the ground, within an altitude which varies from zero to a height approximately equal to the wingspan. There is no simple explanation, but there is a compressive force between the ground and the wing and also a decrease in the downwash angle of the air from the trailing edge of the wing, causing a reduction in *induced drag*.

Ground loop. An uncontrollable violent turn of an airplane while taxiing, or during the landing or takeoff run.

Ground speed. The velocity of an aircraft relative to the earth.

Guidance, inertial. A guidance system which does not depend on information obtained from outside the rocket or missile, and which contains elements sensitive enough to operate on the principle of Newton's second law of motion.

Guidance system. A system that measures and evaluates flight information, correlates it to the expected destination, and converts the results into parameters necessary to achieve the desired flight path. A guidance system may be self-contained within the rocket, or the guidance function may be performed by various combinations of ground and airborne components.

Gusset. Any generally triangular brace used to strengthen the corners of a structure.

Gyroscope. A gyroscope consists of a well-balanced flywheel, universally mounted, and having three degrees of freedom about its center of gravity, which always remains in a fixed position. A gyroscope exhibits the characteristics of rigidity as long as the wheel is revolving at a high speed—it tends to remain in the same position and plane of rotation.

Hand-launched glider. A glider that is thrown into the air.

Hatch. A door in the side of a spacecraft.

Headwind. A wind that blows approximately parallel to the line of flight of an aircraft and retards the ground speed of the airplane.

Heat shield. Any device that protects something else from heat.

Helicopter recovery. Rocket recovery system in which vanes on the rocket are activated by the engine's ejection charge. The vanes are airfoil surfaces mounted on the rocket in such a way that air flowing over them generates lift, causing the rocket to rotate (like a helicopter) safely to the ground.

Higher powered rocketry. Model rockets that use engines (or combinations of engines) that are rated higher than 20 newton-seconds (D engine or higher).

Horizon. The line where the earth and sky apparently meet.

Horizontal stabilizer. A structural component of an aerodynamic vehicle consisting of a fin mounted on the vehicle so that its largest surface is parallel to the plane of the horizon.

Hypersonic. Supersonic velocities having a *Mach number* of at least 5.

Ignite. To begin the combustion process of a rocket engine.

Igniter. An electrical device that initiates the combustion process in a rocket engine.

Igniter plug. A specially shaped plastic piece that holds the *igniter* securely into the nozzle of the rocket engine.

Impact area. The area where an errant rocket lands.

Impulse. The product of a force and the brief time during which the force is applied.

Impulse, total. The product obtained by multiplying the thrust from the motor by the burning time in seconds.

Indirect staging. Any staging technique in which the hot ejection charge gases of the booster engine do not ignite the *sustainer engine*. This usually requires an onboard ignition system to ignite the sustainer engine.

Induced drag. The part of drag that results from the generation of lift of the wing.

Inertia. That property of matter by which a body at rest tends to stay at rest and a body in motion tends to continue in motion unless acted upon by some external force.

Infinite-span wing. In aerodynamic theory, a wing of endless span, thus having no tip vortices or induced drag, assumed for purpose of simplification.

Inherent stability. Stability of an aircraft due solely to the disposition and arrangement of its fixed parts, i.e., that property which causes it, when disturbed, to return to its normal attitude of flight without the use of controls.

Instability. The opposite of *stability*.

Interference drag. When two parts of an object or parts of an airplane are in close proximity to each other their combined drag is greater than their respective drags if tested individually.

Interior ballistics. Deals with the rocket's behavior in reaction to gas pressures inside the rocket, escapements, and the shift in the center of gravity as propellants are consumed.

Interlock. Any safety device inserted in an electrical circuit that must be correctly position or removed for the circuit to be completed. Used in launch control systems to prevent accidental ignition. An example of an interlock is a *safety key*.

Interstage section. A section of a rocket that lies between stages.

JATO. Abbreviation for "jet-assisted-takeoff"; an auxiliary rocket device for applying thrust to an aircraft to help it take off with heavier loads, shorter runs, and greater accelerated speeds.

Jet. The high-velocity, hot gas stream that rushes out from the rocket nozzle at supersonic velocity.

Jig. An accurately constructed framework used as an aid in assembling and aligning structural parts of an airplane or rocket.

Kicker. A liquid applied to *cyanoacrylate* adhesives to make them harden quicker.

Kinetic energy. Energy due to the motion of a mass. It is equal to one-half the mass times the velocity squared. Kinetic energy = $1/2mV^2$

Kushnerik effect. A loss of engine thrust and total impulse caused when a rocket engine is recessed inside a rocket's body.

Laminar flow. Smooth flow of air in which no crossflow of fluid particles occur between adjacent stream lines; hence, a flow conceived as made up of layers—commonly distinguished from turbulent flow.

Laminated wood. A product formed by gluing or otherwise fastening together a number of laminations of wood with the grain substantially parallel. (Differs from plywood in that in the latter the grain of alternate plies is usually crossed at right angles; also the plies of the latter are usually made up of veneer.)

Lateral axis. An imaginary line running through the *center-of-gravity* of a model, parallel to the wingspan of a glider. The model will pitch up or down about this axis.

Launch. To send off a rocket vehicle under its own rocket power.

Launcher. A mechanical structure for controlling the initial flight path of a rocket without providing any propulsion in itself.

Launch angle. The angle between a vertical plane and the longitudinal axis of a rocket being launched.

Launch controller. An electrically operated device used to ignite rocket engines from a remote location.

Launch lug. A round hollow tube that slips over the launch rod to guide the model during the first few feet of flight until stabilizing velocity is reached.

Launch lug standoff. A pylon on which the launch lug is attached. Used on models where the diameter of the nose is larger than the rest of the rocket.

Launch pad. The load-bearing base or platform from which a rocket is launched.

Launch rail. A type of *launch rod* that, instead of a circular cross section, has a cavity that will accept a post attached to the rocket. Launch rails are stiffer than launch rods and won't flex as much.

Launch rod. A cylindrical rod used to guide a rocket in its first few feet of flight.

Launch tower. see *Tower launcher.*

Leading edge. The front edge of a wing or fin.

Lift. The force that occurs when air moving over the top of a moving object travels faster than the air under it, producing uneven pressures. The pressure on the top of the object (wing) is lower than under it, sucking the object upward. That component of the total aerodynamic force acting on a body perpendicular to the undisturbed airflow relative to the body.

Lift coefficient. A dimensionless number found by:

$$\frac{Lift}{Coefficient} = \frac{Total\ Lift\ Force}{1/2 \times Air\ Density \times Velocity^2}$$

Abbreviation: CL. It allows direct performance comparison of two different airfoils.

Liftoff. The action of a rocket as it separates from its launch pad in a vertical ascent.

Liftoff mass. The entire mass of the model at the moment of ignition, not including the small mass of the igniter or igniter plug.

Lift-to-drag ratio. The lift generated by a wing divided by the drag produced, expressed as a ratio. Abbreviation: L/D.

Lite-ply. The name given to a low-density plywood. Sometimes also called "wop-pop."

Longitudinal axis. An imaginary line through the *center-of-gravity* of a model parallel to the fuselage or boom. The model rolls left or right about this axis.

Mach number. The ratio of the velocity of an object to the velocity of sound under the same atmospheric conditions. A speed of Mach 1 means the speed of sound, regardless of altitude.

Maneuverability. That quality of any vehicle that determines the rate at which its attitude and direction of movement can be changed.

Mass. Quantity or amount of matter of an object. *Weight* depends on mass.

Mass-burning rate. The rate at which a mass or bulk of solid propellant is consumed per unit time while enclosed in a combustion chamber under known conditions of pressure, ambient grain temperature, and gas-flow velocity.

Mass flow rate. The rate at which exhaust gases travel through a rocket nozzle measured in kilograms per second.

Mass ratio. The ratio of the liftoff mass to the final burnout mass. The larger the number, the higher the rocket will go.

Maximum thrust. See *Peak thrust.*

Mean aerodynamic chord. The chord of an imaginary rectangular airfoil that has pitching moments throughout the flight range the same as those of an actual airfoil or a combination of airfoils under consideration; calculated to make equations of aerodynamic forces applicable to nonrectangular wings.

Micro balloons. A powder or paste made from microscopic, hollow glass spheres. Typically used as finishing putty for filling gaps in a rocket or as a thickener for epoxy.

Micro clips. Small spring-loaded clamps for connecting the electrical launch system to the igniter inserted into the rocket motor.

Mid-body ejection. A method of ejecting the recovery system out of the rocket near the middle of the body tube. The tube is separated at that point instead of near the nose cone as a drag reduction technique and to reduce the chances of the *zipper effect* .

Minimum-diameter rocket. The smallest diameter rocket than can be built for a given type of rocket engine. For "mini" engines the minimum-diameter rocket would use a BT-5 (13 mm diameter) tube as the main body. Minimum-diameter rockets are used to achieve the highest possible altitude.

Module. A combination of components contained in one package or so arranged that together they are common to one mounting, which provide a complete function or functions to the subsystem in which they operate.

Moment. A tendency to cause rotation about a point or axis. The object will rotate around a point called the "center-of-mass," or "*center-of-gravity*." The measure of this tendency is equal to the product of the force and the perpendicular distance between the point of axis of rotation and the point of application.

Momentum. The property of a moving object which is the product of its mass multiplied by its velocity.

Monocoque (mo'-no-kok) construction. A type of construction in which the skin or shell carries all the bending and shear stresses. Monocoque construction has vertical bulkheads as its only reinforcement.

Monokote®. Brand name of heat-shrinkable plastic used as a covering for *built-up* wings on airplanes.

Motion. Movement of an object in relation to its surroundings.

Motor. See *Engine.*

Motor mount. See *Engine mount.*

Multi-stage rocket. A rocket vehicle having two or more rocket units, each firing after the preceding unit has exhausted its propellant. Normally, each unit, or stage, is jettisoned after completing its firing. Also called a multiple-stage rocket or, infrequently, a step rocket.

Music wire. A high grade, uniform variety of steel used for the manufacture of springs. It is known for its great stiffness. Also called "piano wire."

Mylar®. A type of sheet plastic known for its high strength. It is optimal for making strong parachutes and streamers.

Nacelle (na-sel'). An enclosure fastened to the wing for fairing an object that is larger than the boundaries of the airfoil section.

Neutral stability. A neutral stable airplane is one that if disturbed from a state of steady flight will not return to its original flight attitude but may seek any new flight attitude and state of steady flight.

Newton. A force or measurement of force. The amount of force needed to move a mass of one kilogram with an acceleration of one meter per second per second; one newton is equal to 0.225 pounds of force. Abbreviation: N.

Newton-second. Metric measurement of a rocket engine's total impulse. The metric equivalent of "pound-second." Abbreviation: N-s.

Nose cone. The foremost surface of a model rocket. Smooths the airflow around the rocket.

Nose block. A solid cylinder of balsa or plastic used to connect two body tubes and prevent ejection charge gases from passing through to the upper tube. See also *Tube coupler.*

Nose blow recovery. A type of streamer in which where the shock cord acts as the streamer so no other recovery device is needed. This method is only used on small and low mass models.

Nose heavy. The condition of an airplane in which the nose tends to sink when allowed to seek its own attitude.

Nozzle. Carefully shaped aft portion of the thrust chamber of a rocket engine that controls the expansion of the exhaust products so thermal energy produced in the combustion chamber is efficiently converted into kinetic energy, thereby imparting thrust to the vehicle.

Ogive. The shape commonly given to nose cone of a rocket. In geometrical terms, it is the surface of revolution generated when a line segment and the arc of a circle are rotated about the axis parallel to the line.

Optimum weight. The ideal mass of a model rocket, which will yield the maximum altitude for a given rocket engine. It is related to the velocity and the inertia of the rocket, which overcome gravity and aerodynamic drag. Factors that determine optimum weight are the thrust curve of the rocket engine, the size of the rocket, and the drag coefficient of the model.

Oscillation (parachute). The swinging of the suspended load under the parachute.

Outboard. The direction perpendicular to the centerline of an airplane and parallel to the airplane's *lateral axis*.

Oxidizer. A rocket propellant component, such as oxygen, that supports combustion when in combination with a fuel.

Pad. See *Launch pad.*

Parabola. An open curve, all points of which are equidistant from a fixed point, called the focus, and a straight line. Nose cones are often shaped like parabolas, which yield lower drag in rockets flying at subsonic speeds.

Parabolic. Pertaining to, or shaped like, a parabola.

Parachute. A flexible fabric, umbrella-like device, used to retard the descent of a falling body by offering resistance to its motions through the air.

Parachute canopy. The plastic sheet or fabric top of a parachute.

Paraglider. A flexible-winged, kite-like vehicle designed for use in a recovery system for model rockets.

Parasite drag. The total drag minus induced drag. Consists of *form drag* (due to shape) *skin friction drag*, *interference drag*, and other drag not associated with the production of lift.

Parasite glider. A small glider that rides piggy back on a rocket during the boost phase of the engine.

Payload. The cargo of a rocket or airplane.

Payload section. The section of the rocket that carries the cargo.

Peak altitude. The highest elevation reached by a rocket; its *apogee*.

Peak thrust. The maximum thrust level that a rocket engine produces.

Pendulum stability. Stability such as is due to a pendulum's center of mass acting at a considerable distance below the pivot point. In an airplane, pendulum stability is achieved by positioning the center of mass below the main wing.

Performance. A measure of the ability of a rocket to accomplish some specific task.

Perigee. The lowest point to the center of the earth in a satellite's orbit.

Permeability. The measure of the rate of diffusion of gas through intact fabric. Used in rocketry to determine how fast a parachute will fall, because the lower the permeability, the slower it will fall. Plastic sheet has a very low permeability, while any woven fabric has a higher permeability.

Pilot parachute. A small auxiliary parachute attached to the apex of the main parachute, designed to pull the latter out of its pack or compartment.

Piston. A closely fitting disk moving to and fro inside a hollow cylinder.

Piston ejection. The method of ejecting a recovery device from a rocket with a solid, sliding bulkhead. This bulkhead protects the recovery device from the heat of the ejection charge without the use of recovery wadding or ejection baffles.

Piston launcher. A special apparatus used to increase liftoff velocity by increasing the pressure at the base of a rocket at liftoff. Usually used with a *tower launcher* or *launch rod* until stabilizing velocity is reached.

Pitch. The up or down rotation about the *lateral axis*.

Pitching moment. Force applied to an aircraft that causes a tendency to rotate up or down about the lateral axis. A positive pitching moment causes an upward rotation, or an increase in *angle-of-attack*.

Planer. A device used to shave thin layers off the surface of a piece of wood.

Planform. The geometric shape of a wing or fin, as seen from above.

Plastic model cement. A type of adhesive used to join parts made from styrene plastic.

Plastic model conversion. A reconfiguring of a static plastic model into one capable of being flown as a model rocket.

Plugged engines. Special rocket motors that have a solid bulkhead in the front end, which prevents the release of ejection charge gases into the rocket.

Plywood. A board made up of two or more thin layers of wood (called veneer) cemented together with the grain direction of each layer perpendicular to the adjacent layers.

Polygon. A plane figure having more than four sides or angles.

Polyhedral. A form of *dihedral* in which the wing is cut into more than two panels to give the upward tilt of the wing tips.

Pop-lug. A launch lug that detaches from the rocket as the model leaves the launch rod. Since launch lugs produce a lot of drag, eliminating the lug for most of the flight allows the rocket to fly higher into the sky.

Pop pod. An engine mount, for forward-engine boost gliders, that detaches from the *fuselage* so that the *center-of-gravity* of the glider moves rearward over the wing.

Porosity. Usually refers to what is technically known as permeability. The ratio of void or interstitial area to total area of cloth expressed in percent. Refers to the amount of air that will pass directly through the cloth of a parachute canopy. See also *permeability*.

Potential energy. A form of stored energy that can be fully recovered and converted into *kinetic energy*.

Powered flight. See *Boost phase*.

Pressure. The normal or perpendicular component of force per unit area exerted by a fluid on a surface.

Pressure relief hole. A small hole to equalize the internal pressure inside a body tube with the external air pressure. Used on *higher-powered rockets*.

Primer. An underlying paint applied directly to the surface of a part. It allows successive layers of paint to adhere better to the part.

Probe. Anything used to explore, examine, and test the nature of something.

Profile. The outline of an object as viewed from a side or the outline of any cross section.

Profile drag. The sum of the surface friction drag and the form drag, usually associated with a two-dimensional airfoil section.

Projectile. A body accelerated to a velocity by the application of mechanical forces, which continues its motion along a ballistic trajectory.

Propellant. A material carried in a rocket vehicle that releases energy during combustion and thus provides thrust to the vehicle.

Propulsion. Act of driving forward or propelling.

Prototype. An original model from which copies are made at a later time.

Pseudo scale model rocket. A fantasy-type model rocket resembling a military or scientific rocket vehicle.

Pylon. A stand-off that mounts part(s) of the model away from the main body tube. Useful for glider pop-pods and for launch lug stand-offs.

Reaction. A movement in the opposite direction of an action. Also used to describe a chemical combustion process such as that occurring in a rocket's combustion chamber.

Rear ejection or deployment. A type of recovery method in which the parachute exits out the back end of the rocket. Is useful as a drag reduction technique eliminating the small gap at the base of the nose cone. See also *Core ejection*.

Red baron. The name given to a non-flying, falling glider when the *pop-pod* doesn't fully release from the glider, or when the recovery device wraps itself around the glider.

Recoverable. Of a rocket vehicle or one of its parts, so designed or equipped as to be located after flight and recovered without damage.

Recovery. The procedure or action that occurs when the whole rocket or other part of a rocket vehicle is recovered after a launch.

Recovery pod. A tube attached externally to a model rocket or glider that carries the recovery system for the rocket engine.

Recovery system. A device incorporated into a rocket for the purpose of returning it to the ground safely by creating drag or lift to oppose the acceleration due to gravity.

Recovery wadding. A flame retardant, biodegradable paper that prevents the hot ejection charge gases from damaging the parachute or streamer recovery system in a model.

Reducer. See *Boattail*.

Redundancy. Having an extra backup part or system that can be used after the primary part or system fails. Many high-powered rockets use an extra deployment system as part of a redundant system for the primary engine ejection charge.

Reefed parachute. A parachute mechanically restrained so it won't open fully,. usually by tying the shroud lines together near the bottom of the *parachute canopy*.

Reflexed airfoil. A specific type of airfoil on which the trailing edge is permanently bent upward. This airfoil is used mainly on *flying wings*.

Regular polygon. A class of polygons with equal sides and angles.

Reinforce. To add strength to a part so it can withstand greater forces.

Reliability. Dependability; probability that a device will perform as intended.

Relative wind. The motion of air in relation to an object. It may be caused by an object moving through still air.

Reloadable rocket engine. A model rocket motor designed to be reused. Typically, the grain, nozzle, and ejection charge must be replaced prior to each flight.

Remote control. Control of an operation from a distance, especially by means of telemetry and electronics.

Rest. The absence of movement of an object in relation to its surroundings.

Retro rocket. A rocket engine that gives thrust opposite to the direction of an object's motion to slow it down or separate a section from the remaining body.

Reynolds number. A nondimensional coefficient used as a measure of the dynamic scale of a fluid flow. It is a correction factor that takes into account the linear dimensions of the model and the speed at which the tests are run. It allows for increasing the density of the air in the wind tunnel, so the results of the wind tunnel tests compare favorably with those that would be obtained if the tests were run with full-sized models at air speeds equal to flight speeds.

Rib. A fore-and-aft structural member of an *airfoil* used for maintaining the correct covering contour of a built-up wing or built-up fin.

Rigid wing. A type of glider that uses a stiff airfoil instead of a flexible fabric one. This airfoil may have ribs for support of the airfoil covering.

Rocket cluster. A group or cluster of rocket engines.

Rocket engine. One that carries its own oxidizer and fuel and operates according to the principles of jet propulsion.

Rocket glider. A type of rocket-launched free-flying glider that does not separate into two or more pieces after engine burnout. The glider changes its mass distribution to create a stable glide by moving parts of itself or by changing its shape. See also *Boost glider*.

Rocket launcher. A device used for launching rockets.

Rocketry. The art and science of designing, developing, building, testing, and launching rockets.

Rogallo. Term used to describe almost any flexible wing glider using a delta configuration. Named after Francis Rogallo, whose experiments in the 1950s let to the modern flexwing.

Roll. Movement about the longitudinal axis of a rocket or glider.

Root edge. The edge of a fin or wing that is attached to the main body of the model.

Rotation. The turning of a body about its axis.

Rotor blades. The lifting surfaces on a helicopter recovery model that slow the

descent of the model and cause the model to spin.

Rotor disc (helicopter). The plane described by the route taken by the tips of the rotor blades.

Rotor hub (helicopter). That portion of the support to which the rotor blades are attached.

Rudder. A vertical stabilizer on a glider used for yaw control. It may be totally fixed or it may have a hinged section to control direction of flight.

Ruddervator. One of a pair of control surfaces set in a V, each of which combines the function of both rudder and elevator.

Rupture. See *Case rupture*.

Safety key. A special removable key used to arm a launch system. No power can get to an *igniter* without the use of a safety key in the *launch controller*.

Safety factor. An intentional, added increase in strength or stability of a rocket beyond expected flight requirements. This increase improves the chances for a successful launch and to accommodates unexpected conditions during the flight.

Sailplane. A performance glider.

Satellite vehicle. The rocket vehicle used to place an earth satellite in orbit.

Scale data. Documentation, including size, details, and markings, of a full-size rocket from which a scale model is created.

Scale model. An exact miniature replica of a real flying rocket or missile.

Schematic. A diagram of an electrical circuit.

Scissor wing. A position-changing, variable geometry wing, consisting of a single wing that rotates at its centerline.

Screw eye. A threaded piece of metal shaped in a loop.

Scoop. Any opening to allow entry of the airstream flowing over the vehicle.

Scrub. To cancel a scheduled rocket firing, either before or during the countdown.

Sealer. Any substance applied to wood or other porous material to fill any voids, yielding a smooth surface.

Section. A cross sectional view at a certain point.

Semimonocoque construction. A variation of the *monocoque* structure in which stiffening members are attached to the *skin* to assist in resisting stresses.

Separation, aerodynamic. The phenomenon in which the flow past a body placed in a moving stream of fluid becomes detached from the surface of the body.

Servo or servomechanism. A small proportional electric motor used in remote control systems to operate the control surfaces of an airplane.

Shell. The outside covering or wall of a thin-walled structure. See also *Skin*.

Shims. Thin pieces of paper, metal, wood, or plastic placed between loosely fitting parts as an emergency method of achieving a tight fit.

Shock cord. A rope or ribbon that absorbs the kinetic energy of a nose cone forced from the rocket by the ejection charge. This cord prevents the nose from falling to the ground separate from the rest of the model.

Shock cord mount. A paper or mechanical fastener used to attach one end of the shock cord to the inside of the body tube.

Shoulder. An *adapter* that is oriented with the smaller diameter toward the front of the rocket. Sometimes called a "reducer." See also *Boattail* and *Adapter*. Also part of the nose cone that fits into the body tube.

Shred. The ripping or tearing of the recovery system during parachute deployment. Term is also applied to the nose cone, wings, or fins being stripped off the rocket during boost.

Shroud, transition. An adapter made from paper or other stiff but flexible material.

Shroud line. The strings on a parachute that attach its canopy to the payload, often the nose cone of the rocket.

Silo. A missile shelter that consists of a reinforced vertical hole in the ground with facilities for launching the rocket.

Sink rate. The vertical downward component of velocity that a glider or parachute has while descending in still air.

Skin. The outward sheet covering of a wing or fin.

Skin friction drag. Resistance, tending to slow the vehicle, which is caused by air particles in the airstream being slowed down by surface roughness of the vehicle.

Slenderness ratio. A dimensionless number expressing the ratio of a rocket vehicle length to its diameter.

Snap nack (nose cone). A sudden reversal of direction of the nose cone as it fully extends the length of shock cord.

Snap swivel. A latching device for the screw eye to which the shroud lines of a parachute are attached. This makes interchanging parachutes quick and easy.

Snuffer tube. A small metal tube into which a dethermalizer wick is inserted. When the wick burns down inside the tube, it is extinguished by lack of oxygen.

Soar. To fly without engine power and without loss of altitude.

Soft landing. A landing on a spatial body at such a slow speed as to avoid a crash or destruction of the landing vehicle.

Solar sail. A device for utilizing solar radiation to supply thrust for spacecraft.

Solid propellant. A rocket propellant in solid state consisting of all the ingredients necessary for sustained chemical combustion. They burn on their exposed surface, generating hot exhaust gases to produce a reaction force.

Sonic barrier. A term for the large increase in drag that acts upon a aircraft approaching the speed of sound. Also called the "sound barrier."

Sonic boom. A concussion-like sound heard when a shock wave generated by a aircraft flying at supersonic speed reaches the ear.

Sonic speed. The speed at which sound propagates through the air.

Sounding rocket. Term used for research rockets that obtain data on the upper atmosphere. These rockets fly on suborbital trajectories.

Spackle. A type of filler paste used in home construction that can be used on model rockets to fill gaps and seams or to make fillets.

Span. The maximum distance, measured parallel to the lateral axis, from tip to tip of an airplane wing.

Spar. A rod or beam that is the main load-bearing structural member in a wing or fin.

Specific gravity. The ratio of the density of some substance to that of water.

Specific impulse. The ratio of the thrust to the propellant mass flow in a rocket engine. Used for determining relative performance of a rocket engine.

Spill hole. A hole cut in the top of a parachute canopy to allow for a quicker descent or for decreased parachute *oscillation*.

Spinerons. Small angled tabs added to the base of fins to cause rotation about the lateral axis of a rocket. Used to increase the stability of the rocket.

Spin stabilization. A method of rotating the rocket during the boost phase of the flight by canting the fins or creating a cambered airfoil so the spinning evens out the forces acting on the rocket. This allows the rocket to fly in a nearly straight line.

Splashdown. The term used for a water landing of a rocket.

Sport model. A typical model rocket that is built primarily for the fun and enjoyment of the hobby. Compare with *Competition model*.

Spot landing. A landing by a model airplane or rocket at some predetermined location.

Spruce wood. A high-density hardwood of very great strength. Commonly used to make fuselage booms of gliders.

Stability. The property of a glider or rocket to maintain its attitude or resist displacement; if displaced, to develop forces to restore the original condition.

Stabilizer. A fixed (horizontal or vertical) tail control surface on a glider, whose primary function is to increase the stability of the aircraft.

Staging. Separating a stage or set of stages from a spent stage of a launch vehicle. See *Multi-stage rocket*.

Stall. The condition of an airfoil or airplane in which it is operating at an *angle-of-attack* greater than the angle of attack of maximum lift. It is a loss of flying speed and in many cases temporary loss of *lift* and control of the airplane.

Static firing. The firing of a rocket engine in a hold-down position to measure thrust and accomplish other tests.

Step rocket. A rocket with two or more stages.

Stick and tissue construction. A term given to a *built-up* wings and fuselages of an aircraft covered with tissue paper.

Stiffeners. Any slender rod added to a large, relatively flat part as a reinforcement to make the part more rigid.

Streamer recovery. Rocket recovery system in which a paper or plastic streamer is attached to the top of the rocket. When deployed by the engine's ejection charge, the streamer creates enough drag to return the rocket safely to the ground.

Streamlining. The act of reducing aerodynamic drag by adding or removing parts to give the model a slim, teardrop shape.

Strength. The ability of a material to resist stress without breaking.

Strength-to-weight ratio. Ratio of the strength of a member to its weight.

Stress. A resultant internal force in a body that resists the tendency of an external force to change the size or shape of the body.

Structural design. The process of determining the arrangement and sizes of parts of a *structure* required to carry loads imposed upon it.

Structure. The load-carrying components that are designed to resist the external loads acting upon the structure as well as to transmit local loads due to weight items.

Stuffer tube. A smaller tube inside a larger body tube that leads the ejection charge gases to the recovery device section of a higher-powered rocket.

Styrofoam®. A brand name of expanded polystyrene foam. A lightweight material that is easily cut or shaped, but does not have a lot of bending strength.

Sub-orbital trajectory. The *flight path* of a rocket that lifts off from the ground but does not reach sufficient velocity to attain orbit about the earth. The flight path will have a parabolic shape and will touch down at some point on the earth.

Supersonic. Faster than the speed of sound. A speed having a Mach number greater than 1.

Sustainer engine. A model rocket engine that sustains or increases the velocity of the rocket. Sustainer engines usually have longer delays than typical engines. They are used for models that coast for long periods of time (i.e., the top stage in a staged rocket, or an ultra-streamlined, low-drag, and low-mass model rocket).

Sweepback. A wing or fin design in which the tips slope backward from the longitudinal centerline of the airplane or rocket.

Swing test. An experiment used to gauge confidence in a models' flight *stability*. It involves attaching a string to the model's CG location and rotating it at a high speed in a large circle around the modeler. A stable rocket assumes a streamlined position, with the nose pointed in the direction of rotation.

Swing wing. A position-changing, variable-geometry wing consisting of two airfoils pivoting independently from each other.

Tab. An auxiliary airfoil or similarly shaped surface attached to a control surface.

Tail boom. A spar or outrigger connecting the tail surfaces and the main supporting surfaces of an airplane.

Tail-heavy. The condition of an airplane in which the tail tends to sink when the longitudinal control is released. Tail heaviness is dangerous because the airplane will likely stall when the wing is flying at too high an angle-of-attack.

Tailless airplane. An airplane in which the devices used to obtain stability and control are incorporated in the wing. The term is used with the same meaning as *flying wing.*

Tail skid. A skid for supporting the tail of an airplane on the ground.

Taper. To narrow gradually toward one end.

Taper ratio. The ratio of the root chord length to the tip chord length.

Target drone. An unmanned aircraft or rocket used as a target for testing interception equipment.

Telemetering. Technique of recording data associated with some distant event, usually by radioing the instrument reading from the vehicle to a recording machine on the ground.

Temperature. The degree of hotness or coldness measured on a definite scale based on some particular system or phenomenon.

Template. A flat pattern sheet used to construct multiple parts quickly and accurately.

Terminal velocity. The equilibrium speed at which a body falls through the air when resistance to air equals the pull of gravity.

Test stand. A platform at which some mechanism or engine is tested.

Test vehicle. A rocket or aircraft used in testing components of proposed aerospace systems.

Theodolite. An instrument used for measuring angles during tracking operations to determine how high a model flies.

Thermal. A rising current of warm air.

Throat. In rocket and jet engines, the most constricted section of an exhaust nozzle.

Through-the-wall. The strongest method of attaching fins to the rocket. A tab on the root edge of the fin fits through a slot cut into the wall of the body tube.

Thrust. The propulsive force created by the rocket engine during the burning and expulsion of gases through the rocket engine's nozzle.

Thrust decay. When a rocket motor burns out or is cut off, propulsive thrust does not fall to zero instantaneously, but progressively declines over some fraction of a second. This graduated reduction and loss of thrust is known as thrust decay.

Thrust phase. See *Boost phase.*

Thrust ring. A bulkhead with an open center mounted within the engine tube, just in front of the engine. Used to transfer the force of thrust to the structure of the vehicle. It also prevents the engine from moving forward in the engine mount, but still allows the ejection charge gases to pass through the engine tube.

Thrust-to-weight ratio. A quantity used to evaluate engine performance. Obtained by dividing the thrust output by the engine weight, less fuel or propellant.

Tip. The edge of a fin or wing the farthest away from the main body of the model.

Tip-off. A errant direction change produced by the launcher. Tip-off can be produced by flexing of the launch rod or by a sudden gust of wind as the rocket leaves the launch rod.

Total impulse. The product of thrust and the time that an engine is firing.

Touchdown. The (moment of) landing of rocket or other aerospace vehicle on the surface of the earth.

Tower launcher. A mechanical structure with guide rails inside that hold the model centered. The rocket does not need a launch lug because the rails guide the rocket, preventing it from shifting in any direction while it is accelerating after ignition. Removing the launch lug lowers the aerodynamic drag on the model.

Tracker. The person taking angular measurements from which the *apogee* of a rocket is determined.

Tracking. Following the flight of a rocket to determine position, altitude, and possibly velocity and distance traveled.

Tracking powder. Any nonflammable powder substance placed inside the rocket to help increase the visibility of the rocket at apogee when the recovery device is deployed.

Trailing edge. The rear edge of a fin or a wing, opposite the direction of travel.

Trajectory. The curved flight path (ballistic portion) of the model rocket prior to the deployment of its recovery device.

Transfer tube. A hollow cylinder that directs ejection charge gases from one location to another. Useful in *direct staging* rocket engines that are separated by a large distance.

Transonic. The region of a rockets flight when the model's speed is just below that of the speed of sound. This region is marked by a sharp rise in aerodynamic drag.

Trigonometry. The branch of mathematics that deals with the sides and angles of triangles and the relationships between them. Trigonometry is used to help determine a rocket's altitude.

Trim. Adjustment of an aerodynamic vehicle's controls to achieve *stability* in a desired flight condition.

Trimming. The act of balancing and setting control surface angles on a glider to achieve a straight, stable glide.

Trim tape. A precolored, adhesive-backed tape used to decorate the outside of a model.

Tube adapter. See *Adapter.*

Tube coupler. A hollow cylindrical tube for joining body tubes of the same diameter.

Tumble recovery. Rocket recovery system in which the balance point of the rocket is moved, causing it to become unstable so it tumbles end over end, creating drag to slow its descent.

Tunnel. A covered channel running longitudinally along a rocket.

Turbulent flow. A type of fluid flow in which there is an unsteady flow of particles. The motion of the particles at any given point varies in no definite manner.

Two station tracking. A method of increasing the accuracy of determining the maximum height a rocket ascends by having two observers taking angular measurements simultaneously.

Umbilical mast. A tower placed next to the launch rod that supports the wire leading to the top of the rocket. These wires may be for igniting the engine (as in the case of a front-engine boost glider) or for some payload that needs to be activated just prior to launch.

Undercarriage. The main landing gear of an airplane.

Unbalanced force. A net force in excess of any opposing forces. An unbalanced force, according to Newton's second law, causes a change in a body's inertia, causing it to accelerate.

Unbalanced thrust. See *Unsymmetrical thrust.*

Unpowered. Without any means of propulsion.

Unsymmetrical thrust. A flight condition arising from either a failure of one engine or an unbalance of engine types, resulting in

thrust loads transmitted mainly on one side of a rocket's plane of symmetry.

Updraft. Rising current of air.

Upper stage. In general the second, third, or later stage in a *multi-stage rocket.*

Vacuum. A region of exceedingly low pressure, more specifically a region in which the gas pressure is a great deal lower than atmospheric pressure.

Vanes. A long set of fins used to straighten the airflow before it reaches the main fin unit at the aft end of the rocket.

Variable geometry. When all or a portion of the glider's lifting surfaces change shape or position (i.e., swing wing and scissor wing gliders).

Vehicle. In general an aerospace structure (such as a rocket) designed to carry a payload through the atmosphere.

Velocity. The rate of motion or speed in a given direction measured in terms of distances moved per unit time with a specific direction.

Veneer. Thin sheets of wood.

Ventral fin. A short airfoil mounted on the belly, or underside, of an aircraft.

Vernier engine. An auxiliary rocket engine, smaller than the main thrust unit, used to obtain adjustments in velocity and trajectory of a missile.

Vertical axis. An imaginary line that runs through the *center-of-gravity* of a model and is perpendicular (out the top) to the fuselage or boom of a glider. The model yaws left or right about this axis

Vertical stabilizer. A structural component of an aerodynamic vehicle consisting of a fin and rudder assembly.

Voltage. Electromotive force or potential difference.

Wadding. see *Recovery wadding.*

Warp. A twist in the wing or fin of a rocket.

Washin and washout. A permanent warp of the wing tips of an airplane. Washin increases the angle of incidence toward the tip, and washout is a decrease. Washout is incorporated in both wing tips for the purpose of delaying tip stall.

Weathercock. The tendency of a rocket to turn into the wind, away from a vertical path.

Wedging. A fin attachment method for models with a cluster of two or more body tubes, where the fins are glued into the gaps between the tubes.

Weight. The force that results from the earth's gravitational attraction of the mass of an object. An object's weight is found by multiplying its mass by the acceleration due to gravity.

Wind. Moving air, especially a mass of air having a common horizontal direction and motion.

Wind tunnel. A tubelike structure or passage in which a high-speed movement of air is produced, as by a fan, and within which objects are placed to investigate the airflow about them and the aerodynamic forces acting upon them.

Wing. The main lifting surface of a glider.

Winglets. Small, nearly vertical aerodynamic surfaces mounted at the tips of airplane wings.

Wing loading. The total mass of the flying glider divided by the planform area of the wing. It represents the average force per area that is exerted on a wing.

Wing tip. The outer end of an airplane wing.

Wood grain. The arrangement of particles or fibers of wood which determines its roughness, markings, or texture.

Wood grain direction. Having an orientation parallel to the fibers in a piece of wood.

Yaw. Rotation (nose to the left or right) about the vertical axis of a glider.

Zipper effect. A slicing of the forward end of a rocket's body tube caused by the tendency of the shock cord and the nose cone to travel in a different direction from the main body.

Index